Believing in the Resurrection

The Meaning and Promise of the Risen Jesus

Gerald O'Collins, SJ

Paulist Press
New York / Mahwah, NJ

Cover design by Sharyn Banks
Book design by Lynn Else

Cover image: Zvonimir Atletic/Shutterstock.com

Appendix, "Easter Appearances and Bereavement Experiences," reprinted by kind permission of *Irish Theological Quarterly*, 76:3 (2011): 224–37.

Library of Congress Cataloging-in-Publication Data

O'Collins, Gerald.
    Believing in the Resurrection : the meaning and promise of the risen Jesus / Gerald O'Collins.
        p. cm.
    Includes bibliographical references (p.   ) and index.
    ISBN 978-0-8091-4757-1 (alk. paper)—ISBN 978-1-61643-133-4. 1. Jesus Christ—Resurrection. 2. Catholic Church—Doctrines. I. Title.
    BT482.O36 2012
    232'.5—dc23
                                                                2011039182

Published by Paulist Press
997 Macarthur Boulevard
Mahwah, New Jersey 07430

www.paulistpress.com

Printed and bound in the
United States of America

CONTENTS

PREFACE

Is Jesus merely a great but dead hero, or is he a risen, living presence? That troubling question of enormous significance has been around for two thousand years.

Christians claim that the crucified Jesus had been raised from the dead and remains powerfully present in our world—a claim that deserves serious attention from any thoughtful person. If we accept this claim as true, it should radically change the way we live our lives as well as the hopes that we entertain for ourselves and for our world. We are not destined at death to lose consciousness forever and return our bodies to the pool of cosmic matter. The resurrection promises us a glorious personal future beyond this life, a future that, in "a new heaven and a new earth" (Rev 21:1), will bring a radical transformation not only for our bodily existence but also for our material world. This is an extraordinary claim and an extraordinary promise, both centered on someone who died as a criminal on a cross, abandoned by nearly all of his followers, and seemingly abandoned by the God whose kingdom he had preached.

From the start of Christianity, this resurrection claim and promise involved a remarkably new assessment of the person of Jesus. He was now identified with the divine name, "Lord" or *Kyrios,* "the name / that is above every name" (Phil 2:9). He was understood to share in God's creative activity and sovereign rule over all things (for example, 1 Cor 8:6; Col 1:15–17). His resurrection from the dead had set him "at the right hand of God," and he now rules from the divine throne in heaven—a belief reflected in the twenty-one quotations from or allusions to Psalm 110:1 to be found in the New Testament: "The LORD says to my lord, / 'Sit at my right hand / until I make your enemies your footstool.'"

Jews of that period showed little interest in this text, whereas for the first Christians it was supremely significant (for example, Rom 8:34). They believed that the risen Jesus participated in the unique divine sovereignty over all things (Eph 1:21–22). As the Lord of the universe he merited adoration from everyone (Phil 2:9–11; Rev 5:11–14).

Thus, faith in Jesus' resurrection from the dead had a dramatic aftermath. It prompted a remarkable account of him as the divine Lord of the entire universe. Remember that the life and death of Jesus had occurred no more than twenty years before Paul, the first Christian writer, began composing and sending his letters. It was startling to maintain that someone of such very recent memory was now "sitting" on the divine throne and reigning over the world "at the right hand" of God.

The Book of Acts recalls several religious leaders in the first century who asserted some kind of messianic status, led uprisings, met their deaths, and became mere footnotes in history. Eleven or twelve years after Jesus was born, "Judas the Galilean" rose in revolt against the imposition of new taxes (Acts 5:37). Around forty years later Theudas headed an uprising (Acts 5:36). A little later someone called "the Egyptian" gathered thousands of followers in an attempt to seize Jerusalem from the Romans (Acts 21:38). All three died, as did many of their supporters. It was never claimed that any one of them was raised from the dead, let alone took his place "at the right hand of God" to reign over the universe. Their tragic stories serve to highlight the truly startling message of Christians about Jesus, who had lived only a short time before and was publicly executed as messianic pretender. Unlike Judas the Galilean, Theudas, and "the Egyptian," Jesus led a nonviolent movement. But like them, he died, apparently, as a total failure. What triggered the message of his resurrection from the dead and all that it involved about his sharing in God's sovereignty and ruling over the whole world?

As readers can see, I introduce this book on the resurrection of Jesus by reminding them of how important *and* astonishing was the Christian message: God had not only raised the crucified Jesus from the dead but also set him at his "right hand" to share the divine rule over the universe and, one should add, to join in sending the Holy Spirit into the world (Acts 2:32–33).

What should engage our attention when we reflect in detail on the Easter message? To locate this book in the contemporary scene, I spend the introduction sampling certain works on the resurrection of Christ published in the past decade. What are some representative authors saying about his resurrection?

To place the message of the resurrection in its philosophical and historical setting, we also dedicate a chapter to the question, What worldviews and background theories affect and even shape our responses to the message of the resurrection? And then we should ask, *Who* was proclaimed as raised from the dead? In other words, before taking up issues about what occurred after the death and burial of Jesus, something must be said about his story and what led to his being condemned to death and crucified (chapter 1).

Then follow chapters on the meaning of the resurrection claim (chapter 2), the appearances of the risen Jesus (chapter 3), the discovery of his empty tomb (chapter 4), and other factors that triggered and maintained the Easter faith and hope of the first disciples. These chapters bring us to the question, What was the resurrection believed to have done in redeeming and transforming humanity and the world (chapter 5)?

Against this backdrop, we then ask ourselves, What justifies today's faith in Jesus as risen from the dead and as a living presence in our world? Can one produce a reasonable case for such Easter faith (chapter 6)? We face the challenge of making some sense of the nature of risen life and the final transformation of the whole created universe (chapter 7). Finally, we take up the connection between Easter faith and the liturgical and moral life of Christians. What impact should the resurrection have on their liturgical celebrations and ethical thinking and behavior (chapter 8)? In an appendix, I examine critically a comparison that has been recently made between the disciples' experiences of the risen Jesus and bereavement experiences. Is this analogy truly close and illuminating?

I thank Christopher Bellitto and all at Paulist Press for suggesting that I write this book. With permission, the appendix is reprinted from the *Irish Theological Quarterly*. With sincere thanks and deep affection, this work is dedicated to all who live and work at Jesuit Theological College, Parkville (Australia). For biblical quotations I generally follow the New Revised Standard Version, but, on occasions, I translate directly from the Greek text of the New Testament.

Gerald O'Collins, SJ
Australian Catholic University
Pentecost Sunday 2011

INTRODUCTION

Some Representative Works
on the Resurrection

We would come up with a tediously long list if we were to reply comprehensively to the question, What have they been saying about the resurrection of Jesus in the past ten years? Many authors go over the same ground and do not add very much either to the debates about the resurrection or to the conclusions that can be reached. Hence I select nine books that have significant things to say, either positively or negatively, about the resurrection and the possibility of Easter faith and hope. This representative sample will bring readers into the current state of resurrection studies.

In presenting these nine works, I do not intend to take readers through them in complete detail and provide full-length book reports. Instead, I choose and highlight significant features that should interest students of the resurrection.

SOME POSITIVE CONTRIBUTIONS

Anthony Kelly, *The Resurrection Effect:*
Transforming Christian Life and Thought (2008)

Anthony Kelly deserves to lead the team of those who have contributed positively to the study of resurrection.[1] He brings together biblical, theological, and philosophical thinking to show how the resurrection of Jesus "saturates" the whole of Christian faith and should transform the life and thought of believers. As *the* key to God's relationship with Jesus and human beings, the resurrection eludes any precise definitions that would pin it down. Rather it provides the broadest horizon within which we can recognize what human life ultimately means, how we should live, and what we can expect from the God who raised Jesus from the dead.

This latest plea for the utter centrality of Easter faith follows earlier attempts to focus Christian thinking and life on the resurrection of the crucified Jesus. In the run-up to the Second Vatican Council, François-Xavier Durrwell helped to "rehabilitate" Easter as the central mystery of Christianity.[2] In the postconciliar years, some writers, like the Lutheran Wolfhart Pannenberg and myself,[3] tried again to revitalize theology and its various specializations by recalling where they should continually go to draw meaning, values, and guidelines: the light of the first Easter Sunday.

But the strange neglect of the resurrection persists. Sadly, leading figures in liberation theology have reflected only a little on Christ's rising from the dead.[4] Themes other than the resurrection continue to engage the attention of Catholic moral theologians, and, even more surprisingly, the resurrection can be seriously neglected by those who write in the area of sacramental theology.[5] We return later in this book to ways in which Easter faith should enliven those two branches of theology, as well as liberation theology itself. Here I only endorse Kelly's call to engage ourselves much more fully with the resurrection of Jesus from the dead.

N. T. Wright, *The Resurrection of the Son of God* (2003)

A magisterial volume by N. T. Wright offers more than eight hundred pages in response to basic questions about the origins of Christianity and the resurrection of Jesus.[6] What did the first Christians mean when they proclaimed that Jesus of Nazareth had been raised from the dead? Where does the historical evidence lead us when we investigate what precisely happened at the first Easter? What should be said about believing today in Jesus' resurrection?

The historical and biblical strength of this book emerges right from the first two hundred pages that map ancient beliefs about life beyond death in both pagan and Jewish worlds. Wright takes us through a panorama of what Greeks and Romans held about where souls went after death. The pagan world assumed that resurrection was impossible. Among the Jews, earlier hints (for example, Isa 26:19; Ezek 37:1–14; and Hos 6:1–2; 13:14) developed, and, in response to the deaths of those martyred in God's cause, became a full-blown belief in coming resurrection (Dan 12:2–3; 2 Macc 7). Of course, some like the Sadducees rejected any life beyond death worth speaking of, and others expected only a disembodied immortality. But by the time of Jesus "most Jews believed in resurrection."[7] They expected a general resurrection at the end of the present age: that is to say, a newly embodied life at the end of history. But no one imagined that any individual had already been raised from the dead or would be raised in anticipation of the last day. Here one should note that Hosea 6:1–2 ("us") and 13:14 ("them") speak in the plural and of a community resurrection and not in the singular or of an individual's resurrection. Nor was there any agreement among those who believed that (general) resurrection would eventually happen as to what it would be like. Would it involve being woken from the sleep of death to "shine" forever like the stars and "the brightness of the sky" (Dan 12) or to enjoy a reassembled body and the restoration of limbs cut off by executioners (2 Macc 7)?

On two scores, as Wright shows, Christian faith in resurrection had no strict precedent even in Judaism. First, it proclaimed that one individual (Jesus) had been raised from the dead in anticipation of the general resurrection at the end of all history. Belief in Jesus' resurrection could not have been generated by prior Jewish beliefs or by study of the biblical texts expressing those beliefs. Second, the other striking difference appears in a distinctively Christian consensus about the nature of resurrection. The newly embodied life of the resurrected Jesus involved a glorious transformation of his human existence, the "spiritual body" of 1 Corinthians 15. That made Christians agree in their expectation of *that* kind of risen existence for themselves. Thus when compared with Jewish hopes for resurrection, the Easter message of Paul and other early Christian witnesses contained two strikingly new elements.

Through the heart of his book Wright deploys the historical data that support the appearances of the risen Christ and the discovery of his empty tomb. Those two events prompted the resurrection faith in Jesus as the messianic Son of God, a faith that set Christianity going and provided the essential shape that Wright traces to the third century of the trajectory of Easter faith and resurrection hope triggered by Jesus' own victory over death.

In such a monumental study different readers will have their own favorite sections. I was particularly struck by what Wright wrote on the Easter stories we read in the closing chapters of the four Gospels. They contain surprising, even strange, features.[8] For example, up to the death and burial of Jesus, all four Gospels quote and echo the Jewish scriptures. A familiar theme in Matthew is his "All this took place to fulfill what had been spoken by the Lord through the prophet(s)," to which the evangelist then attaches one or more biblical citations. Surprisingly such biblical "embroidery" does not show up in his final, Easter chapter. The other evangelists also leave their Easter narratives biblically "unadorned." A second unexpected feature is the absence of personal hope in the Easter stories. Elsewhere the New Testament writers repeatedly express their own hope for risen life when they refer to the resurrection of Jesus. A classic example of this connection comes in 1 Corinthians 15, a letter written years before any of the Gospels took their final shape. These and further strange silences and unexpected features of the Easter chapters in the Gospels should encourage us to agree with Wright that the substance of these chapters represents a very old telling of the discovery of the empty tomb and of Jesus' encounters with the disciples—a time before biblical and theological reflection began working on connections and implications to be drawn from that discovery and those appearances. There is a haunting, ancient simplicity in the Easter stories that speaks for their credibility.

Richard Swinburne,
The Resurrection of God Incarnate (2003)

Like Wright, Richard Swinburne is concerned to put a case for faith in Jesus' resurrection from the dead.[9] A philosopher rather than a biblical scholar or historian, he takes a broader approach and concludes that there is a high probability that Jesus rose from the dead. This broad approach involves four major steps: (1) God, being perfectly good and perfectly powerful, had serious reasons for "intervening" in human history by becoming incarnate. (2) Since the life and teaching of Jesus show him to have been the incarnate Son of God, we can conclude that he was uniquely the kind of person God could be expected to have raised from the dead. (3) In making his case, Swinburne paints with broad sweeps of the brush, but also introduces some specific questions and arguments. (4) He draws together his case by concluding with a calculus of logical probability. It expresses in a formal manner his previous steps and aims at showing how it is very probable that the resurrection happened. I know of no other book on the resurrection that ends in such a mathematical way, with twelve pages of axioms, theorems, and an apparatus of calculus.

Let me comment on each of the four steps. As regards step 1, the suffering and sinning of human beings make it plausible that in his infinite love God would act by personally coming on the scene to set right a tragic situation. After all, John wrote, "God so loved the world that he gave his only Son, so that everyone who believes in him may not perish but may have eternal life" (John 3:16). Nevertheless, the incarnation did not *have to happen.* God might have dealt in other ways with the tragedy of human sinning and suffering, or—to use Swinburne's way of putting things—have "fulfilled" the divine "obligations"[10] in ways other than the incarnation. In the light of the divine freedom, may one allege that, given the human predicament, the incarnation was highly probable? Here I express a quibble about the language of intervention that Swinburne (and others) continually use. To call the incarnation an "intervention" can too easily suggest an "outsider" God, even a kind of "meddlesome" God, who comes on the scene for the first time. This is inappropriate language; God is always intimately present everywhere and in every situation, from moment to moment sustaining in being everything that is. It would be less misleading to characterize the incarnation as a "special divine act," or, together with the resurrection, as "*the* special divine act" that differs qualitatively from other special divine acts, like miracles.[11]

5

Here too I protest against Swinburne reducing the resurrection to the category of miracle and describing miracles as "violations of natural laws."[12] First, the resurrection of Jesus should not be called a miracle or even a super-miracle. Miracles, like the healing miracles of Jesus, are, to be sure, signs of what he wishes to do for us in the final kingdom (in the perfect bodily "healing" of the resurrection). Nevertheless, they happened and happen within our historical world of space and time, even if they point to what is to come. The resurrection of Jesus goes beyond any such miracles; it was and is the real beginning of the world to come, the event that initiates a sequence of final events that will fulfill and complete his personal rising from the dead (1 Cor 15:20–28). Second, *violate* has four meanings, all of them negative and even ugly: (1) disregard or fail to comply with; (2) treat with disrespect; (3) disturb or break in upon; (4) assault sexually. Presumably Swinburne uses *violate* in sense 1. But when working miracles occasionally and for good reasons, God is surely better described as suspending or overriding the normal working of natural laws. Since it is God who created the precise shape and functions of the laws of nature, it seems odd to speak of God "disregarding" or "failing to comply with" them. *Suspending* or *overriding* seems more appropriate language.

As regards Swinburne's second step, what he calls "the marks of an incarnate God," or "the life required of an incarnate God," are found exemplified in Jesus. He was the one and only prophet to satisfy the requirements for being and being recognized as God incarnate. Obviously Swinburne cannot go into much detail about the life, preaching, claims, and miraculous deeds of Jesus and what that all implied about his personal identity. But, as I argue in chapter 1, a good case can be made for concluding that, when revealing the divine mystery and working for the salvation of human beings, Jesus gave the impression of claiming to be on a par with God. To put matters the way Swinburne does, Jesus was indeed the kind of person whom God could be expected to raise from the dead. I prefer to say that Jesus, while being rejected and crucified as a blasphemer and threat to the public order, was in fact so truly identified with God and the divine cause that one would expect God to vindicate him in resurrection. Luke draws on Psalm 16 to indicate what one might, or even should, expect from God after the execution of Jesus: "You will not abandon my soul to Hades, or let your Holy One experience corruption" (Acts 2:27).

In step 3 Swinburne introduces something valuable in certain questions and arguments. He names, for instance, the new celebration of *Sunday* as a question to be answered. Why did the Jewish disciples of Jesus, his first disciples, no longer give priority to the Jewish Sabbath or Saturday and turn "the first day of the week" or Sunday into *the* day for meeting and celebrating the Eucharist (which, after all, was instituted at the Last Supper seemingly on the day that we call Thursday)? What made them hold Sunday so special that they changed not only their manner of worship (1 Cor 11:23–26) but also their special day for worship? An obvious answer is close at hand for this momentous switch away from the Sabbath, the day that God was understood to have assigned for rest and worship. Sunday was the day when the tomb of Jesus was discovered to be open and empty and the day when the disciples first encountered him risen from the dead.

Swinburne spends a chapter examining and refuting five rival theories of what happened to Jesus: for instance, that Jesus did not die on the cross but was taken down alive and recovered, or that he did die and was buried but his body was then removed by friends. As regards the first theory, which sensationalist but totally unscholarly writers revive every year or so, Swinburne points to several large difficulties it faces: for example, if Jesus continued to live on, "is it really plausible to suppose that he would have taken no further interest in the mushrooming movement which his passion and apparent resurrection had inspired? Would he (in view of what we know about him from the Gospels) really have colluded with such massive deception?"[13]

What of the theory that friends (for example, the female disciples) removed the body of Jesus from the tomb where Joseph of Arimathea had given him burial, took the body for proper burial elsewhere (for example, in Nazareth), and concealed this act from most of the disciples? But why would such disciples have wanted to conceal from the other disciples what they had done out of devotion to Jesus? Even more important, could they have been able to keep secret their actions in removing the body from the tomb, transporting it somewhere else, and giving it honorable burial there? As Swinburne remarks, "Even if they had tried to keep the theft secret from the other disciples, it is most unlikely that they would have succeeded."[14]

In an appendix Swinburne assigns numerical values to the various probabilities involved in his four-step argument. He maintains that, if these values do not "exaggerate the force of the arguments by which they are supported,…it is indeed very probable that Jesus was God incarnate who rose from the dead."[15] In view of the Trinitarian faith that Swinburne accepts, it would be preferable to speak of Jesus being *the Son of God incarnate* who rose from the dead. But, more important, while appreciating Swinburne's vigorous defense of the resurrection, I wonder how many people could come to believe in the resurrection simply on the basis of numerical values that they might assign to probabilities constituting various steps in the arguments that they develop from the historical testimony of the New Testament. Personal factors and experience, not to mention the influence of the Holy Spirit, feed into the making of Easter faith, as I argue in a later chapter.

Sandra Schneiders, *Written That You May Believe: Encountering Jesus in the Fourth Gospel* (2003)

Unlike the three authors we have just examined, Sandra Schneiders did not write her acclaimed book on John's Gospel precisely as a work on the resurrection.[16] But the subtitle could easily have been "Encountering the *Risen* Jesus in and through the Fourth Gospel" (emphasis mine). The book shares the aim of John's Gospel: to prompt its readers into encountering and believing in the risen Jesus. To be sure, the Fourth Gospel assigns only two chapters out of twenty-one to the Easter story. But, as Schneiders points out, "The Johannine resurrection narrative is one of the literary jewels of the New Testament."[17] What is more, the Jesus of the entire Fourth Gospel is no mere historical memory but a living presence. Right through the whole text and especially in the stories of various representative individuals who meet Jesus, readers are invited not to return to the past but to relate here and now in faith to the risen Jesus. The story of the man born blind (John 9:1–41), in particular, synthesizes the challenge of seeing the risen Christ with the eyes of faith and committing oneself to him.[18] In the text such episodes belong to the history of the pre-Easter Jesus, but they move beyond the past to put the timeless questions, Do you here and now experience in Jesus the One who is utterly true and good and brings us the face of God? If so, are you willing to become his disciple, and so "have life in his name" (John 20:31)?

The presence of the risen Christ permeates the Fourth Gospel, not least the story of the raising of Lazarus (John 11:1–53).[19] It is faith in Jesus as the resurrection and the life (John 11:25) that allows Martha, Mary, and other disciples to face and cope with death in their own families and the prospect of death themselves.

The risen and glorious Jesus remains intimately present in and among his community of friends (John 15:15). In the struggles and disappointments of their lives and ministry, experiences of the glorified Jesus will be actualized again and again when they hear the word proclaimed, "It is the Lord," and sit down at table with him (John 21:1–14).

Schneiders joins forces with the Fourth Gospel to remind us that the resurrection of Jesus is something much more than a matter of historical debate; it involves an existential issue, a spiritual challenge, and a personal relationship. In the haunting words with which Albert Schweitzer ended his 1906 classic:

> He comes to us as One unknown, without a name, as of old, by the lakeside, He came to those men who knew Him not. He speaks to us the same word: "Follow thou me!" and sets us to the tasks which He has to fulfil for our time. He commands. And to those who obey Him, whether they be wise or simple, He will reveal Himself in the toils, the conflicts, the sufferings which they shall pass through in His fellowship, and, as an ineffable mystery, they shall learn in their experience Who He is.[20]

In recent years the Western world has witnessed a growing interest in personal religious experience and various forms of spirituality, including alternative spiritualities not embodied in nor often addressed by traditional religion. Reading Schneiders's book on encountering Jesus and rereading what Schweitzer wrote a hundred years ago suggest that, unless we take up again the experiential reference of resurrection faith as proposed by John's Gospel, we will fail to provide what is urgently needed: a revival of that Easter spirituality that can provide life and life in abundance.

T. Peters et al., eds., *Resurrection: Theological and Scientific Assessments* (2002)

The fifth and final book to be considered among "the positive contributions" is a theological and scientific study of bodily resurrection produced by an international team.[21] In 1987, after a study week at the papal summer residence in Castel Gandolfo involving theologians, philosophers, and scientists, John Paul II wrote to the director of the Vatican Observatory encouraging such dialogue and raising a series of striking questions on how the findings of modern science might enrich our understanding of some Christian beliefs. What, for instance, are the implications of science for faith in the life of the world to come? *Resurrection: Theological and Scientific Assessments* responded to this question by bringing together distinguished scientists and theologians to explore, in the light of the laws of nature, belief in bodily resurrection.

Through a meeting in Heidelberg in 2001 and a series of conferences elsewhere, the three editors gathered a seminar team that represented research and teaching faculty in physics, biology, neuroscience, biblical studies, Egyptology, church history, philosophy, and systematic theology. The eighteen contributors (ten from Germany, six from the United States, and one each from England and South Africa) pursued the question, How should we assess the resurrection of Christ and our own future resurrection religiously and scientifically?

One of the editors, Ted Peters, not only skillfully introduces the book by summarizing the issues to be handled but also draws together in a conclusion some major conceptual challenges. How, for instance, can faith in the resurrection present (1) the nature of the risen body and (2) the preservation of personal identity in the resurrection? Peters quotes at the end the radiant lines of Rabindranath Tagore: "Death is not extinguishing the light; it is only putting out the lamp because the dawn has come."[22]

While the "Big Bang" cosmology seems to favor the biblical doctrine of the first creation, two major scientific scenarios for the future threaten the Easter promise of the new creation to come. In a masterly chapter, "Bodily Resurrection, Eschatology, and Scientific Cosmology," Robert Russell faces the two scenarios for cosmic death: the universe will either freeze itself out of existence or collapse back into a dense fireball. But we may not presume that the laws of nature that have governed the past and continue to govern the present will also necessarily govern the future. In the ongoing history of the cosmos, God is free to act in new ways and transform the laws that he has created. Christian hope rests on something radically new, which we have already glimpsed in the resurrection of Christ himself.

John Polkinghorne, familiar to many through his work on science and religion and for his win of the Templeton Prize in 2002, shows how the final hope of Christians cannot be truly maintained by those who play down the empty tomb and bodily resurrection. That hope involves, along with a personal and spiritual continuity, some element of material continuity between the pre-resurrection and the postresurrection Jesus. Those who disagree end up arguing for a "full" tomb, which means an "empty" Christian faith. They also have to reckon with the clear evidence that all four Gospels found it very important that the tomb of Jesus was empty. In some real sense, a genuine resurrection must be bodily. The message of the empty tomb also reinforces the sense of a redemption that enjoys a cosmic scope; in other words, the resurrection brings the well-founded expectation of a "new heaven" and a "new earth."

Among the many fine chapters in this book, let me also mention those by Brian Daley (on early Christian ways of articulating faith in the resurrection), Nancey Murphy (on the resurrection and personal identity), and Noreen Herzfeld. Herzfeld demolishes as science fiction the thesis of cybernetic immortality that reduces the human self to mere information patterns.

All in all, this valuable dialogue between scientists and theologians illuminates the Christian hope that the end of the world will bring the healing and transformation of our personal history and the renewal of all things. It translates into modern terms the link St. Paul had drawn in Romans 8 and 1 Corinthians 15 among (1) the resurrection of Jesus, (2) the bodily resurrection of human beings, and (3) the new creation of the whole universe.

The five books chosen for this sample of positive contributions to resurrection studies represent distinct fields: theology (Kelly), biblical studies (Wright), philosophy (Swinburne), spirituality (Schneiders), and science (Peters, Russell, and Welker). Before turning now to two works that fail to advance the cause of resurrection studies, let me first recall two learned but ambivalent books that provoke a "Yes, but" reaction.

BETWIXT AND BETWEEN

Dale Allison, *Resurrecting Jesus: The Earliest Christian Tradition and Its Interpreters (2005)*

After coauthoring a major commentary on Matthew's Gospel and publishing other significant works on the New Testament, Dale Allison long ago established himself as not only a notable, learned biblical scholar but also a provocatively independent interpreter. Not surprisingly he was chosen to write the entry on Jesus for the 2006 edition of the *Encyclopedia of Religion*.[23] His *Resurrecting Jesus*,[24] despite its title, also contains essays on other topics. But it belongs in this introduction, since it contains nearly two hundred pages on the Easter appearances, the empty tomb, and the whole question of historical research and belief in the resurrection.

After the death of Jesus, something happened to set the Christian movement going. What was it? After stating the orthodox belief that defends the reality of the empty tomb and the objectivity of Jesus' postresurrection appearances, Allison takes us through six rival theories (for example, hallucination, deliberate deception, and so forth), indicating their exponents and noting various difficulties that tell against these theories.[25] He skillfully groups together these hypotheses and alerts readers to their origins, import, and weaknesses.

Over specific questions connected with the resurrection, Allison engages with N. T. Wright and Richard Swinburne, as well as with me (mainly on the issue of bereavement experiences, of which I speak following). He probes Wright's claim that the resurrection of Jesus is the best historical explanation of the biblical evidence.[26] Like many others (including myself in *Easter Faith*),[27] Allison insists that we all evaluate questions about the resurrection from within our own worldviews. Background theories (about such matters as accepting or denying the possibility of special divine actions and, indeed, about the existence and nature of God) can be decisive.[28] Hence Allison "understands" why Swinburne, "in his recent defense of the resurrection, commences by first seeking to establish the existence of a certain sort of God and the likelihood of such a God communicating with and redeeming the human race."[29] Allison also joins with Swinburne in asking the question, Was Jesus someone who "should have been raised from the dead"?[30] In other words, when reflecting on the resurrection, we also need to assess the teaching and actions of Jesus. Allison draws together the two requirements: "If judgment about the resurrection cannot be isolated from one's worldview, it equally cannot be isolated from one's estimation of the pre-Easter Jesus."[31]

In some sections Allison shows himself at his incisive best: for instance, in an excursus eliminating the arguments of John Dominic Crossan (and others) and defending the historicity of the burial story and Joseph of Arimathea's central role in it.[32] He rightly observes that the historicity of the burial story always plays some role in evaluating the historicity of the empty tomb story. It is not that the former "proves" the latter. But, as Dan Kendall and I wrote, "For a critical assessment of the New Testament traditions about the empty tomb much depends on one's evaluation of the burial story."[33] Our article took aim at the questionable case Crossan made against the historicity of the burial story that we find in Mark 15:42–47. As Allison was to do, we concluded that Crossan "has done nothing to undermine its historical credibility, which remains accepted by very many biblical scholars from Bultmann to Fitzmyer and beyond."[34] As far as I know, my article with Kendall and then Allison's excursus are the only detailed examinations and rejections of the way Crossan dismissed the story of Jesus' historical burial by

Joseph of Arimathea. Given Allison's penchant for adequate and even extensive documentation, it is a little strange that he made no mention of the article I published with Kendall.

In general, Allison's documentation is breathtaking: 692 footnotes for his 178 pages on the resurrection, and many of these footnotes contain multiple references. Unlike some scholarly books, his index of names includes the authors of books and articles that appear only in the footnotes. Again unlike some modern scholars, Allison does not limit himself to recent years when citing writers who meet with his approval or disapproval. His exceptionally wide reading enables him to quote nineteenth-century or even earlier works that express with clarity, and at times elegance, notions that Allison endorses or deplores.

But, regrettably, when comparing the postresurrection appearances with reports of people experiencing their beloved dead and, in particular, alleged collective experiences of that kind, he introduces in an undifferentiated way references to a mass of literature, some of it unreliable popular publications, some it coming from parapsychologists of the nineteenth and twentieth centuries, and some of it not dealing, at least directly, with the matter in question, the experiences of *bereaved* persons.[35] It almost seems as if the sheer quantity of the references replaces the quality of the argument. Apropos of "reports of collective apparitions," Allison notes that they are "prominent in the literature of parapsychology but not in normal psychology."[36] That should have warned him against introducing, as he does, references to a number of long-discredited parapsychologists. Very many scholars, including professional psychologists, find only pseudo-science in the works of parapsychologists.

But let me come to the heart of my quarrel with Allison. He scrutinizes carefully the New Testament data about the appearances of the risen Jesus (or, as he and others call them, "christophanies"[37]) and the discovery of the empty tomb.[38] As regards the former, he states what "appears to be the facts": "Several people reported christophanies" and "Jesus ostensibly appeared on more than one occasion to more than one person."[39] Reviewing the arguments *against* and *for* the historicity of the empty tomb,[40] he tentatively concludes that the story of the empty tomb is "more likely to be history than legend."[41] As a biblical scholar, Allison feels himself at an impasse: historical reasoning cannot by itself decide the issue and produce certain conclusions about the alleged resurrection of Jesus. The evidence seems inconclusive. In Allison's words, "Historical criticism cannot judge the extraordinary experiences of the disciples to be true or false, or attribute them either to the Spirit of God *or to psychology.*"[42] Yet it is to psychology and reports of bereavement experiences that Allison himself turns.

Encouraged by his own experience of a deceased friend and by experiences of his deceased father that occurred to several members of his immediate family,[43] Allison moves to interpret the postresurrection appearances of Jesus as instances of such bereavement experiences. He presses "the similarities between reports of postmortem encounters with Jesus and visions of the recently departed"[44] and never pauses to review the dissimilarities.[45] He ignores, for instance, the way the bereaved who have enjoyed such visions do *not* claim that their dear departed are risen from the dead and that their graves have been found empty. Where the Easter narratives do not supply some alleged feature of the bereaved disciples' mourning experience (for instance, the anger that they "must" have felt), Allison supplies it himself: they "would not have been human if they had not felt anger and resentment toward those they held responsible for crucifying the man to whom they were devoted."[46]

Allison concludes his book with twelve pages on "the disciples and bereavement."[47] Some final words sum up his thesis: "Shortly after his death, the followers of Jesus saw him again, sensed his invisible presence, overcame their guilt by finding sense in his tragic end, idealized and internalized their teacher, and remembered his words and deeds."[48] This summary reduces all that happened after the death and burial of Jesus to what happened on the side of the bereaved disciples, to their subjective experience, and to their activity. They "saw him again" and "sensed his invisible presence," rather than the risen Jesus himself taking the initiative to "appear" to them (1 Cor 15:5–8). They "overcame their guilt by finding sense in his tragic end," rather than the risen Jesus and the Holy Spirit conveying to them forgiveness (for example, John 21:15–19) and insight (for example, John 16:13). They "idealized and internalized their teacher," rather than their risen Lord encountering them and enabling them to "live in him" and "abide" in his love (for example, John 15:1–10). They "remembered his words and deeds," rather than the Holy Spirit coming to "teach" them everything and "remind" them of all that Jesus had said and done (for example, John 14:25).

This one-sided privileging of the disciples' experience and activity runs dead contrary to the primacy of the divine initiative that pervasively shapes the Easter narratives and theology of Paul and the evangelists. It also leaves behind Allison's own theological tradition.[49] The leaders of the Protestant Reformation rightly highlighted God's prior activity in Christ and the Holy Spirit over anything that human beings, including the first disciples, might by themselves see, sense, overcome, find, idealize, internalize, and remember. In Allison's version of things, the coming to Easter faith and the foundation of the Christian Church looks very much like a human work. Allison properly recognizes that the findings of historical research, even that practiced by someone as expert as himself, are insufficient in themselves to bring him or anyone else to faith in the risen Jesus. Once or twice he recalls the setting in which such faith flourishes and grows, the Christian community at worship on Easter Sunday.[50] The Easter faith of generations of worshiping and practicing believers provides what Allison looks for: the experiential and religious "warrant" for accepting that God has raised Jesus from the dead.[51] A pity that he did not turn in that direction rather than use (or misuse?) psychology and engage in what amounts to a serious "reduction" of the New Testament's message of the resurrection. If one might adapt some words of St. Paul (1 Cor 15:54–55), "Resurrection has been swallowed up in psychology. Where, O resurrection, is your victory? Where, O resurrection is your sting?"

Allison begins with a moving "confession" in which he shows his longing to endorse a faith that holds that Jesus was truly resurrected from the dead.[52] But, bewitched by possible analogies with bereavement experiences, he ends with his own version of psychological reductionism. In the appendix of this book I explore the bereavement analogy, which is both like and unlike the Easter experiences of the first disciples.

Daniel Smith, *Revisiting the Empty Tomb: The Early History of Easter* (2010)

In a recent book Daniel Smith takes on a more limited project than Allison but practices a similar (yet not identical) form of reductionism: he draws not on modern psychological research into the experiences of bereaved persons but on a mass of "assumption" stories from Greco-Roman and Jewish sources that are supposed to unlock the "real" meaning of the empty tomb story in Mark 16:1–8.[53] Let us see some of the details.

Smith limits himself to (1) exploring the tradition of Jesus' empty tomb (as he reconstructs its religious background) and the tradition of the postresurrection appearances, and to (2) accounting for the differences of perspective between these two traditions. He explains the differences by arguing that the empty tomb tradition did not originate as a way of stating that Jesus had been raised from the dead but as a "disappearance" tradition or a way of expressing that Jesus had been assumed from the tomb into heaven and would be seen again at the Parousia. He associates the earliest form of the disappearance tradition as he finds it in Mark 16:1–8 with, for instance, the disappearance of Elijah in 2 Kings 2. One might raise a doubt here: Elijah, unlike Jesus, had not died and been buried before being assumed.

Smith has studied assiduously many ancient texts that seem relevant to his argument, along with modern authors who comment on them. He notes significant differences between Jewish accounts of assumption (through which Elijah and others escape from death by being "taken up" with a view to their eschatological functions to come) and Greco-Roman stories. The latter usually involved an apotheosis in which some hero was taken alive into the presence of the gods or else his spirit ascended while his dead body was buried.

Smith recognizes that we have something unique in the case of Jesus: Christian belief in him involved *both* resurrection *and* assumption/ascension (for example, Phil 2:9; 1 Tim 3:16). But he never acknowledges a key difficulty thrown up by the cases he cites of Heracles, Romulus, and other such heroes and heroines. Unlike Jesus (who lived and died shortly before the New Testament came into existence), these heroes and heroines were understood to have lived in a very distant past, and—one can reasonably maintain—most probably never existed at all. A similar difficulty also affects the way in which Elijah and other ancient biblical figures might be pressed into service as parallels for the traditions that arose about what happened to Jesus. Whatever one's verdict on the historical reality of these ancient figures, they certainly did not exist, as Jesus did, within living memory.

Smith does not refer to Richard Bauckham's *Jesus and the Eyewitnesses*,[54] a work that might have qualified his willingness to credit the New Testament authors and their sources with a high degree of "creativity." Bauckham recognizes that the period between Jesus and the final composition of Mark and the other Gospels was spanned by the continued presence and testimony of some who had participated in the history of Jesus: namely, such original eyewitnesses as Peter, Mary Magdalene, and the sons of Zebedee. They played a central and authoritative role in guiding the transmission of the traditions about Jesus and would not have tolerated "creative" innovations. Bauckham's historical reconstruction of the role of the original eyewitnesses does not allow for the kind of imaginative developments Smith alleges. Smith imagines Mark and/or his sources fashioning—on the basis of a saying from Q: "You will not see me" (Matt 23:39; Luke 13:35)—an empty tomb tradition that involved not resurrection from the dead but Jesus being taken up into heaven.

Dealing with this and other texts from the sayings-source used by Matthew and Luke, Smith (like many others) writes of those (in the plural) who compiled Q and to support his theory of an assumption speculates about their theology and community life. But surely it was entirely possible that it was only one individual who put Q together? After all, it was only one individual, Luke, who put together the third Gospel—not to mention the cases of other Gospels.

Smith offers various helpful insights when treating details in the Easter chapters of Luke and Matthew. But the arguments in favor of his central theme (that, as we move from Mark to John, we see a progressive accommodation of a disappearance/assumption

18

tradition, first found in Mark, to an appearance/resurrection tradition) do not convince.

First, the Greco-Roman material used to support Smith's
interpretation of Mark 16:1–8 as a disappearance/assumption
story seems largely irrelevant to a Gospel that most scholars interpret against a Jewish background. This evangelist sets the story of
Jesus within the framework of Jewish salvation history; his text is
permeated with quotation and echoes of the Jewish scriptures as
he goes about illustrating how Jesus fulfilled various Jewish
motifs. Greco-Roman motifs do not provide a key, let alone a
master key, for interpreting what Mark wrote either in his final
chapter or in the rest of his Gospel. Paul Danove, in a literary and
rhetorical study of this Gospel, finds little or no evidence of
Greco-Roman influence.[55] Years ago, in a paper that anticipated
the thesis of Smith's book, Adela Yarbro Collins "explained"
Mark's empty tomb story largely on the basis of Greco-Roman
ideas of a notable figure being translated into heaven. But she had
to admit that "it is hard to find" in Mark much influence from
Greco-Roman sources.[56]

Second, as we move from Mark to John, we find a progressive linking of two traditions. But it is one that links the tradition
of the discovery of the empty tomb (entailing Jesus' resurrection
from the dead, not his assumption into heaven) with the tradition of his appearances to individuals and groups.

Third, the central statement in the Easter chapter of Mark is
"He has been raised" from the dead (along with "He is going
before you into Galilee and there you will see him"), not "He has
been taken up into heaven" (and "You will see him again at the
Parousia"). Smith tries hard to explain (or explain away?) Mark's
text in favor of his disappearance/assumption thesis, but the arguments seem contrived. The language of assumption or ascension
turns up elsewhere in the New Testament (for example, Phil 2:9;
1 Tim 3:16), but not in Mark 16.

TWO BOOKS ON THE FRINGE

Geza Vermes, *The Resurrection* (2008)

Geza Vermes secured his place in the modern history of biblical studies through (1) *Jesus the Jew*, which prompted many Christian scholars to take seriously the Jewishness of Jesus and the Gospels, and (2) *The Complete Dead Sea Scrolls in English*,[57] which helped curb bizarre theories that misuse the scrolls. But *The Resurrection* fails on two accounts.[58] First, Vermes is a less reliable guide to Jewish views on the afterlife than are Jon Levenson and Alan Segal.[59] Second, Vermes's thesis, that Jesus "rose" only in the sense of being loved by his followers who "felt" that he was still with them, is no more convincing now than what his friend Paul Winter (whom Vermes cites on this point) wrote years ago.[60] According to this thesis, what happened after the death and burial of Jesus was merely a change in the disciples, not a new, transformed life for Jesus himself. In these terms, resurrection is not a fact about Jesus himself, but simply a fact about his disciples, past and present.

The basic problem with any such change-of-heart thesis is that it must deny the obvious meaning of what the New Testament authors repeatedly say, and say in a variety of ways. Let me take just one example, the formula of proclamation cited by Paul: "I handed on to you…what I in turn had received: that Christ *died* for our sins in accordance with the scriptures, and that he *was buried*, and that he *was raised*…, and that he *appeared* to Cephas [Peter], then to the twelve" (1 Cor 15:3–5). In this formula, Christ is the subject of all four verbs, the last two ("was raised" and "appeared") just as informative as the first two ("died" and "was buried"). In the case of both pairs of verbs, the second verb explains and supports what the first claims. We know that Christ died because he was buried; burial is a pointer to death. We know that Christ has been raised because he appeared bodily alive to a number of individuals and groups; dead persons do not appear like that.

For all the moving sincerity with which Vermes and his dead friend Winter have put forward their thesis, they must suppose that Paul and other New Testament writers, although seeming to claim some new fact about Jesus (his personal resurrection from death to new life), were using a deceptive form of discourse and merely talking about a fresh love that now possessed their hearts. They spoke only of themselves, not of a new event affecting Jesus himself.

En route to his epilogue ("Resurrection [Merely] in the Hearts of Men"), Vermes not only illustrates his rich historical knowledge but also makes judgments that invite challenge. First, while rightly observing that the theme of resurrection does not enjoy a central place in the preaching of Jesus, he ignores some texts that *imply* resurrection: "Many will come from east and west and will eat with Abraham and Isaac and Jacob in the kingdom of heaven…" (Matt 8:11). How will the patriarchs and those many others who join them at the final feast of the kingdom do so unless they have been raised from the dead? The longest passage explicitly concerned with resurrection comes in Jesus' debate with some Sadducees (Mark 12:18–27). Vermes asserts that "most critical commentators rightly assume" that this story is "inauthentic" and "probably reflects by anticipation" later conflicts between Sadducees and Christians.[61] Sampling some critical commentators on Mark, I found that, while Adela Yarbro Collins agrees with Vermes, John Donahue, Joel Marcus, John Meier, and Francis Moloney hold that the dispute on resurrection goes back in its substance to the historical ministry of Jesus. In any case all five scholars argue for their position and do not simply assume that the passage is authentic or inauthentic.[62]

Vermes spends a chapter on the predictions made by Jesus about his coming death and resurrection and concludes that they are "authentic" (he meant to write "inauthentic").[63] In so joining Rudolf Bultmann and dismissing the historicity of the three predictions in Mark (8:31; 9:31; 10:33–34) as prophecies after the event, Vermes fails to notice that one early and pervasive Christian interpretation of Jesus' death is missing. It is *not* stated that "the Son of Man must suffer and be killed *for us and for our sins* and then rise again." Nor do these three predictions include one enormously important detail: the killing by crucifixion. These omissions support the (now widely held) view that the passion predictions are by no means free inventions and contain an historical kernel:

Jesus anticipated his violent death and hoped for a divine vindication through resurrection.

When discussing a resurrection text from late in the first century, John 6:54 ("Those who eat my flesh and drink my blood have eternal life, and I will raise them up on the last day"), Vermes speaks of "eating of blood" (surely it should be "drinking of blood"?), dismisses this as a "cannibalistic allegory" (introduced by a Gentile Christian), and appeals to a council held in Jerusalem around 50 CE and its injunction about "abstaining…from blood" (Acts 15:20).[64] But Vermes says nothing about a letter from the 50s in which Paul, a Jewish Christian *par excellence*, provides the earliest account of the Eucharist and writes of "drinking" the Lord's "blood" (1 Cor 11:25–26).

For an historical account of the resurrection in the New Testament, it is better to read N. T. Wright's *The Resurrection of the Son of God* (dismissed by Vermes as "faith wrapped in scholarship"[65]) and query the claim made on the dust jacket that Vermes has been "the greatest Jesus scholar of his generation." Such praise belongs rather to Raymond Brown, John Meier, or others.

Philip Pullman, *The Good Man Jesus and the Scoundrel Christ* (2010)

Every year or so sensationalist books debunking the resurrection of Jesus are published. They often make a great splash but normally leave hardly a ripple. Some of them rehash an old theory about Jesus being taken down alive from the cross. They differ by dispatching him to continue his life in various parts of the world, like France, Rome, the Dead Sea Community, or India. Apropos of the Indian connection, with his 1894 book, *The Unknown Life of Jesus Christ*, Nicolas Notovitch fashioned the first part of the legend: Jesus, he alleged, spent some preministry years in India.[66] The second half of the legend was created by Mirza Ghulam Ahmad; in an 1899 work (in Urdu) he asserted that Jesus was saved from the cross, went to Kashmir, and died there at the age of 120 in Srinagar, where tourists are still shown his "grave." Without a shred of evidence in its support, this whole story was simply made up, spread among a gullible public, and is due to be rehashed any year now.

Let me, however, speak of a book that was the talk of the town at Easter 2010 and eliminated the resurrection of Jesus as a case of deliberate deception: Philip Pullman's *The Good Man Jesus and the Scoundrel Christ*.[67] Pullman invests Jesus with a twin called "Christ" who becomes more and more alienated from his brother and led astray by a mysterious, demonic "stranger." Eventually Christ plays the part of Judas in being paid to lead a guard to Jesus and identify him with a kiss. In Pullman's version, Christ does not then give way to remorse but agrees to do something worse by masquerading as his dead brother and deceiving people into thinking that Jesus has risen from the dead. After Jesus has been buried by Joseph of Arimathea and Nicodemus, "the stranger" organizes several men to remove the body of Jesus during the night of Saturday/Sunday. He persuades Christ to return the next morning and play the part of the risen Jesus.

Mary Magdalene, who has discovered the tomb to be open and empty, then meets and talks with the twin brother of the dead Jesus. She thinks she has seen the risen Jesus and runs to announce the wonderful news to the other disciples. Later the same day, the disciples set off as a group for a village called Emmaus. Christ joins them on the road. They reach the village at night and invite him to join them for a meal. A disciple called Cleopas brings a lamp close to the face of Christ and takes him to be the risen Jesus. Christ plays out the deception and encourages the disciples to identify him as his twin brother raised from the dead.[68]

Many of those who reviewed Pullman's book found little plausibility in the way he explains the empty tomb and the Easter appearances. Right from New Testament times, skeptics have repeatedly accounted for the emptiness of Jesus' tomb by alleging that his body had been removed by friend or foe (for example, Matt 28:11–15). The only new twist added by Pullman comes when he attributes the removal of the corpse to a sinister "stranger" who is intent on creating organized Christianity.

As regards the postresurrection situation presented by Paul and the Gospels, Pullman ignores the appearances of the risen Jesus in Galilee (Matt 28:16–20; John 21; and implied by Mark

16:7), the appearance to Peter (1 Cor 15:5; Luke 24:34), the appearance to "more than five hundred" disciples (1 Cor 15:6), the appearance to James and then to "all the apostles"(1 Cor 15:7), and the appearance to Paul (1 Cor 9:1; 15:8; Gal 1:12,15–16; Acts 9; 22; 26). Pullman selects the appearance to Mary Magdalene (John 20:11–19) and the Emmaus story (Luke 24:13–35) and rewrites them. He not only remains silent about so much testimony to postresurrection appearances but also leaves us with a strange puzzle. Could the early Christian witnesses have lived such heroic lives and spread the message of Jesus with so much effective devotion if all that lay behind their missionary outreach were two episodes in which first a credulous woman (Mary Magdalene) and then a group (the disciples at Emmaus) mistook the identity of someone they met?

Pullman's version of what happened after the death and burial of Jesus is so contrived and plays so fast and loose with the evidence that it loses even its superficial plausibility. At the end, does he turn the greatest story ever told into the greatest puzzle ever imagined? The reconstruction proposed by Pullman, the body of Jesus being spirited away and then one individual and one group misidentifying his twin as if he were Jesus risen from the dead, is historically speaking quite implausible. To be sure, Pullman has written a work of historical fiction. But, by its nature, *historical* fiction should be plausible, even and especially from an historical point of view.

History shows us an *effect*, the propagation of the Christian message and community throughout the world, a propagation that took place despite ruthless persecutions and other terrible setbacks. If Christ did not personally rise from the dead, what else might have *caused* this visible and public effect in world history, the development and massive presence of the Christian religion? Pullman asks us to believe that this effect was brought about by (1) fraud (namely, the theft of Jesus' body), and (2) a mistaken identification, deliberately provoked by a twin of Jesus masquerading as his dead brother brought back to life. That such an odd turn of events was sufficient to cause the rise and spread of Christianity will convince only the credulous and those who cannot imagine that there is a God who raised Jesus from the dead and gave him a new and glorious life.

Such then are nine works that have been published in the first decade of the twenty-first century and that represent current writing on the resurrection. Against this background, I now turn to what I want to say about Easter faith, both biblically and theologically.

PART I

THE BIBLICAL TESTIMONY

Chapter 1

OUR WORLDVIEWS AND THE LIFE AND DEATH OF JESUS

Before moving to examine directly the resurrection of Jesus, I pause and respond, at least briefly, to two major issues. What background theories about the existence and nature of God, human beings, and their universe affect our thinking and the positions we reach on the resurrection? How might worldviews decisively shape our judgments about what happened to Jesus? Second, why and how did the teaching and activity of Jesus lead to his crucifixion? What qualified him as someone who should be raised by God to a new and transformed life?

BACKGROUND THEORIES

The worldviews that come into play and filter our historical judgment when reflecting on the resurrection of Jesus are large and complex. A full treatment of this topic would require an entire book. I illustrate here the role of worldviews or background theories by offering three examples: (1) the issue of special divine activity; (2) the presence of presuppositions in historical research; and (3) the role of evidence in making personal relationships.

Special Divine Activity

Those who hold that God has created the world but subsequently has never done (and never does) anything special have excluded in advance the possibility of Jesus' resurrection from the dead. Having made the universe with its physical laws, God, they argue, always respects those laws and never acts in ways that suspend or override them. Hence, when discussing the resurrection and miraculous deeds reported by the New Testament, they either dismiss them as legendary accretions that appeal only to the credulous or interpret them in ways that omit any special divine activity. Such a mindset could never accept that the tomb of Jesus was found to be empty because God had raised him to a final life of glory.[1] The "scientific" picture of the world endorsed by Gerd Lüdemann, for instance, excludes the miraculous and so rules out in advance the possibility of a special divine action that brought about Jesus' rising from the tomb.[2]

But should one accept such a ban on special divine activity and view the universe as a closed continuum of causes and effects over which God exercises no control? Does this ban come from a flawed philosophy about the world as a rigidly uniform system? Does it come from "scientism" rather than from science? The all-powerful, omnipresent God from whom the created world, its laws, and their operations depend from moment to moment can presumably override at times such laws for very good reasons, which may not, or may not yet, be clear to us. While usually respecting the natural order of the world and its functioning (and so not indulging in frequent exceptions to the laws of creation), God is not blocked from performing such special or even unique actions as that of raising Jesus from the dead. In such cases, God acts in ways that are qualitatively distinct and different from the ordinary divine "work" of creating and sustaining the world.

Before examining the case of God possibly raising Jesus from the dead, we need to check our view of divine activity, including the possibility of special or even unique divine acts. Here Denis Edwards offers valuable leadership by reflecting on how God acts. Edwards's well-thought-out "background theory," which draws on philosophy, science, and theology to present an account of divine activity, allows him to conclude that the resurrection of Jesus gives meaning and direction to the whole universe, to all its laws, and to its future.[3]

Historical Knowledge

Before scrutinizing in detail any historical evidence in support of Jesus' resurrection from the dead, we consider the general nature of knowledge provided by historical evidence and its limits. What is involved when human beings know things, above all in the area of history? In this context the background theory of Lüdemann exposes itself to serious criticism. In a "ruthlessly honest quest for truth," he wants to "take an undistorted look" at the resurrection, one that "will look in a purely historical and empirical way at the historical context of the testimonies to the resurrection." Inevitably, those he disagrees with tend to be charged with "dogmatism," "prejudice," and even with knowing "a priori what needs to be proved."[4]

Lüdemann's view of human knowledge exemplifies that naïve realism criticized by Bernard Lonergan and others for presuming knowledge to be merely a matter of taking "an honest look." The profession of ruthless, undistorted honesty repeats what many scholars have long ago challenged: namely, the claim to make a purely historical, neutral, and "scientific" approach to some controversial issue or person from the past, as if the resurrection of Christ were something "merely" historical to be kept at arm's length and weighed up dispassionately.

Standing head and shoulders above Lüdemann, Dale Allison, as we saw in the introduction, recognizes that all biblical and historical research takes place on the basis of a whole network of prior judgments and elaborate systems for evaluating and explaining what is "real." There is no such thing as a view from nowhere or research with no presuppositions. It is neither desirable nor even possible to undertake such research. Lüdemann, however, alleges that he is pursuing a totally honest inquiry and doing something that others fail to do: he looks without any bias at the evidence, or rather at the evidence that he allows to count. Any debate with him should begin with his flawed background theories about knowledge in general and historical knowledge in particular.

What I missed in the case of Allison, however, was a clearer sense of the way in which historical conclusions do not fall merely into two categories: historically certain (for example, the Gettysburg speech of President Abraham Lincoln) and the indeterminate (for example, for Allison and others, the discovery of the empty tomb), in which case one is always justified in hesitating to embrace any conclusion. Surely one should recognize the huge number of historical conclusions that responsible scholars firmly hold even if they do not allege that they reach the status of utter certainty? Thus J. N. D. Kelly marshaled evidence to draw the conclusion that what we know as the Nicene-Constantinopolitan Creed (used by all Christians at the Eucharist) does in fact come from the First Council of Constantinople (381 CE).[5] There had been considerable diversity of views on this matter. That did not lead Kelly to conclude that no one really knows with certainty where the creed came from and how it fell into its final shape.

Historical studies teem with such examples of leading scholars making a solidly probable case and reaching firm conclusions that they believe do better justice to the evidence currently available. Although they cannot pretend to have reached the kind of utter certainty that discounts the possibility that further evidence might come to light and qualify or even disprove their conclusion, they continually refuse to throw up their hands and declare that the issue in which they are interested is "indeterminate." One needs to recognize the range of possibilities for conclusions in historical research: from the utterly certain, through the highly probable, the solidly probable, the probable, and various shades of possibility, right down to the genuinely indeterminate. Apropos of the empty tomb, for instance, has Allison been too stringent in imposing conditions that can rarely be satisfied, especially when we are dealing with events or alleged events of two thousand years ago?[6]

In the city where I live, a courier service for parcels advertises itself as "delivering certainty." The firm uses *certainty* in the sense of "may be relied on." They deliver punctually and can be trusted not to lose or misdirect any parcels. The firm does not claim to deliver certainty in the sense of always providing some "undoubted fact" that should command our unqualified assent: that is to say, an utter certainty that allows us to discount the possibility of further evidence ever emerging that would challenge, seriously modify, or even disprove some fact or conclusion that we have accepted. Historical investigation does not always "deliver certainty" in that sense, by providing conclusions that are not only undoubted but also can never be doubted. *Delivering probability*, even high probability, describes more accurately the business of competent historians.

Personal Relationships

A third area for which background theories seem highly relevant for a study of the resurrection can be put this way: How far does historical evidence contribute to the making or unmaking of personal relationships? Can historical investigation alone and by itself, on the one hand, first create faith in a person, or, on the other hand, undermine such faith?

Here we need to insist that accepting the resurrection of Jesus from the dead involves entering into a personal relationship with him. It would be odd, to the point of bizarre, if someone were to allege, "Yes, I genuinely and sincerely accept that God raised Jesus from the dead, but that makes no difference whatsoever about what I do with my life or with what I hope for personally. His resurrection is a fact to which I give my assent, but it is not a fact that involves my becoming and remaining his follower." Such a position would seem extraordinarily inconsistent: professing the resurrection in theory yet not allowing that profession in practice to flower in a personal commitment to Jesus.

Entering into personal relationships typically involves going beyond the evidence, as when people pledge themselves to each other in the lifelong commitment of marriage. Background checks into the previous activities and history of someone could never provide the necessary and sufficient grounds for such a profound commitment. In fact, most people would, I believe, find it insulting even to think of founding loving commitments on the basis of background checks. We do not verify and justify our faith in another person simply on the grounds of historical investigation and rational argument.

Something like that comes into play when believers give their allegiance to the risen Jesus, whom they experience as invisibly, yet truly, present in their lives. When they come to faith in Jesus by accepting the external testimony of the Christian community to the crucified and resurrected Jesus and the internal promptings of the Holy Spirit, they are taken beyond the evidence—specifically, the mere historical evidence. They do not base belief in the resurrection—that is to say, in the risen Jesus—on historical grounds alone. Their faith is not irrational, but it is not reducible to reason.[7]

The analogy I have drawn from engagement and marriage also suggests the mutual interaction between knowing and loving. We are dealing with a two-way street. While knowledge makes it possible to love someone, such knowledge is also facilitated by love. As St. Augustine of Hippo remarked, *"nemo nisi per amicitiam cognoscitur"* (*De diversis questionibus*, 83.71.3), which could be unpacked and paraphrased as "You need to be a friend of someone before you truly know him or her." We see with our hearts and not merely with our heads; the eyes of love allow us to discern and know what is truly there.

This principle holds good of believers. They commit themselves to Jesus in loving faith because they know something of him and his history. Yet at the same time they acknowledge the historical truth of Jesus and see meaning in his history, because they love him and find in him the object of their deepest hopes and desires. In a way that resembles our relationship with cherished relatives and friends, we love Jesus because we know him, and we also know him because we love him.

We could press on to expound other background theories that can affect our reflections on Christ's resurrection: for instance, the nature of *analogy* and the need to distinguish between close (and useful) analogies and more remote (and less helpful) analogies. Do the experiences of Christian (and other) mystics throw light, for example, on the nature of the appearances of the risen Jesus?[8] But enough has been said to establish the decisive role for the study of the resurrection played by items that make up our worldviews.

Our study of Jesus' resurrection also involves first recalling some features of his life and death. Who was it that God raised from the dead? Why was this "appropriate"?

LIFE AND DEATH OF JESUS

Proclaiming the message "God has raised the crucified Jesus to new life" should prompt three initial questions: (1) Who was this Jesus during his lifetime? (2) How did he come to be executed? (3) What did he anticipate would be achieved through his violent death? In the introduction we saw that Swinburne, like very many others before him, understands the resurrection as God's vindication of Jesus, the divine signature on the life, teaching, and death of Jesus. In other words, God endorsed the life of Jesus, the values he embodied, and the identity he claimed for himself. If God raised Jesus because of who he was and what he did, we need to offer some account of who Jesus was and what he did.

The Preaching of Jesus

When drawing here and later on the Gospels, I use the widely accepted scheme of *three stages* in the transmission of testimony to Jesus' deeds and words: (1) the initial stage during his earthly life when his disciples spoke about him, quoted his teaching, and began interpreting his identity and mission; (2) the handing on by word of mouth or in writing (including the use of "notebooks") of testimony about him after his death and resurrection; and (3) the authorial work of the four evangelists later in the first century. One can use such criteria as multiple (independent) witness in arguing that testimony to particular words and deeds derives substantially from the first stage: that is to say, from the history of Jesus himself. When I draw on the Gospels, I indicate whether I understand some passage to testify to what Jesus said or did at stage 1, or whether the passage seems to illustrate rather what a particular Gospel writer at stage 3 (and/or the tradition behind him at stage 2) understood about Jesus' work and identity. I cannot stop to justify my reasons for holding some deed or saying to have originated historically in what Jesus said or did. But I cite only examples for which such justification is available from commentators.[9]

Few claims are more historically certain about Jesus than that he proclaimed a message that was rare in first-century Judaism (and for that matter would be rare in the New Testament outside the Synoptic Gospels): the kingdom or royal reign of God. He announced that "the time is fulfilled, and the kingdom of God has come near; repent, and believe in the good news" (Mark 1:14–15). The "time" that is fulfilled, "the kingdom" that has come near, and "the good news" that is to be believed may seem less than fully personal. But the very next episode in Mark's narrative provides the fully personal element. Jesus begins to call to individuals, "Follow me" (Mark 1:17).

In proclaiming the kingdom as already *present* (for example, Matt 12:28 = Luke 11:20; Luke 17:20–21) or as to come in the *future* (for example, Matt 6:10 = Luke 11:2; Mark 9:1), Jesus talked of God as Lord of the world and of God's decisive action in liberating sinful men and women from the grip of evil and giving them a new and final age of salvation. The telling of parables and the performing of miracles characterized Jesus' work for the kingdom. Both in his preaching and in his miraculous deeds, Jesus presented himself as inseparably connected with the divine rule that was breaking into the world. In his person and presence, God's rule had come and was coming. He was "the kingdom in person," as the third-century Christian writer Origen put it.[10]

Jesus was aware of fulfilling a (1) prophetic (for example, Mark 6:4; Luke 13:33) and (2) messianic mission. Claim 1 is less controversial, but many have challenged claim 2. At times, admittedly, Jesus seems to have taken his distance from talk of being "the Messiah" or anointed and promised deliverer sent by God (for example, Mark 8:27–31). But it is quite implausible to argue that Jesus was oblivious of performing a messianic mission. He gave some grounds for being perceived to have made such a claim. Otherwise it is very difficult to account both for the charge against him of being a messianic pretender (for example, Mark 14:51; 15:2,26) and for the ease with which his followers began calling him "the Christ" immediately after his death and resurrection. He had disclosed messianic consciousness by a key saying about his miraculous activity (Matt 11:2–6 = Luke 7:18–23) and implied something about himself when contrasting "mere" Davidic descent with the higher status of being the Messiah (Mark 12:35–37).

But there was more to his self-disclosure than that. At times he went beyond the prophetic (or messianic) "I was sent" to say

"I came" or "I have come." On the one hand, he was remembered as having taken a small child in his arms and declaring, "Whoever welcomes one such child in my name welcomes me, and whoever welcomes me welcomes not me but him who *sent* me" (Mark 9:36–37; italics mine). In a parable about the wicked tenants of a vineyard, Jesus obliquely referred to himself as "the son" who had finally been *sent* (Mark 12:6). Yet, on the other hand, he sometimes went beyond the normal prophetic self-presentation "I was sent" to affirm "I came": "I have come to call not the righteous but sinners" (Mark 2:17); "I came to bring fire to the earth, and how I wish it were already kindled!" (Luke 12:49).

This "coming" language is also connected with another, enigmatic self-designation: "The Son of Man came not to be served but to serve…" (Mark 10:45). Occasionally the language of "coming" and "sending" is combined (for example, Luke 13:34–35). Without insisting that every "sending" and "coming" saying derives from the historical Jesus, we can argue that they are numerous enough to support the conclusion that he understood his mission both as the Son sent by the Father and as the One who had come from heaven to earth. The Jewish prophets disclosed their sense of having been sent by God but never purported to come in their own name. Furthermore, they never presented themselves as "sons of God," nor were they ever called that. None of them ever explained his mission as a personal initiative, "I have come."

Over and above such sayings, Jesus showed that he so identified himself with the message of God's kingdom that those who responded positively to this message *committed themselves to him* as disciples. To accept the coming rule of God was to become a follower of Jesus. To be saved through the kingdom was to be saved through Jesus. With authority Jesus encouraged men and women to break normal family ties and join him in the service of the kingdom (for example, Mark 10:28–31; Luke 8:1–3). By relativizing in his own name family roles and relationships, Jesus was scandalously at odds with the expectations of his and other societies. All of this raised the question, Who did Jesus think he was if he made such personal claims?

Either by what he said or by what he did (or both), Jesus claimed authority (1) over the observance of the Sabbath (for example, Mark 2:23–28), (2) over various regulations of the Torah, and (3) over the Temple (for example, Mark 11:15–17)—three divinely authorized channels of salvation. Apropos of (1), when setting priorities for Sabbath observance, Jesus taught on his own authority and not out of traditional sources of authority. (2) While Jesus never aimed at abrogating or annulling the Mosaic Law as a whole, he took it upon himself not only to criticize the oral law for running counter to basic human obligations (Mark 7:10–12) but also to set aside the written law on such matters as retribution, divorce, and food (Matt 5:21–48; Mark 7:15,19; 10:2–12). For instance, he "absolutely forbade divorce and branded divorce and remarriage as the sin of adultery." Here Jesus rejected something "accepted and regulated by the Torah."[11] This was to make a startling claim to a personal authority that put him on a par with the divine Lord who had prescribed for these matters through Moses. We might state what was at stake as follows: "Of old it was said to you by God speaking through Moses, but I say to you." After examining teaching concerned with the Sabbath, divorce, food laws, and Jesus' abolition of oath taking, John Meier concludes about Jesus and his claims: "he and he alone" could "tell Israel how to interpret God's law as befits members of the kingdom." Jesus taught with his own authority, claiming to "know directly and intuitively what God's will is."[12]

(3) Apropos of the Temple and a key saying about the Temple, it is hard to establish the original form of what Jesus said (Mark 14:57–59; Acts 6:13–14). But it involved some claim that his mission was to introduce, between God and the chosen people, a new relationship that would supplant the central place of their current relationship, the Temple in Jerusalem.[13]

Seemingly on a level with Jesus' astonishing assertion of personal authority over the sacred day, the divine law, and the central place for experiencing God's presence was his willingness to dispense with the divinely established channels for the forgiveness of sins (sacrificial offerings in the Temple and the mediation of priestly authorities) and to take God's role by forgiving sins in his own name. He did this by word (for example, Mark 2:1–11; Luke 7:47–49) and by table fellowship with sinners (for example, Luke 15:1–2).

All in all, Jesus claimed or at least implied a personal authority that should be described as putting himself on a par with God.
Since he gave such an impression during his ministry, one can
understand why members of the Sanhedrin charged him with
blasphemy. They feared that he was not merely a false prophet but
was even usurping divine prerogatives (Mark 14:64).

These (explicit and implicit) personal claims made by Jesus
also involved his uniquely authoritative role in bringing others to
share in the *final reign* of God. Using his enigmatic self-designation
as Son of Man, he asserted that the coming salvation of human
beings depended upon their relationship to him: "I tell you,
everyone who acknowledges me before others, the Son of Man
also will acknowledge before the angels of God; but whoever
denies me before others will be denied before the angels of God"
(Luke 12:8–9).[14] Jesus identified himself with the Son of Man
who was to come "with the clouds of heaven" (Mark 14:62) and
"with great power and glory" (Mark 13:26), who would "send out
the angels and gather his elect" (Mark 13:27), and who, sitting
upon "his throne of glory" (Matt 19:28; 25:31), was to judge all
the nations (Matt 25:31–46). This language about the coming Son
of Man represented Jesus acting in a final scenario of human salvation as supremely authoritative—in fact, as divine judge.

Finally, knowing and naming God in a new way, as "Abba"
("Father dear" or even "Daddy"), formed a striking feature of Jesus'
message of the kingdom. Jesus showed that he personally experienced a unique divine sonship (for example, Matt 11:25–27), a filial relationship that gave him the right to invite others to share in
the life-giving fatherhood of God (for example, Matt 6:9; Luke
11:2). Jesus preached the kingdom of God, but at the heart of this
kingdom was the divine "Abba," not the divine "King."[15]

These (explicit and implicit) claims about who he was and
what he was doing for human beings obviously posed the question, Was all this true? If it was, it clearly pointed to him as someone who deserved to be raised by God. Yet two further questions
are also relevant: How and why did Jesus get himself into the situation of being crucified? Did he expect anything to come about
through his violent death?

The Opposition to Jesus

The single-minded devotion with which Jesus proclaimed the kingdom, the "scandalous" claims he made about his own identity, and the loving freedom with which he reached out to the sinful and suffering led him into conflict with groups of Pharisees, Sadducees, and others. As Mark tells the story, that opposition showed itself from the start (Mark 2:1–3:6). At the end, some highly placed Sadducees joined forces with one of Jesus' disciples (Judas Iscariot) and Pontius Pilate, the Roman governor of Judea, Samaria, and Idumea (26–36 CE), to bring about the crucifixion.

Undoubtedly the religious authorities in Jerusalem took Jesus' entry into Jerusalem (with its perceived messianic significance) and cleansing of the Temple to be major challenges to the way they understood faith and conducted affairs at the heart of Jewish life. Add too the dramatic "sign" of Lazarus's resurrection from the dead (John 11), which had a profound impact on the Jerusalem public and prompted the Sanhedrin, the Jewish council, presided over by the high priest Caiaphas, to proceed with the arrest of Jesus and his execution (John 11:45–57).

We can add a fourth episode that fueled official hostility to Jesus in the days leading up to his death: the messianic anointing that expressed Jesus' subversive claim to kingship (Mark 14:3–9; John 12:1–8). Judas apparently reported the episode of the anointing to the chief priests (Mark 14:10–11), who had already decided to arrest Jesus and have him killed (Mark 14:1–2). The messianic anointing must have seemed the last straw to the religious authorities. They may well have feared that Jesus and his disciples were dangerously intent on a messianic uprising. The anointing at Bethany also led Judas, whatever the motives for his final defection, to make his definitive break with Jesus. Thus the anointing provided "both added cause for the chief priests to take swift action against Jesus and also the means to do so in the shape of Judas' offer."[16] They had clinching motivation for their decision and further evidence of Jesus' seditious behavior. All this supported the case they could present to Pilate about Jesus' challenge to Roman rule: Jesus was claiming to be the king of the Jews and

40

planning an uprising. The sequence of events reported by John may well have been correct: first, the messianic anointing in Bethany and then, the very next day, Jesus' messianic entry into Jerusalem (John 12:12–15). In the politically charged atmosphere of Jerusalem, the sequence of those two episodes strengthened the resolve of the chief priests to do away with Jesus.[17]

How did Jesus face his coming death? At some point in his ministry, and not simply at the very end, Jesus began to anticipate his own violent death. He referred to himself as "the bridegroom" whose presence gave joy to the wedding guests and the groom's close attendants. But, as he ominously added, the bridegroom would be "taken away" from them. This picture of himself as a tragic bridegroom alluded to his violent end (Mark 2:18–20).

Jesus saw his ministry as standing, at least partially, in continuity with the prophets, right down to John the Baptist, the prophetic precursor from whom he received baptism. In his prophetic role Jesus had a premonition that he would inevitably die a martyr's death and apparently expected that to happen in Jerusalem, the city that "kills the prophets and stones those who are sent to it" (Luke 13:33–34; see 11:47, 49–51). Not only past history but also contemporary events had their lessons to teach. The execution of John, whose prophetic activity directly prepared the way for the ministry of Jesus, showed how perilous such radical religious activity was in the Palestine of those days. Jesus would have been remarkably naïve not to have recognized the danger.

In this connection we should cite the Parable of the Vineyard and the Tenants (Mark 12:1–12), which came from a controversy between Jesus and some religious leaders. It was the only parable in which Jesus spoke clearly of his own mission.[18] What does the parable indicate about Jesus' sense of his coming end? The "servants" stood for the prophets who, on God's behalf, had over the centuries confronted the religious and political leaders of Israel. Jesus thought of himself as "the son" through whom "the owner of the vineyard" made a final bid to the "tenant farmers," the leaders of Israel. But a violent death overtook the son—a clear pointer to the fate that Jesus anticipated for himself. Who were the "others" to whom the property was to be given and not merely leased? Seemingly they were the Jewish disciples of Jesus and the

Gentiles, who together would form the reconstituted Israel. Yet the identity of the beneficiaries was not clarified, nor did any resurrection from the dead appear as the aftermath of the violent death suffered by the son.

The major conclusions we draw should be limited to four. First, Jesus understood himself to be in person the climax of God's dealings with the chosen people. Second, he found himself in dangerous controversy with some of the leaders of Israel. Third, the outcome of that unflinching conflict would be Jesus' violent death, the nature of which was not specified. Fourth, there would be a dramatic change in God's relationship with his vineyard, Israel.

Even before reporting the Parable of the Vineyard and the Tenants, Mark has inserted three predictions in which Jesus announced the suffering and death of "the Son of Man" and his subsequent vindication through resurrection (Mark 8:31; 9:31; 10:33–34). Frequently these predictions have been dismissed as "prophecies after the event," created by early Christians who wanted to show that the death of Jesus belonged to the divine plan. To be sure, some precise details of Jesus' passion, especially those in the third prediction (for example, about being "mocked," "spat upon," and "scourged") look like items that were later added to that prediction because of episodes that occurred in the course of the passion. Nevertheless, even if the predictions were to some extent embellished during the post-Easter tradition, their essential content could well derive from the earthly Jesus. In particular, the second passion prediction, the shortest and the vaguest of the three, seems likely to be an authentic saying: "The Son of Man is to be betrayed into human hands, and they will kill him, and three days after being killed, he will rise again" (Mark 9:31).[19]

Let us pull matters together. We can reasonably conclude that (at least to the core group of his disciples) Jesus announced his coming death and expressed his hope that God would quickly or "in a short time" (in that less precise, biblical sense of "after three days") vindicate him through resurrection. Jesus contrasted a human verdict passed on him with a divine verdict passed on him. A rejection on the human side would be reversed by a resurrection on the divine side. But what did Jesus make of the value *for others* of his impending death? What did Jesus expect that his fate would bring to others, even to the whole human race?

The Expectations of Jesus

The theme of God's kingdom can help us appreciate how Jesus understood his death. From the outset he announced the divine rule to be at hand. He saw suffering and persecution as characterizing the coming of that kingdom (for example, in the Beatitudes and the concluding petition of the Lord's Prayer [Matt 6:13]). The message of the kingdom involved a period of crisis and distress that would move toward "the day of the Son of Man" (Mark 13), the restoration of Israel (Matt 19:28), the banquet of the saved (Luke 14:15–24),[20] and the salvation of the nations (Matt 8:11–12). Thus the arrest, trial, and crucifixion of Jesus dramatized the very thing that totally engaged Jesus: the rule of God that was to come through a time of ordeal.

At the Last Supper Jesus linked his imminent death with the divine kingdom: "Truly I tell you, I will never again drink of the fruit of the vine until that day when I drink it new in the kingdom of God" (Mark 14:25).[21] It is widely agreed that this text derives from something Jesus himself said during his last meal with his friends. Death is approaching; he will have no occasion again to have a festal meal of any kind. But after his death God will vindicate the cause of Jesus by fully establishing the divine kingdom. Jesus looked forward with hope to the time when he would be seated at the final banquet—obviously with others at his side—and drink "the fruit of the vine." This closing kingdom saying, a saying that connects the kingdom with his coming death, should be interpreted in the light of what Jesus had already said.

Jesus had continually preached the future reign of God, which would be *the* saving event for all human beings. By linking his approaching death with the coming kingdom, Jesus implicitly interpreted his death as salvific for all. Through his preaching he had promised salvation for human beings at large.[22] Now he associated his death with that future salvation and communion at the final banquet in the coming kingdom of God. The kingdom saying at the Last Supper may be laconic. But it was charged with meaning through what Jesus had already said about the coming reign of God.

It is hardly surprising that Jesus made such a positive integration between the coming kingdom and his death. The message about the divine reign was inseparable from the person of Jesus. This essential connection between the message of Jesus and his person meant that the vindication of his person in and beyond death entailed the vindication of God's kingdom and vice versa— a vindication that entailed salvation for all humanity.

The strongest evidence for Jesus' own understanding of his coming death, its saving import, and its "beneficiaries" comes from the Last Supper and the institution of the Eucharist.[23] The breaking of the bread, identified as his body, and the pouring of the wine, identified as his blood, imaged forth the sacrificial surrender of his life, the action of total self-giving that was to take place in his violent death. Clearly those followers present at the Last Supper shared in his body that was being given up to death and in his blood that would be shed. They were invited to participate in Jesus' destiny and enjoy a new, permanent communion or covenant with him. Whether Jesus spoke expressly of a "new covenant" (1 Cor 11:25; Luke 22:20) or only of a "covenant" (Mark 14:24; Matt 26:28) that was being instituted through his "blood," he inevitably evoked key biblical passages (for example, through a cultic link to Exodus 24:3–8 and through an eschatological link to Jeremiah 31:31–33) that illuminated his actions and words. He was making a new and final covenant with God, sealed and ratified by the shedding of his blood.

But whom did Jesus (according to 1 Corinthians 11:23–26; Luke 22:14–20) intend to be the beneficiaries of his death and the new covenant? The "for you" of the Pauline and Lucan tradition was not limited to those who shared the common cup at the Last Supper. Since Jesus called for a *future* repetition of the bread ritual ("Do this in remembrance of me," according to both Paul and Luke) and of the cup ritual ("Do this in remembrance of me," only in Paul), he clearly wanted to confer on an indefinite number of others the saving benefits of his life and impending death. Even if Jesus did not literally express the directive, "Do this in remembrance of me," one can argue that this addition rendered explicit his intentions. He wanted to establish for countless others his continuing presence in the meal fellowship that he had instituted with a small, core group of disciples.

Mark 14:24, followed by Matthew 26:28, has Jesus speaking of his blood poured out "for many," an inclusive, Semitic expression for a great multitude or countless number: that is to say, "for all." Paul offers a spectacular case of *many* meaning *all* when he contrasted the impact of Adam and Christ: "Just as one man's trespass led to condemnation *for all*, so one man's act of righteousness leads to justification and life *for all*. For just as by the one man's disobedience, *the many* were made sinners, so by the one man's obedience *the many* will be made righteous" (Rom 5:18–19; emphasis mine). The apostle passes seamlessly from "all" to "the many" as equivalent terms.

But what of Jesus himself? By *many* did he mean not only all Jews but also all Gentiles? If we understand "for you" and "for many" as both pointing to an indefinitely large group, we are still left with the question, Did Jesus intend the benefits of his violent death and the covenant to be conferred on all those and only on all those who were sharing and would share in the ritual and fellowship he was creating? Would the benefits of his sacrificial death "for many" be passed on only to the new covenant community, the fellowship of those who would draw on the saving power of Jesus' death by eating his "broken body" and drinking from the common cup?

Here we should recall the meals Jesus shared with all manner of people, not least with the disreputable. That table fellowship conveyed forgiveness to sinners and celebrated in advance the happiness of the heavenly banquet to come, a banquet to which all were invited. The practice of Jesus during his ministry threw light on his inclusive intentions at the Last Supper. It was intended to be "the last" supper or climax of a whole series of meals that revealed his saving outreach to everyone.[24]

Israel was the context for the ministry of Jesus; yet that ministry had a universal dimension.[25] His message of the kingdom reached beyond the frontiers of religious and ethnic separations. God's reign here and hereafter was for all human beings. The parables of Jesus reveal this universal horizon. Even in the Parable

45

of the Tax Collector and the Pharisee (Luke 18:9–14), the only parable located in the most Jewish of settings, the Temple, the universality showed through. Jesus asserted that the full extent of God's generosity had hitherto been ignored: the divine pardon was offered to all.

By rejecting or at least relativizing dietary laws and merely external purity regulations (Mark 7:14–23) that established and preserved the boundaries between Jews and Gentiles, Jesus implied that these distinctions had no ultimate significance before God. What mattered was the internal state of the "heart"— its purity or corruption.[26] Hence Jesus' vision of Israel's future involved many coming "from east and west" and eating "with Abraham and Isaac and Jacob in the kingdom of heaven" (Matt 8:11). The ministry of Jesus envisaged salvation for the nations. Having lived and preached such a vision, at the end Jesus, one can reasonably suppose, accepted that in some sense he would die for all people.

The activity and claims made by Jesus right through to their climax at the Last Supper raise the crucial question, Did all of this point to him as someone who would be vindicated by God and raised to a new, transformed life?

Chapter 2

THE MEANING OF THE RESURRECTION CLAIM

What do the authors of the New Testament and subsequent Christians mean by their claim that God raised Jesus from the dead or that Jesus rose from the dead? When Paul, for instance, quotes a four-part formula about Christ's death, burial, resurrection, and appearances (1 Cor 15:3–5), what does he intend when he speaks of the resurrection? (1) Does this statement offer information? If so, about what and/or about whom? (2) Or does Paul in no way intend to state facts but merely to encourage a fresh understanding or a new way of looking at things? If the evidence pushes us to settle for (1), are we facing an explanation ("Christ has been raised from the dead") that rests upon several descriptions (above all, "He died," "He was buried," and "He appeared")? Is the picture this: people experienced and reported his death, burial, and postmortem appearances; the appearances, together with the discovery of the empty tomb, triggered the explanation "He has been raised"?

A METAPHOR BUT NOT "MERELY" A METAPHOR

Before taking up these questions, we need to clarify the status of resurrection language as a metaphorical expression. A metaphor involves an extended use of language that, while being false in the literal sense, makes a true statement about reality. While not literally being a shepherd, God behaves with such loving concern toward "me" that the metaphor found in Psalm 23:1

is justified and puts us in touch with reality: "The LORD is my shepherd...." The new world of electronics abounds in metaphors. An oblong gadget alongside my desktop is not a small rodent, but the way it can be moved around legitimates its name, and certainly the "mouse" keeps me in touch with (and partially controls) what is going on inside my computer. If we pause to think about *hard drive, software,* a computer *crashing,* the *World Wide Web,* the *Internet, surfing the Net, Twitter, Facebook,* and further jargon in current electronic vocabulary, we should recognize that these terms are literally false. There is, for instance, no such thing as a gigantic piece of open-meshed fabric (or "World Wide Web") that covers the planet. Yet such language, while being used in an extended sense, puts us in touch with reality or what is objectively "out there."

I have taken an example from Psalm 23. But one could endlessly pile up further examples from religious and secular literature, science, and technology to illustrate the way metaphors let us contact what is truly "there" in our world. If someone says, "It's raining cats and dogs," we know that, literally speaking, a number of domestic animals are not being hurled from upper floors of the building where we work. While false in the literal sense, the statement can be verified as true if we glance out the window of our office and see that it is raining heavily. Metaphors, while using language in extended ways that are false in a literal sense, are continually informative and true.

Hence we should avoid at all costs talking about something being "merely" a metaphor or "only" a metaphor. That implies that literal talk constitutes first-class language and that metaphors belong to a second-class use of language that can be safely set aside. This is to ignore the pervasive use of metaphor in everyday language, not to mention scientific and technological language. In the brave new world of electronics, we would never dream of dismissing so much of the terminology as "merely metaphorical." We need to accept, understand, and apply it if we want to stay in touch with people and reality "out there."

The *literal* and the *metaphorical* differ simply in their use of language and not in their capacity to communicate objective truth. The former takes words in their primary or usual sense. The latter imaginatively applies names (for example, "the mouse"), descriptive terms (for example, "a glaring error"), or phrases (for example, "raining cats and dogs") to objects or actions to which they apply, not literally but imaginatively. Both the literal *and* the metaphorical usage of language talks about reality.

When Paul quotes from the tradition the verb *egēgertai* ("He has been raised"), he uses in an extended sense *egeirō*, a verb that in its literal (transitive) sense means "to wake up" or "to rouse from sleep." Paul, as well as the Book of Acts, takes another verb in an extended sense when applying *anistēmi* to the resurrection of Jesus (for example, 1 Thess 4:14; Acts 2:24, 32; 3:26). Used transitively, this verb means "to set upright, set erect, or make to stand up," and, intransitively, "to stand up." Metaphorically these two verbs apply to the dead Jesus: (1) he has been woken from the sleep of death; (2) he has been made to stand up and put back on his living feet, or, in an intransitive usage, he stood up after being laid low by death. I illustrate this using my own translations.

In the New Testament the two verbs sometimes take the form of a "divine passive" that understands the unspoken agent of resurrection to be God. In 1 Corinthians 15:4, we should complete the "He has been woken up/raised" and add "by God." In Romans 4:25, we should likewise complete the clause "[He] was raised for our justification" and add "by God." Paul, as well as the very early tradition behind him, explicitly presents the resurrection as "God (or the Father) woke up/raised Jesus from the dead" (for example, Rom 10:9; 1 Cor 6:14; 15:15; Gal 1:1; 1 Thess 1:10). Likewise Acts speaks of God making the dead Jesus "stand up" (for example, Acts 2:24; 13:33).

To signal the metaphorical sense in which Jesus was "woken up," "made to stand up," or "stood up" himself, Paul sometimes adds "from the dead": "God raised him [Jesus] from the dead" (Rom 10:9; see Gal 1:1). The apostle also draws attention to the way he uses language metaphorically by adopting the conventional description of the dead as "those who have fallen asleep" (1 Cor 15:6; 1 Thess 4:13). Hence he can call Christ "the first fruits of those who have fallen asleep" (1 Cor 15:20). Many cultures express death through the metaphor of "falling asleep." In the metaphorical language of the New Testament, Christ has been woken from the sleep of death.

Paul's language about the resurrection forms a metaphorical way of speaking about an event that remains hidden from him in its inner nature. (Something similar happens when scientists use metaphors to speak of the subatomic world that is hidden from their sight or accessible only indirectly.) Paul understands the resurrection of Jesus, as well as the (coming) general resurrection of the dead, not as a mere resuscitation of a corpse but as involving radical transformation. It means entering a new life freed from corruption and definitively removed from death (for example, Rom 6:9–10; Phil 3:21). Through resurrection the bodily existence of Christ and human beings becomes "glorious," "spiritual," and transformed in ways that Paul struggles to elucidate through various comparisons and negations (1 Cor 15:35–57).

We can summarize what Paul and other New Testament witnesses claim about the fate of Jesus as follows: after this crucifixion and burial, through a special divine action[1] that set the ultimate seal of approval on his life and work, Jesus was personally delivered from the state of death. With his earthly body transformed and taken up into a glorified existence, he initiated the end of all things for human beings and their world. The postresurrection appearances (with the mission that they entailed and the new life of the Holy Spirit that they brought) showed how the resurrection of Jesus was not only primarily "for him" (*pro se*) but also secondarily "for us" (*pro nobis*). This version of the Easter claim has often been disputed, both explicitly and implicitly, both in whole and in part.

DISPUTING THE CLAIM

In modern times various writers have argued that the "real" resurrection claim is simply that Jesus rose in the hearts of his disciples, his cause continued, and the disciples came to a new consciousness about life and their position before God. In other words, these writers maintain that after his death nothing at all happened to Jesus himself. In using resurrection language,

Christians were not talking about Jesus but only about themselves. The disciples had come to see that Jesus was right in what he said about God. In that sense *they* had risen from their spiritual death.

In the introduction we saw that Dale Allison edges toward this position by his one-sided privileging of what the disciples experienced after the crucifixion. Certainly Geza Vermes follows his long-dead friend, Paul Winter, by adopting this view. Jesus "rose from the dead" only in the sense of being loved by his followers, who "felt" that he was still with them. Winter expounded the view that resurrection was an event that affected (and continues to affect) the disciples, not Jesus himself. The "something" that happened after his death and burial was a change only in them, not a new, transformed life for Jesus. "Crucified, dead, and buried," Winter wrote, Jesus "yet rose in the hearts of his disciples who had loved him and felt he was near." He added, "He is rising again, today and tomorrow, in the hearts of men who love him and feel: he is near."[2] In these terms resurrection was not a fact about Jesus himself but simply a fact about the love and feelings of his disciples, past, present, and future. After the crucifixion a new beginning was to be found—but only with those disciples, not with Jesus. Something happened and continues to happen to the original and later disciples, not to the dead Jesus.

One could cite others who, during the past fifty years since Winter's book appeared, have redefined the resurrection by interpreting it as merely an expression of early Christian consciousness, love, and renewed discipleship.[3] Whatever form this redefinition takes, it remains, however, quite implausible to decode the New Testament language about the resurrection by purging it of any claim about the personal, postmortem existence of Jesus. Such redefinition fails to face the richly complex way in which the message of his resurrection is conveyed and converges.

What the New Testament has to say about the resurrection of Jesus is communicated through a variety of idioms:

- Formulas of preaching about the resurrection
  (for example, Rom 4:25; 1 Cor 15:3–5)
- Professions of Easter faith (for example, Rom 10:9)

- A new attribute for God as the God who raised the dead Jesus (for example, Gal 1:1)[4]
- The Easter narratives of the four Gospels
- A long, theological argument developed by Paul (1 Cor 15:12–58)
- Speeches in Acts that center on the resurrection (for example, Acts 2:31–32; 3:15; 4:10)

Thus the New Testament brings into play a wide range of expressions to proclaim that Jesus himself has been raised from the dead and now enjoys a new, transformed *life* (for example, Luke 24:15, 23; Rom 14:9; 1 Cor 15:35–50). The first Christian authors fill out this language about Jesus' resurrection by speaking of his being "alive" (for example, Luke 24:23; Rom 14:9), of his "entering into" or being "assumed" into "glory" (for example, Luke 24:26; John 7:39; 12:6; 17:1; 1 Tim 3:16) and "exalted" (for example, Phil 2:9) to "the right hand" of God (the Father) (for example, Acts 2:33; Rom 8:34).

In all this language the primary claim was not that Jesus' cause continued or that the disciples had been raised to a new consciousness and life of faith by coming to see that Jesus had been right about God. The primary claim concerned the crucified Jesus himself; he had been personally brought from the state of death to new and everlasting life. Of course, the early formulas recognized that his resurrection had also taken place in order to change and "justify" us before God (for example, Rom 4:25). The resurrection led the disciples and others to a new, graced life of faith and initiated our final resurrection from the dead (for example, 1 Cor 15:20). Nevertheless, first, the resurrection claim referred to what had happened to Jesus himself. He *also* rose in the minds and hearts of his disciples, precisely because he himself had first been raised from the dead and then appeared to them. They would not have been "justified" unless he had already been raised.

The four-part formula quoted by Paul makes that clear by naming four events in which Jesus was involved (1 Cor 15:3–5).[5] It was he who died; it was he who was buried; it was he who has been raised from the dead; it was he who appeared to Peter and then to the Twelve (that is to say, to the Eleven, after the defection and death of Judas). Jesus (named as "Christ") is himself the subject of the four verbs. The last two verbs ("was raised" and "appeared") are just as informative as the first two ("died" and "was buried"). The one who died and was buried is the one who has been raised and appeared. In both pairs of verbs, the second verb supports what the first claims. We know that Christ died because he was buried; burial is a sure pointer to death. We know that Christ has been raised because he appeared bodily alive to a number of individuals and groups; dead persons do not appear like that. In short, the formula cited by Paul primarily asserts something that happened to Jesus, a "something" that, also and secondarily, happened "for our sins in accordance with the scriptures" (1 Cor 15:3).

In these and many other instances, had the first Christians, although seeming to claim a new fact about Jesus (his resurrection from the dead), misidentified their experience, falsely described it, or even deliberately used a deceptive form of discourse? Were they talking *only* about some new, seminal idea that now possessed their hearts and minds? Such an explanation, proposed by Winter, Vermes, and others, involves the conclusion that the basic Easter message of the first Christians has been fundamentally misunderstood for many centuries. Their propositions about Jesus' personal resurrection from the dead—so it is asserted—expressed a hidden meaning that one can now see to have differed drastically from the conventional meaning of the words they used. They were speaking only of themselves, never of a new, postmortem event affecting Jesus himself.

This position is quite far-fetched and unconvincing. When Paul quotes an early Christian formulation about "Jesus Christ and God the Father, who raised him from the dead..." (Gal 1:1), the ordinary conventions covering the use of language indicate that this formula primarily pointed to Jesus and offered some information about what had happened to him after his death. A new event, subsequent to and distinct from the crucifixion, brought him from the condition of death to new and lasting life. To allege that the true primary referent in the proposition "The Father raised Jesus from the dead" was not Jesus but the disciples is to open up a surprising gap between what Paul (and other New

Testament witnesses) wrote and what they meant. They wrote, "The Father raised Jesus from the dead," but—in defiance of general usage and public conventions governing the recognition of meaning—they primarily meant "The Father raised us to a new life of faith."

When dealing with other ancient texts from the Mediterranean world (for example, those coming from Julius Caesar, Cicero, Josephus, Plutarch, and Tacitus), no reputable interpreter would dream of attributing to them a liberty in switching the referent and expressing a hidden meaning that differs from the conventional sense of the words they used. Here any differences between secular and religious classics from the antiquity are irrelevant. The question is one of basic grammar and meaning. The New Testament authors introduced Jesus as the object ("God raised Jesus") or subject ("Jesus was raised" or "Jesus rose") in their central claim about the resurrection. Did they write down the name "Jesus" but secretly intend some other object or subject ("the disciples") in these sentences? That would mean explaining Paul's four-part formulas as follows: "The disciples 'died' for their sins; they were 'buried' spiritually; they have been 'raised' to a new life; they 'appeared' gloriously committed and confident."

Are we to imagine that the first Christian authors were deliberately deceptive in their use of language? Or were they remarkably incompetent? These are the only plausible alternatives open to us if we allege that their assertions about Jesus' resurrection were merely assertions about themselves.

Those who feel free to redefine the original Easter claim are, in effect, claiming to know better than the New Testament authors what those authors meant when they wrote what they did. This may be too severe. Perhaps the problem with those who redefine the Easter claim comes to this. They fail to distinguish between people holding something to be true and the effects of this claim on those who make it. In proclaiming his resurrection, Jesus' followers primarily claimed a new fact about Jesus himself. Holding his resurrection to be true had deep, transforming effects on them. These effects depended, however, on the fact that they held something to be true: namely, that Jesus himself had passed from the state of death to a new and final life.

54

Or perhaps the basic problem concerns very simply the activity of God and background views of it. The New Testament proclaims that Jesus (1) was crucified by men and then (2) raised by God. Some of those who redefine the Easter message seem reluctant to admit that God might act in such a strikingly special way. Hence the New Testament texts *must* mean something else, something that they can believe. Yet their way of dealing with (2) does clear violence to the New Testament texts and claim. It also allows us to deal freely *with their texts*. The freedom they allow themselves when interpreting the New Testament's Easter message provides us with the license to make what we want of their assertions. Thus we might comment, "They appear to be excluding the personal resurrection of Jesus, but 'really' they are only talking about themselves—about their own persistent spiritual suffering and ways of coping with it."

DERIVING RESURRECTION FROM ASSUMPTION?

Our introduction to this volume reviewed a book by Daniel Smith, who argues for the primacy of "assumption" or "apotheosis" language. The earlier form of the empty tomb story (Mark 16:1–8), he proposes, was a way of expressing that the dead Jesus had been assumed into heaven and would be seen again at the Parousia. He likens this "disappearance" tradition to that of Elijah in 2 Kings 2:1–13, even though he is aware of a major difference: unlike Jesus, Elijah had not died and been buried before being taken up in a fiery chariot. Smith also introduces Greco-Roman stories involving an apotheosis in which some hero was taken alive into the presence of the gods, or else his spirit "ascended" while his dead body remained buried. As I noted, Heracles, Romulus, and other such heroes and heroines, unlike Jesus, were supposed to have lived in a very distant past and most likely never existed at all. This is a difficulty that also touches the case of Elijah and other ancient biblical figures. Whatever one holds about their historical reality, they certainly did not exist within living memory, as Jesus did. Smith wishes to prove that, as we move from earlier to later traditions, the New Testament develops claims about Jesus being resurrected and appearing to his disciples that replaced, or at least were associated with, the primary claims about the disappearance of Jesus and his being assumed into heaven. Smith does not stand alone in developing this thesis; we noted something similar being proposed, for example, by Adela Yarbro Collins.

What then is primary? Obviously the language of disappearance and assumption is less specific than that of a resurrection after death and burial followed by postmortem appearances. While Roman emperors after their death were alleged, like Romulus, to have been taken up to the gods and deified, Elijah's passage to heaven did not involve death and burial. In and of itself, assumption language was more flexible and vaguer. Did less precise assertions about Jesus' being exalted and ascending into heaven gave rise to more specific claims about his being raised from the dead and appearing to groups of disciples or individuals? Did the notion that at his death Jesus was "taken up" to God constitute the older claim, from which the resurrection claim derived? Could belief in Jesus' resurrection have been a subsequent, pictorial expression of an earlier, vaguer conviction that God had somehow "exalted" Jesus after or even at his crucifixion?

To "exalt" (*hypsoō*) means, literally, to raise on high or lift up and, metaphorically, to ennoble, place high in rank or power, or enhance in position. Clearly this term and related expressions enjoy a broader range of meaning than the two verbs for resurrection we examined earlier. As the narrower term, *resurrection* implies exaltation but not vice versa. To be raised from the dead is necessarily to be exalted. But, as we have seen, Elijah could be portrayed as having been exalted without his dying and being raised from the dead. The two concepts also diverge inasmuch as resurrection includes a certain horizontal element, while exaltation suggests simply a vertical movement. Christ is lifted from the world below to heavenly glory above. But resurrection first directs our attention backward: the one who is raised must first have died. Only after this prior event of death can he be resurrected either to resume in some fashion life on earth or to be taken up into heaven.

Was the more inclusive concept (exaltation) the primary one from which the claim about Christ's resurrection evolved? Paul and Mark register a crushing difficulty for Smith's hypothesis. The very early formula quoted by Paul runs, "Christ died for our sins, was buried, has been raised [perfect tense], and appeared to Cephas, then to the Twelve" (1 Cor 15:3–5). The apostle and the tradition on which he draws do *not* say, as Smith would prefer, "Christ was buried and assumed into heaven, and will appear again at the Parousia." The interpreting angel in Mark announces, "Jesus was raised [aorist tense]….Tell his disciples and Peter that he is going ahead of you into Galilee; there you will see him" (Mark 16:6–7). The angel does *not* proclaim, "Jesus has been assumed into heaven; you will see him again at the Parousia." The oldest version of the empty tomb story involves resurrection and appearance to Peter (Cephas) and the disciples, not an assumption story involving eventual appearance at the Parousia.

Originally resurrection and exaltation seem to have been relatively independent interpretations of the same event. The resurrection claim was *not* derived from the less specific assertion that God had exalted Jesus in or after his death. This conclusion emerges when we distinguish the following four patterns in New Testament accounts of Jesus' destiny.

1. Death is followed by resurrection (for example, 1 Cor 15:3–4; Mark 9:31).
2. Death is followed by heavenly exaltation (for example, Phil 2:8–9) or entering into glory (for example, Luke 24:26).
3. Death is followed by resurrection and the effective continuation of resurrection by enthronement at "God's right hand" (for example, Rom 8:34).
4. Resurrection and exaltation are used interchangeably to describe what followed Jesus' death (Luke 24:26 = 24:46).

When we examine these and further examples, we fail to find that death-exaltation texts occur *early* in the New Testament, while the pattern of death-resurrection surfaces only *later*. If a pattern exists, it is rather the opposite. The theme of exaltation emerges as an interpretation of resurrection. The death-resurrection model appears in Paul's earlier works and often in passages that seem to be drawn from earlier formulations (for example, 1 Thess 1:10; 1 Cor 15:3–4; Gal 1:1; Rom 10:9); the death-exaltation pattern turns up subsequently (for example, Luke 24:26) and in one of the apostle's later letters (Phil 2:8–9).

John, of course, writing toward the end of the first century, develops the theme of exaltation. The Son of Man who descends from heaven through the incarnation ascends back to the Father by way of being "lifted up" on the cross. Thus the crucifixion is both a physical raising up and the divine exaltation of Christ (John 3:14; 6:62; 8:28; 12:32–33). The model has ceased to be death leading to exaltation. John speaks rather of a death that is Christ's exaltation and passage to the Father. Nevertheless, the fourth evangelist does not dispense with the pattern of death-resurrection-exaltation (through ascension). When Christ meets Mary Magdalene, he is portrayed as already risen from the dead but still on his way to the Father (John 20:17). When he eventually speaks to a group of the disciples, he does so on the far side of the exaltation (John 20:19–23).

John has good reason for not portraying Jesus as ascending into heaven at the moment of his death on the cross. That would lead to a docetic position that only the spirit of Jesus ascends into heaven while his body remains behind on the cross. Such an ascension of Jesus' spirit would run counter to John's affirmation that "the Word became flesh" (John 1:14). Perhaps John's vision can be best stated as follows: the exaltation implied by Jesus being lifted up on the cross is manifested through the reality of the resurrection and ascension.[6]

However we interpret the details of the exaltation theology found in John, evidence is lacking to show that the original conviction about Christ's exaltation in death came first and only later this vaguer belief was crystallized into the specific claim that he had been raised from the dead. We may not evade in that way the basic task of examining the credibility of the testimony offered by Paul and the evangelists. Did Jesus appear gloriously alive after his death to certain individuals and groups? Did Mary Magdalene (accompanied probably by other women) discover his tomb to be open and empty on the third day? But before tackling these questions, we need to face one further way of "underinterpreting" the meaning of resurrection.

RESURRECTION NOT INVOLVING THE BODY?

Can you have a personal resurrection that is not bodily? That was the proposal of the late Arthur Peacocke: the new, personal life of the crucified Jesus did not involve any physical continuity between his body laid in the tomb and his risen life.[7]

Peacocke offered a one-sidedly spiritual version of our human existence and future. He expressed the hope that the purposes of God may "finally achieve their fulfillment *beyond space and time* within the very being of God himself."[8] This future existence "beyond space and time" will entail the Creator bringing "created personalness *out of materiality* into the divine life."[9] Peacocke seemed to fall into a radical and final dualism. The matter of Christ's crucified body was left behind, just as our matter and our material world will be left behind when we are finally brought "out of materiality" and beyond space and time into the very being of God. For Jesus and for us, this entails a transition from the created, material order into "a state of unity with God" and an existence in "an entirely new mode" of being.[10]

This version of the resurrection seems to turn it into an escape from the world of matter, a kind of "disembodying" phenomenon. By dispensing with the empty tomb, Peacocke ends up holding a position that looks scarcely distinguishable from the immortality of the soul and reduces it to the survival of Jesus' inner self, which brings a total break with his former bodily existence so that he can enjoy an immortality beyond the grave in another world. According to Peacocke, Jesus was and we ourselves will be, so we may hope, "brought out of materiality" into the very being and life of God.

Peacocke kept the language of resurrection but radically changed its meaning. His version of a personal, but non-bodily, resurrection was nothing less than a disguised version of the immortality of Jesus' inner self or soul. Christians of the New Testament and those Jews at that time who hoped for resurrection could not have made sense of a personal but non-bodily resurrection. They would have told Peacocke, "Since your account of the resurrection excludes anything bodily, you should use another term: namely, immortality of the soul."

Chapter 3

THE APPEARANCES OF
THE RISEN JESUS

Some of the early followers of Jesus claimed to have seen him gloriously alive after his death. We know this from the New Testament, which reported his appearances to groups and to individuals:

- To "the twelve" (1 Cor 15:5)
- To "the eleven and those with them" (Luke 24:33–49)
- To "those who came up with him [Jesus] from Galilee" (Acts 13:31)
- To "the disciples" (John 20:19–23; Mark 16:7)
- To "all the apostles" (1 Cor 15:7; obviously in Paul's list a distinct and larger group than the Twelve)
- To Simon Peter and six others (John 21:1–14)
- To "more than five hundred brothers and sisters" (1 Cor 15:6)
- To Cleopas and his companion (Luke 24:13–35)
- To Mary Magdalene and "the other Mary" (Matt 28:9–10)
- To Mary Magdalene (John 20:11–18; Mark 16:9–11)
- To Cephas/Peter (1 Cor 15:5; Mark 16:7; Luke 24:34)
- To James (1 Cor 15:7)
- To Saul/Paul (for example, 1 Cor 9:1; 15:8; Acts 9:1–9)

These sources diverge on secondary matters. Who was the first to see the risen Lord? Mary Magdalene or Simon Peter? Where did these appearances take place—in Galilee (for example, Mark 16:7) or in and around Jerusalem (Luke 24)? Yet the sources agree on the primary fact of appearances to certain individuals and to groups, in particular, the core group of disciples, "the Twelve" (for example, 1 Cor 15:5), as well as indicating that the encounters depended upon the risen Jesus.

The key verb here is *ōphthē* (for example, 1 Cor 15:5–8; Luke 24:34; Acts 13:31), which should be translated as "he appeared" or "let himself be seen," rather than "was seen by." All the contemporary translations that I have checked (in English, French, German, and Italian) render the verb as "appeared" (or its equivalent in other languages). The use of this verb, along with other items in the Easter accounts, indicate that, according to the New Testament testimony, the appearances depended upon the initiative of the risen Lord.

THREE OTHER FEATURES OF THE APPEARANCES

The objective reality of the postresurrection appearances has been challenged in various ways. But before examining some typical challenges, let us observe three characteristics of the appearances.[1]

Ordinariness of the Appearances

First, there is a notable "ordinariness" about the Easter appearances, as reported very briefly by Paul and narrated by the Gospels. Unlike other communications from God, they do not take place in ecstasy (as happens, for example, in Acts 10:9–16; 2 Cor 12:2–4), nor in a dream (as happens, for example, in Matt 1:20; 2:12–13, 19–20, 22), nor—with the seeming exception of John 20:19–23—by night (as happens, for example, in Acts 16:9; 18:9–11; 23:11; 27:23–24). The appearances occur under normal, daytime circumstances and without the traits of apocalyptic glory that we find elsewhere (for example, Mark 9:2–8; Matt 28:3–4). The one exception comes when Acts describes Paul's experience on the Damascus road: he faces "a light from heaven, brighter than the sun" (Acts 26:13; see 9:3; 22:6, 9). But there is no mention of this luminous phenomenon when Paul himself refers to his encounter with the risen Christ (1 Cor 9:1; 15:8; Gal 1:12, 16). Perhaps the apostle alludes to his meeting outside Damascus when he writes of "the light of the knowledge of the glory of God in the face of Jesus Christ" (2 Cor 4:6). Yet he stresses "the inward phenomena" or shining in human hearts, not the outward, luminous phenomena of the Damascus road encounter that Acts narrates three times.[2]

Against this notion of the appearances being ordinary, one might appeal to John of Patmos's vision of the risen Christ (Rev 1:9–20). That account talks of the Lord's eyes being "like a flame of fire" (Rev 1:14) and his face being "like the sun shining with full force" (Rev 1:16). But what we read here is not a description in the ordinary sense. Rather it is a comparison in which "the feel or value, the effect or impression of one thing is compared with that of another." John of Patmos is "not giving a visual image which a skilful painter might reproduce." Rather, "he is telling his readers that if, for example, they will think of the feelings that they have before a torrent in spate or beneath the brilliance of the midday sun, they will have some inkling of the sense of majesty and sublimity which he experienced in the presence of the heavenly Christ." In short, this passage from Revelation does not purport to describe, let alone describe in detail, the Lord's appearance. Drawing on traditional imagery from Daniel, Ezekiel, and other sources, it provides an "affective comparison" expressing the visionary's reaction to Christ's majestic presence.[3]

This opening vision "in the spirit" (Rev 1:10) or in a state of prophetic illumination differs radically from the original and much earlier appearances that made the visionaries eyewitnesses of the risen Jesus and, in the case of some of them, official founders of Christianity. The Book of Revelation does not suggest that John of Patmos is now becoming such a witness to the risen Christ and thus receiving a basic qualification for taking up a foundational, apostolic ministry. The opening vision functions in quite a different way: to introduce and communicate messages to seven churches in Asia Minor (Rev 1:17—3:22) and, more broadly, to introduce the revelatory experiences that make up almost the whole of the book. So far from describing some vision that qualifies the visionary to become an apostle, Revelation looks back to the apostles who have already completed their work as founders (Rev 22:14). In short, the opening vision does not aim at describing the risen Christ, nor can it be appropriately compared with his original Easter encounters with Peter, Paul, and the other founding fathers and mothers of Christianity.

Language of Sight

Despite a certain ordinariness about the Easter appearances, the New Testament attributes a transformed life to the risen Jesus. His new, embodied existence is no longer subject to the normal limitations of the material universe; he now exists "beyond" and "lives to God" (Rom 6:10). Yet he freely emerged from the other world to enter into contact with people in this world, (1) revealing himself to them, (2) calling them to faith and mission, and (3) doing so in a way that included some kind of external perception. Apropos of (1) and (2), Paul understands his encounter with the risen Jesus as bringing revelation and a call to faith and mission (1 Cor 9:1; 15:8–11; Gal 1:1, 12, 15–16). Paul's language suggests some analogy to the vocations of Old Testament prophets (Isa 6:1, 5; 49:1; Jer 1:5). The controversial issue is (3), the extramental perception. Did the Easter appearances involve an objective vision in space? Was there someone "out there" to be seen?

In reporting or referring to the encounters with the risen Christ, the New Testament authors privilege the language of sight. He "appeared" to some people (for example, 1 Cor 15:5–8; Luke 24:34) and they "saw" him (for example, 1 Cor 9:1; Mark 16:7; Matt 28:17). Occasionally in the New Testament the Greek verb "see" (*horaō*) can be used of intellectual perception, just as blindness is a metaphor for incomprehension. Thus, "for those outside, everything comes in parables; in order that / they may indeed look [see] but not perceive, / and may indeed listen [hear] but not understand…" (Mark 4:11–12). But normally, seeing and appearing involve some visual component (for example, Mark 9:4; Luke 5:12; John 1:29; Acts 2:3). Instances like Mark 4:11–12 deal with the intellectual perception of some truth (that is very relevant to one's human existence and destiny) or the failure to comprehend such a truth. One can "see" truth in a purely interior, noncorporeal way.

But with the Easter encounters we are dealing with a claim about a bodily resurrected person appearing to other persons who exist within our space-time world and see him. In that case it is difficult to imagine how a purely spiritual, interior seeing could be reconciled with the New Testament terminology of the appearances. This is not to argue that when the risen Jesus appeared he was an exterior object to be perceived and recognized by anyone who happened to be present, irrespective of their personal dispositions.

Yet one must admit that Paul and the evangelists show little interest in describing, let alone explaining in detail, the nature of the appearances. I simply point out that some visual component seems implied by the language that the New Testament uses for the encounters with the risen Jesus. Unlike the Old Testament prophets, the apostolic witnesses to the resurrection typically saw the risen Lord rather than heard his word.

Here, of course, we recall how the New Testament often fills out "seeing" with a meaning that includes but goes beyond a merely literal and everyday sense. When Jesus saw Simon and his brother Andrew and then saw the sons of Zebedee (Mark 1:16, 19), it was a significant look. The connotations of "calling" were close at hand; that was true also in the case of Jesus' seeing Levi in Luke 5:27. The desire of Zacchaeus to see Jesus (Luke 19:3–4) likewise included but went beyond simple physical perception and seemed to hint at the way in which the tax collector sensed that Jesus could bring him salvation. Zacchaeus's eagerness to see Jesus was no "mere expression of curiosity" but "something more," a "vague discernment of something special about this person who was passing through and of whom he had heard."[4] Add too the way *seeing* in John's Gospel includes but goes beyond its simple everyday meaning, so as to suggest a passage to faith (for example, John 1:39; 12:21). *Seeing* is almost a synonym with *believing* (for example, John 9:37–38). "Opening the eyes" (seven times in John 9:1–41) is tantamount to being brought to believe.

Since *seeing* could enjoy this richer sense during the story of Jesus' ministry, we should all the more insist that normal, everyday perception by itself does not do justice to what "seeing" the risen Lord entailed (for example, John 20:28; 1 Cor 9:1). That seeing included but went beyond mere visual perception.

65

Claims to Authority

Obviously *some* of the appearances are connected with the *leadership* role of particular Christians. This raises a third question. To defend his apostolic mission and freedom, Paul puts the rhetorical questions: "Am I not an apostle? Have I not seen Jesus our Lord?" (1 Cor 9:1). Yet the New Testament also recalls men and women to whom the risen Lord appeared who were not specially commissioned to be apostolic witnesses, as Paul, Peter, and others were. The two disciples on the Emmaus road (Luke 24:13–35) and the more than five hundred followers of Jesus (1 Cor 15:6) met the risen Lord but were not thereby authorized for leadership roles.

The Twelve were reconstituted when, in the presence of around 120 followers of Jesus, Peter supervised the election of a replacement for the dead Judas (Acts 1:15–26) and mentioned two requirements. The candidate must not only have been associated with Jesus during his earthly ministry but also have seen the risen Lord. Two candidates were proposed, Matthias and Joseph, who was "called Barsabbas" and also "known as Justus." Chosen by lot, Matthias joined the ranks of the Twelve. The story implies that there were some, perhaps many, others from among the 120 who met the two requirements, in particular, that of having seen the risen Jesus. Yet only Matthias, and none of these others, was chosen for the authoritative, leadership role that belonged to the Twelve.

Every now and then writers dismiss the resurrection appearances as merely claims to legitimate the authority of Paul and others within the Christian community. But such a reductive explanation does not do justice to the evidence. As we have just seen, the New Testament reports and implies that the risen Jesus appeared to many people who seemingly played no special leadership role in the emerging church. Claims about such appearances can be made without any reference to these people exercising particular authority. In the case of Paul himself we have, to be sure, the case of a major leader who derived his apostolic authority from his encounter with the risen Lord. But that encounter led Paul to join an *existing* Christian community. How do we account for the origin of that community that was already in place several years before Paul became a Christian and asserted his apostolic authority? The New Testament points us toward the postresurrection appearances as the major trigger creating the Christian movement.

THE APPEARANCES CHALLENGED

Since the second century, the objective reality of the postresurrection appearances of Jesus has been questioned. We look at two such attempts to discredit the appearances: first, the thesis that we deal with hallucinations and, second, the attempt to reduce the appearances to "mere" bereavement experiences.

Hallucinations?

Celsus, a pagan philosopher whose *True Discourse* is the oldest literary attack on Christianity, argued that the alleged witnesses to the risen Jesus were hysterical and hallucinated (Mary Magdalene) and in the case of "some other one" (presumably Peter) either hallucinated or was an ambitious liar: he "either dreamt in a certain state of mind and through wishful thinking had an hallucination…or, what is more likely, wanted to impress the others by telling this fantastic tale."[5] By branding Mary Magdalene as a hysterical woman, Celsus began a long tradition of gratuitously alleging that the disciples of Jesus, both male and female, were temperamental, even unbalanced by character, and prone to visions. Every now and then they are depicted this way, even though there is not a shred of evidence that they were more prone to be hallucinated than anyone else.

In modern times various authors have dismissed the appearances as hallucinations or the experiences of hallucinated persons who, after his death and burial, were anxiously expecting to see Jesus risen from the dead and, through a kind of chain reaction, mistakenly imagined that they saw him present to them. They misattributed to an external source what they had produced themselves: "the presence" of the risen Christ. In an attempt to discredit in this way the appearances, Gerd Lüdemann developed the hallucination theory and other claims about the psychohistory of Peter and Paul.[6] The postresurrection "appearances" would then be merely internal, psychological events that took place totally in the minds of the first disciples and were not produced by any external stimulus. In short, those appearances were purely subjective visions, with no external reality corresponding to them.

The evidence that we have from the four Gospels does not support any picture of Jesus' disciples excitedly expecting to meet him risen from the dead. Instead of persuading themselves into thinking that they saw him, they had to be persuaded that he was gloriously alive again (for example, Matt 28:16–18; Luke 24:36–43; John 20:24–25). What the Gospels record seems credible: the crisis of Jesus' arrest and disgraceful death on a cross left the disciples crushed. Only by ignoring the evidence can we picture them anxiously awaiting his return from the dead and out of their imaginations hallucinating his appearances.

Furthermore, the thesis of an ecstatic group hallucination might be more feasible if the New Testament had reported only one appearance and that to a particular group on a particular day. Instead, it reports appearances over a period of time and to different groups, as well as to different individuals (for example, 1 Cor 15:5–8). As regards the groups to whom Jesus appeared, the testimony presents us with at least six distinct groups: the "twelve" (for example, 1 Cor 15:5); "all the apostles" (1 Cor 15:7, who seem in Paul's list to be a more extensive group than the Twelve); Simon Peter and six others (John 21:1–14); "more than five hundred" believers (1 Cor 15:6); Cleopas and his companion (Luke 24:13–35); and Mary Magdalene and "the other Mary" (Matt 28:9–10). The variety of traditions makes it quite implausible to reduce these six groups to one group who, on a particular occasion and by a kind of chain reaction, imagined one after another that they saw Jesus. In short, the hallucination hypothesis offers a psychological explanation but cannot produce historical evidence in support of such an explanation.

Pentecost is the only major ecstatic group experience that the New Testament describes the disciples to have expected and experienced. But that episode involved receiving the Holy Spirit, not seeing the risen Christ. Some have tried to identify the appearance of the risen Christ to more than five hundred believers (1 Cor

15:6) with the outpouring of the Holy Spirit on the 120 followers of Jesus on the day of Pentecost (Acts 1:15; 2:1–13). But, for good reasons, most scholars reject the view that one and the same event came to be reported in two (obviously) different ways: as an appearance of the risen Christ to more than five hundred persons and as the outpouring of the Spirit on 120.[7]

Did Paul deceive himself into thinking that he saw the risen Jesus? As critics have repeatedly observed, the hypothesis of a group hallucination emphatically fails to account for the case of Paul. Far from hoping to meet the risen Christ, he persecuted the first Christians. His encounter with Christ (1 Cor 9:1; 15:8; Gal 1:11–16) took place several years later and in different place from the other Easter appearances (Galilee and in or near Jerusalem). Before the meeting on the Damascus road, Paul was in no way committed to Jesus. Quite the contrary! The appearance to Paul could not be a case of wish fulfillment. Yet might it be that his persecution of Christians disclosed a deep conflict within him, "a Christ complex" that finally resolved itself when he hallucinated the presence of Christ?[8] But do we have any reliable evidence that might let us enter into the state of mind of Paul *before* his Damascus road experience? Years later and with extreme brevity, Paul recalled how, when he persecuted the church, he was blameless and righteous from the standpoint of the law (Phil 3:6; Gal 1:13–14). Here a biblical scholar like Lüdemann seems out of date in his approach. Most historians now view with skepticism attempts to psychoanalyze people long dead, especially someone like Paul, about whose interior, mental life we have little or no data. He left us very little information about his inner state of emotions and tensions as a Christian and nothing at all about that state in his pre-Christian days.

Some writers have introduced both physical and mental details to explain (or explain away?) the Damascus road encounter. Michael Grant, for example, suggested that Paul's experience could have been "stimulated" by "heat, exhaustion [and] thirst." In any case, Paul "was already in an extremely nervous, anxious state, which made him highly suggestible" and "on the ragged edge of consciousness." How did Grant know about Paul's physical condition and "emotional climate," as he called it?

Grant simply invented these details and had no evidence to back them up.[9]

Two *religious novelties* in what the disciples claimed about Jesus create a major difficulty for the hallucination hypothesis. It necessarily reconstructs the sequence of events on the basis of the interior state of the disciples and what they *already* believed and expected before Jesus died. But this hypothesis cannot explain two remarkably new things that the disciples began to proclaim after they saw the living Christ.

First, what options were available for the disciples after Jesus was executed as a messianic pretender and even a blasphemer? Could they have modified their messianic belief in Jesus and proposed him to be another martyred prophet, like John the Baptist and others before him? Hardly, it seems to me. To be crucified was not only to suffer an utterly cruel and humiliating form of execution but also to die under a religious curse (Gal 3:13) and "outside the camp" of God's people (Heb 13:12–13). In other words, crucifixion was seen as the death of a criminal and godless man who perished away from God's presence and in the place and company of irreligious persons. To honor anyone put to death in such a way was an awful and profound scandal (1 Cor 1:23). Given that crucifixion was such a disgrace, could Jesus' disciples have been led through their hallucinations to proclaim him *even as a martyred prophet?*

In fact, they began preaching the crucified Jesus as the divinely endorsed Messiah risen from the dead to bring salvation to all. The notion of a messiah who failed, suffered, was crucified, and then rose from the grave was simply foreign to pre-Christian Judaism and hence could not have shaped any hallucinations on the part of the disciples. Since their previous religious beliefs could not have prompted them into making such startlingly new claims about Jesus, what triggered this religious novelty? Where did it come from, if not from the resurrection of Jesus himself, now made known to them through his appearances and the discovery of the empty tomb?

The second novelty concerned a striking shift in religious expectations. By the time of Jesus, some or even many Jews cherished a hope that the resurrection of all the dead and a general

70

judgment would terminate human history. But no one imagined, as we saw in the section on Tom Wright in the introduction, that one individual would be resurrected from the dead *in anticipation* of the last day. But then the followers of Jesus began announcing that one individual had already been raised to a glorious existence that anticipated the end of all history. What prompted this remarkable change in expectations that had no precedent in Jewish faith and hence could not have fed into alleged hallucinations on the part of the disciples? Once again the plausible cause can only be the actual resurrection of Jesus and his Easter appearances.

Since any hallucination hypothesis depends upon what the disciples *already* believed and expected at the time of Jesus' death, it cannot cope with the two striking novelties in what they began to proclaim. Hallucinating disciples projecting their prior beliefs could not have preached the crucified Jesus as the divinely appointed Messiah, nor could they have claimed that Jesus had been gloriously raised from the dead in anticipation of a universal resurrection of all the dead. Neither they nor anyone else entertained such a belief and such an expectation, which might have led to and shaped their hallucinations.

"Mere" Bereavement Experiences

In recent years a second challenge to the Easter appearances has come from those like Dale Allison (see the introduction to this book) who argue that cases of bereaved people who experience their beloved dead illuminate the experiences of those who claimed to have seen the risen Christ. Some who endorse this approach (for example, Lüdemann) allege that the Easter "appearances" were nothing more than ancient episodes in the psychobiographies of bereaved persons.

The appendix to this book discusses in detail the proposed analogy between the Easter appearances and the experiences of the bereaved. Here let me simply note one decisive difference. Those who have experienced (in visions or in other ways) recently deceased persons do not claim that their dear ones have been resurrected from the dead. Their reports suggest rather the sentiments found in the Book of Wisdom: "The souls of the righteous / are in the hands of God,… / They are at peace" (Wis 3:1,3).

Some psychologists, like Richard Bentall, describe bereavement experiences as hallucinations brought on by emotional stress. It is not that he judges everyone experiencing these (and other "hallucinations") to be suffering from an illness. "Modern surveys," he writes, "have continued to provide evidence that hallucinations are experienced by people who otherwise appear to be normal."[10] The bereaved, who may be thoroughly normal persons, are hallucinated because they experience a living person who is not present at the time.[11] Here Bentall cites the pioneering 1971 study of Dewi Rees, "The Hallucinations of Widowhood."[12] As we see in the appendix, Rees later regretted using the word *hallucination*, a loaded term that judges the experiences of the bereaved as merely imaginary and not real—in the sense of not putting them into objective contact with a deceased person who is really present to them.

In this context the worldview we embrace proves decisive. Whoever does not accept another world that is real but normally invisible will logically describe the experiences of the bereaved as hallucinations. They are not truly being contacted by their dear ones who have gone before them into the other world of God, because there is no such other world. More broadly, all religious experiences can only be hallucinatory, whether those of ordinary people or those of truly saintly men and women. Religious experiences must be hallucinations, facilitated by the (unfounded) beliefs held by people of faith.[13] But researchers like Dewi Rees who reject this worldview regard bereavement experiences as real, not imaginary.

BEYOND THE FRINGE

Sometimes challenges to the postresurrection appearances come in nonscholarly, bizarre forms and belong to what we might call "the frivolous fringe." Sensationalist in nature, they may make a big splash for the moment but hardly leave a ripple. I mention two such "explanations" of the appearances.

A Twin Brother?

In the introduction we saw how Philip Pullman in *The Good Man Jesus and the Scoundrel Christ* "eliminated" the Easter appearances of Jesus by introducing a twin brother ("Christ"), who pretended to be Jesus risen from the dead. Mary Magdalene and other disciples were tricked into believing that a resurrection had taken place. As I argued, only the credulous will find any plausibility in Pullman's reconstruction of what happened after Jesus died and was buried.

The Swoon Theory

In presenting Richard Swinburne's work on the resurrection, in the introduction I summarized his objections to the theory that Jesus was taken down alive from the cross, revived in the tomb, somehow got out, and lived on for several or even many years. Jesus genuinely appeared to his followers. But these were meetings with someone who had not died, not with someone who had been raised from the dead.

In the nineteenth century H. E. G. Paulus and others floated this ingenious "swoon" theory. The cool of the tomb and the aromatic spices revived Jesus, and he managed to escape from the tomb when an earthquake shifted the stone blocking the entrance. He stripped off his shroud and put on the clothes of a gardener that he found lying around. This led Mary Magdalene to mistake him for a gardener. For forty days he lingered on with his disciples and took leave of them in a mist. Versions of a post-crucifixion revival turn up in works by Robert Graves, D. H. Lawrence, George Moore, Barbara Thiering, John Updike, Karl Heinrich Venturini, and others, including those who created the story of Jesus escaping to Kashmir, where he eventually died at the age of 120 (see introduction). Some variants on this "happy ending" to the passion narrative picture Jesus going away to live with Mary Magdalene, as in *Holy Blood, Holy Grail*, authored by Michael Baigent, Richard Leigh, and Henry Lincoln.[14]

Against these different (and often contradictory) versions of the swoon theory, it must be said that their major source, the New Testament itself, contains not a shred of hard evidence in their favor. The Gospels, Paul, and primitive Christian formulas (quoted in 1 Corinthians 15:3–5, the early speeches in Acts, and elsewhere) agree that Jesus genuinely died by crucifixion and was buried as a dead man. Other ancient sources corroborate this. The Jewish historian Flavius Josephus (d. after 100 CE) reports that Jesus was crucified under Pontius Pilate (*Antiquities*, 18:63–64). It appears that some Christian or Christians revised this passage in Josephus by adding material in praise of Jesus, but at least the information about the execution of Jesus goes back to Josephus himself. Writing around 113 CE, the Roman historian Tacitus explains that the name "Christians" came from the founder of their sect, Christ, who was executed by the procurator Pontius Pilate during the reign of the emperor Tiberius (*Annals*, 15:44). In an obscure passage the Babylonian Talmud writes of Yeshu, who led some Israelites astray by his magic but was then "hanged on the eve of the Passover" (*Sanhedrin*, 43a). These Roman and Jewish sources show little historical knowledge about Jesus, but they indicate no doubt whatsoever that he genuinely died by public execution.[15] Like the passion narratives in the four Gospels, these and other documents contain not the slightest hint that Jesus was or could have been alive when the executioners had finished with him.

In the nineteenth century David Friedrich Strauss (1808–74) cast many doubts on the Gospel stories but even so had no patience with the swoon theory. He put his finger on a knockdown difficulty against any hypothesis of a half-dead Jesus reviving in the tomb, emerging, and then appearing to his followers:

> It is impossible that a being who had stolen half dead out of the sepulcher, who crept about weak and ill, wanting medical treatment, who required bandaging, strengthening and indulgence…could have given the disciples the impression that he was a Conqueror over death and the grave, the Prince of Life, an impression which lay at the bottom of their future ministry. Such a resuscitation…could by no possibility have changed their sorrow into enthusiasm, have elevated their reverence into worship.[16]

Add, too, the fact that neither the New Testament nor any other source provides evidence for the existence and activity of a Jesus who had revived from apparent death.

In conclusion, the swoon theory reduces the origin of Christianity not only to a banal story about a bungled execution but also to a gross act of misrepresentation. In place of Jesus truly rising from the dead and appearing to his followers, we are told that he had an incredibly lucky revival from apparent death, an escape that the disciples later misrepresented when they claimed that he had been raised from the dead, "no more to return to corruption" (Acts 13:34). The swoon theory, by granting Jesus only a temporary respite from death after an extraordinarily unpleasant brush with crucifixion, makes the New Testament language about his glorious, new, incorruptible existence (for example, Luke 24:26; 1 Cor 15:20–28, 35–58; 1 Pet 1:11; 1 Tim 3:16) simply incomprehensible or else a bold lie.

THE APPEARANCES REVISITED

To avoid finishing this chapter on a negative note, I end by noting two features of the appearances: the grace of a certain preparation that preceded them and the collaboration they required.

Graced Preparation

Some ancient and more modern critics have cast doubt on the appearances by noting their nonpublic character. Celsus (in *True Discourse*) and Porphyry (in *Against the Christians*), for instance, argued that if the risen Christ truly appeared risen from the dead, he should have made himself known to his Jewish opponents, to Pilate and Herod, and even better to the members of the Roman Senate.[17] Many centuries later Hermann Reimarus (1694–1768) declared the lack of such public appearances to be irreconcilable with Jesus' alleged mission to call all people to a new faith. "If only he had manifested himself one single time after his resurrection in the temple, before the people and the

Sanhedrin in Jerusalem, visible, audibly, tangibly," Reimarus wrote, "then it could not fail that the entire Jewish nation would have believed in him." Hence Reimarus concluded, "Even if we had no other stumbling-block about Jesus' resurrection, this single one, that he did not allow himself to be seen publicly, would itself be enough to throw all its credibility aside, because it cannot agree in all eternity with Jesus' intention in coming into the world."[18]

When responding to Celsus in the third century, Origen argued that the risen Christ could not be perceived in an ordinary way, as if he were just another object in our world. The resurrection brought the revelation of Christ's divine status, something that was not to be seen with the eyes of the old creation.[19] Origen's sense of the new conditions required for communicating between the sender/revealer (the risen Christ) and the receivers (the apostolic witnesses) deserves to be developed.

The resurrected Christ himself constitutes the beginning of the end of the world (1 Cor 15:20, 23), the realized presence of the new creation. Through his risen bodiliness, matter has been elevated to a final, transformed state that goes far beyond the bodiliness we presently experience in this world. "Exalted at the right hand of God" (Acts 2:33), Christ shares in the divine mystery and is not to be manipulated, weighed, measured, or in other ways treated like an ordinary object in this world. He appears where and to whom he wills and disappears when he wills (for example, Luke 24:31).

Those who accept the summary just given about the new status of the risen Christ should find little difficulty in acknowledging what it calls for: graced powers of perception on the part of those who saw him. We might apply to the past a paraphrase from 1 John about the final vision of God: "When Jesus appeared we were like him, for we saw him as he was/is" (1 John 3:2). To see the risen Christ required a transforming grace for the recipients of that experience. To see him they needed to be first made, in some sense, like him, a grace that was not given either to the guards at the tomb (Matt 28:4,11) or to Paul's companions on the road to Damascus (Acts 9:7).

This graced perception of the risen Christ involved some kind of preparation, which, however, should not be exaggerated, as it was by Rudolf Pesch. A 1973 issue of a theological journal was largely dedicated to Pesch's original thesis on the Easter faith of the disciples and to critical evaluations of his interpretation.[20] He denied the historicity of the postresurrection appearances and maintained that the disciples simply applied to Jesus a prior Jewish tradition about the martyrdom and resurrection of godly persons, especially eschatological prophets. To know that Jesus had risen from the dead, the disciples needed no further information or input after the crucifixion and burial. However, the existence of such a prior tradition is quite uncertain. For that and other reasons, in a 1980 lecture that became a chapter in a Festschrift for F.-X. Durrwell's seventieth birthday, Pesch withdrew his earlier hypothesis and accepted the visions of the risen Jesus as real events in history, through which the disciples knew of their Lord's resurrection and exaltation.[21]

To be sure, the evidence, as Pesch himself came to realize, firmly excludes the view that by the time the passion arrived the original disciples were already fully prepared for Easter faith. Nevertheless, one should not go to the other extreme and insinuate a complete discontinuity. Their association with him during his ministry in certain ways prepared such disciples as Peter and Mary Magdalene for their special, personal experience of the risen Christ.

Initially, Paul misunderstood the righteousness given through faith in the living Jesus and persecuted the early church. Yet his faultless rectitude in keeping the law (Phil 3:6) also served as some measure of preparation for his seeing the risen Lord, a preparation that evidently was not shared by Caiaphas, Pilate, Herod Antipas, and the members of the Roman Senate. Of course, it is with unusual passion that Paul states the change he underwent when he moved from a pre-Christian Jewish life to his present life in Christ as a Jewish Christian. He describes his previous piety as so much excrement that should be thrown out (Phil 3:7–9). Certainly he had to change much (but not all) of his thinking about righteousness.[22] In general, it would be a mistake to allege a complete break with his Jewish, religious past. His striking dedication to the scriptures and to prayer, for instance, was not irrelevant in preparing him for the Damascus road encounter. Even though he read the scriptures and prayed differently after that encounter, Paul was already a prayerful, biblical person before he met Jesus.

Collaboration

The appearances of the risen Christ also invited a collaboration that did not leave the disciples in the state of purely passive observers (if there could be such a state). They were not coerced into meeting him, recognizing him, and accepting his resurrection from the dead and their mission to the world. In Matthew's account "the eleven" freely keep the rendezvous on a mountain in Galilee (Matt 27:7, 10, 16). Even so, when Jesus appeared, some remained doubtful. They had to allow these doubts to be dealt with when Jesus drew near and commissioned them (Matt 28:17–20). Luke's Emmaus story portrays a gradual entering into an experience of the risen Lord that brought the two disciples to invite him to stay with them. Only then did they recognize him in "the breaking of the bread" (Luke 24:13–35). In John's account Mary Magdalene first "turned" around physically (20:14) and then, when called by name, "turned to" the risen Jesus and acknowledged him (20:16). This second turning suggests Mary's spiritual collaboration that brought the meeting to its high point. Or perhaps we are to understand that Mary first "turned away from the supposed gardener," and then, "when she recognized his voice, she turned back to him."[23] That too would be an act of collaboration.

Beyond question, much more needs to be said exegetically and historically about these episodes from Matthew, Luke, and John. I simply note how these three Gospels, for all their differences, converge in recalling that the encounters with the risen Jesus invited the disciples to collaborate freely. The appearances were deeply self-involving experiences through which they became dedicated witnesses (for example, Acts 2:32; 3:15; 4:20). From what we know of Caiaphas, Pilate, Herod, and the members of the Roman Senate, one would not imagine them to be ready for such generous and even heroic participation in a personal experience of the risen Lord.

Chapter 5 faces the question that has doubtless entered the reader's mind. What justifies us in joining Peter, Mary Magdalene, Paul, and other Easter witnesses in accepting that Jesus has been raised from the dead? Before reaching that issue, we take up a further question, about a secondary cause that signaled to the first Christians Jesus' resurrection: the discovery of his empty tomb. *Secondary* indicates the order of importance, not necessarily the chronological order of events. The discovery of the empty tomb may well have preceded in time the first appearance of the risen Jesus.

Chapter 4

THE DISCOVERY OF
THE EMPTY TOMB

In the New Testament narratives, the discovery of the empty tomb served as a secondary sign, which was ambiguous in itself—Mary Magdalene jumped at first to the conclusion that someone had taken away the body of Jesus (John 20:2, 13, 15)—but which, when taken with the appearances, served to confirm the reality of his resurrection. But do the Gospel stories of Mary Magdalene alone (John) or with others (Mark, followed by Matthew and Luke) contain a reliably historical core? I deal with a case of multiple attestation: two traditions that report the empty tomb story: the Markan tradition (paralleled partially by Matthew and Luke) and the somewhat different tradition that entered John's Gospel.

In the introduction to this book I discussed that Daniel Smith alleges that Mark and/or his sources, on the basis of a saying from Q, created an empty tomb tradition that was then taken up by the other evangelists. I also noted that, in a paper that preceded Smith's book, Adela Yarbro Collins "explained" Mark 16:1–8 as created by the evangelist on the basis of Greco-Roman ideas of notable figures being translated into heaven. Before presenting a case for the discovery of the empty tomb deriving from an historical event, I reflect on some features in the Easter stories in Mark and the other Gospels that suggest a very early origin for such stories rather than any creative inventions by the evangelists themselves or by others on whom they drew.

VERY OLD TRADITIONS

I recalled in the introduction what N. T. Wright had to say about certain "silences" of the Easter stories that speak against the idea of their coming from later sources. First, up to the death of Jesus, all four Gospels continually quote and echo the Jewish scriptures. Mark's passion narrative, for instance, borrows language from the psalms in telling the story of Jesus' suffering and death.[1] But when he moves to his Easter story and the visit of three women to the tomb of Jesus, he neither cites nor echoes the scriptures. A familiar theme in Matthew is his "All this took place to fulfill what had been spoken by the Lord through the prophet," a formula to which the evangelist then attaches one or two biblical citations.[2] Surprisingly such biblical "embroidery" does not show up in his final, Easter chapter. Possibly the words "All authority in heaven and on earth has been given to me" (Matt 28:18) allude to Daniel 7:14 ("To him was given dominion / and glory and kingship"). Yet, substantially if not perhaps entirely, Matthew follows Mark in leaving his resurrection chapter biblically "unadorned." Luke 24:27, 32, 44–45 and John 20:9 refer to the new understanding of the scriptures that the risen Christ communicates, but neither evangelist cites any passage to show how the resurrection of Jesus fulfilled some biblical promise. This silence prompts the question, If Mark 16:1–8 (followed by the other Easter stories) were fictional creations of the evangelists and/or the sources on which they drew, why did they refrain from producing scriptural proof texts that would lend credibility to their fictional narratives?

A second surprising feature of the Easter stories of Mark and the other evangelists is their failure to describe the risen Jesus with traits of glory. They do not adopt the resurrection language of Daniel 12 and state that Jesus was "shining like the brightness of the sky." A glorious "angel of the Lord" appears in Matthew 28:3, but that figure is at most an angelic double for Jesus, not Jesus himself. The promise in Mark 16:7 is that Peter and the other disciples will see Jesus in Galilee, but not that they will see him "in a glorious state." To be sure, the risen Jesus appears and disappears at will; locked doors do not prevent him from showing himself to the disciples (John 20:26). But, all in all, there is a curious ordinariness to the accounts of the risen Jesus. This can seem more striking when we recall that Paul, who wrote his letters before any of the four Gospels came into its final shape, reflected on the "glory," "power," and other features of the risen bodiliness of Christ, "the man of heaven" (1 Cor 15:42–49).

The mention of Paul recalls a third strange feature of the Easter narratives in all four Gospels: their failure to present believers as sharing or hoping to share in the resurrection of Jesus. Writing in the mid-50s, the apostle spends verses developing what he means by the risen Christ being "the first fruits of those who have died" (1 Cor 15:20). But, when some years later the evangelists composed their Easter chapters, they drew on very early traditions that came from a time when Christians had not yet spelled out for themselves a major implication of Jesus' resurrection: they too would share in that glorious resurrection. This reticence suggests that these chapters represent a very old telling of the discovery of the empty tomb and Jesus' encounters with his disciples—a time before Paul and others reflected on the implications to be drawn from Jesus' resurrection, made known through that discovery and the appearances.

The letters of Paul repeatedly attend to the redemptive significance of the dying and rising of Christ. A lapidary statement sums up that significance: "[Jesus our Lord] was handed over to death for our trespasses and was raised for our justification" (Rom 4:25). In this verse the apostle may be citing a previous formula. He certainly does so when he reminds the Corinthian Christians that "Christ died for our sins in accordance with the scriptures" (1 Cor 15:3). Here a fourth significant absence is noticeable. Mark presents the interpreting angel as calling Jesus simply by his historical name (and not by the title of "Christ" or "Lord")[3] and saying to the three women in the tomb, "You are looking for Jesus of Nazareth, who was crucified. He has been raised" (Mark 16:6). No saving or atoning significance is attached to either his crucifixion or resurrection, as in Romans 4:25. While written later than Paul, Mark's Easter narrative shows a haunting, ancient simplicity that takes us back to the origins of the Christian story.

MARK'S CREATION?

The more we detect such a simplicity that derives from the origins of Christianity, the less plausible we find the theory that the discovery of the empty tomb was not an historical event but merely a later creation, a fictional scenario coming from the evangelist Mark. But it is worth spelling out further reasons that tell against the view of Yarbro Collins, Rudolf Pesch, Smith, and others that Mark 16:1–8 is a fictional narrative.

First, despite all the theological insights and allusions that modern scholars have detected in the Gospel of Mark, he does not seem to have been very creative from a literary point of view. Hence it is hardly to be expected that he would invent out of nothing not only an entire episode but also an episode that centered on something of supreme importance, the resurrection of Jesus from the dead. Joel Marcus, while allowing for some editorial additions made by Mark (for example, Mark 16:7), argues that the evangelist incorporates "an existing narrative" into his final chapter. Marcus also draws attention to the independent witness of John 20:1–2, which "tells the same basic story, and in a way that is in some respects more primitive (e.g., one woman rather than three, no angelic interpreter)."[4]

Second, the thesis that Mark ends his Gospel with a fictional episode involves us in portraying Matthew and Luke as gullible. They used, as the majority of scholars rightly hold, Mark 16:1–8 as a major source in composing their Easter narratives. Matthew and Luke repeat the main lines of Mark's story about the discovery of the empty tomb as if it were a factual narrative. Have they misunderstood Mark and read as history what was intended only as an imaginative fiction about an apotheosis of Jesus? Can a modern scholar presume to evaluate better than those two evangelists the status of their main source?

Third, as I remarked in the introduction, the period between Jesus (crucified around 30 CE) and the final composition of Mark's Gospel (late 60s) was spanned by the continual presence and testimony of those who had participated as eyewitnesses in the history of Jesus. Mark's closing chapter mentions a number of these witnesses: (1) the protagonists at the tomb, who were Mary

Magdalene, Mary the mother of James (the James being presumably "James the younger" or "the small" mentioned by Mark 15:40 and Luke 8:2[5]), and Salome; and (2) those who were directed to Galilee and saw the risen Jesus—Peter and the disciples. These followers of Jesus played a central role in transmitting traditions about him; some, or even many of them, were still alive in the 60s. Presumably, they would not have tolerated such a creative and major innovation as a purely fictional story of three women discovering the tomb of Jesus to be open and empty on the third day. It is hard to imagine that Mark exposed himself to an easy rebuttal of his fiction by putting a number of eyewitnesses into his new story.

Fourth, Yarbro Collins and Smith, as I reported in the introduction, attempt to explain how Mark created his empty tomb story on the basis of Greco-Roman ideas of a notable figure being translated into heaven. But various scholars, as I also noted, find little or no evidence of such Greco-Roman influences either in the final chapter of Mark or in the rest of his Gospel. Such influences do not provide a master key to Mark's text. Rather he set an account of Jesus within the framework of God's saving work for the chosen people. Hence he did not begin his story with Jesus but quoted Isaiah to indicate that what immediately follows (about John the Baptist) continues what God had already done: "See I am sending my messenger ahead of you, / who will prepare your way; / the voice of one crying out in the wilderness: / 'Prepare the way of the Lord, / make his paths straight'" (Mark 1:2–3).

Fifth, Rudolf Pesch proposed that Mark, when composing his final chapter, used an earlier tradition about women discovering the tomb of Jesus to be open and empty. But this tradition did not derive from some actual event in history; it was simply a means of illustrating the earliest Christian proclamation of Jesus' death and resurrection that we find classically expressed in 1 Corinthians 15:3–8. Such a theory holds that Mark 16:1–8 and the tradition behind it (along with the subsequent empty tomb stories in the other Gospels) did not convey any factual information about the state of Jesus' tomb. It was simply a way of announcing the resurrection of the crucified Jesus and his Easter appearances.[6] But may we interpret Mark's final chapter and the tradition behind it as merely an imaginative elaboration of what we already find in 1 Corinthians 15:3–8?

Pesch's thesis has to cope with an even stronger form of the difficulty indicated in our third point. If eyewitnesses still alive in the 60s would have challenged Mark's alleged invention, there would have been more or even many more of them around to challenge a pre-Markan tradition concocted in the 50s if not earlier. Could such a pre-Markan fiction of three (named) women discovering the tomb of Jesus to be open and empty have survived challenges coming from numerous eyewitnesses who were very much alive in the first two decades after the death and resurrection of Jesus?

Then a detailed comparison indicates that the two traditions, the Pauline and pre-Pauline proclamation of the resurrection and the appearances, on the one hand, and the empty tomb story, on the other, have independent origins. Major elements in 1 Corinthians 15:3–8 do not turn up in Mark 16:1–8: the double appeal to the scriptures (1 Cor 15:3,4); the atoning death "for our sins" (1 Cor 15:3); the title "Christ" (1 Cor 15:3), which may have already become a second name for Jesus; and the appearances to more than five hundred followers of Jesus, to James, to all the apostles, and to Paul himself (1 Cor 15:6–8). Mark's empty tomb story promises appearances only to the disciples and Peter (Mark 16:7).

Mark's narrative contains some major items of which 1 Corinthians 15:3–8 knows nothing at all: the discovery of the empty tomb by three (named) women; the dating of this discovery to "the first day of the week" (Sunday) rather than the Pauline "the third day" (1 Cor 15:4); the interpreting angel; and the promise of appearances *in Galilee*. Paul's list provides no locale for any of the appearances. Thus even a cursory comparison between 1 Corinthians 15:3–8 and Mark 16:1–8 shows substantial differences that throw serious doubt on the thesis of a tradition of the resurrection and the appearances leading to the formation of an empty tomb tradition. These traditions seem to have quite different origins; Mark's story does not derive from a Pauline proclamation. But is the empty tomb tradition essentially reliable?

IN DEFENSE OF THE EMPTY TOMB

Apologists for the empty tomb stories as substantially reliable frequently argue from the central place of women in these stories. In the oldest version from Mark 16:1–8, three women were astonished to find Jesus' tomb open and empty on the first Easter Sunday morning. If this story were simply a legend created by Mark or other early Christians, they would presumably have attributed the discovery of the empty tomb to male disciples rather than to women. In first-century Palestine, women and slaves were, for all intents and purposes, disqualified as valid witnesses.[7] The natural thing for someone making up a story about the empty tomb would have been to ascribe the discovery to men and not to women. Legend makers do not normally invent positively unhelpful material. Why would anyone attribute to women the key testimony to the empty tomb unless that was actually the case?

Critics have attempted to rebut this argument in various ways. Some maintain that it was public knowledge that by the first Easter Sunday the male disciples had already fled from Jerusalem and had not yet returned to the city. Hence Mark or whoever made up the story of the discovery of the empty tomb had no choice. The protagonists had to be female disciples, as they were known to have stayed behind in Jerusalem.[8] This explanation leaves us with a curiously mixed picture of the moral constraints felt by Mark or whoever created the empty tomb story. On the one hand, he respected a precise and reliable piece of information that the existing tradition recalled about the whereabouts of the followers of Jesus on a given day: only female disciples were in the city on the first Easter Sunday morning. But, on the other hand, he felt free to invent from nothing the narrative about their visit to the tomb of Jesus and the discovery they made. One wonders how such a story would have struck its contemporary readers. They knew that female disciples had been around on that morning, but they had hitherto not known anything whatsoever about three of those women visiting the tomb and finding it to be open and empty.

Other critics dismiss the significance of the point about women being invalid witnesses. Yes, they agree, that point would tell in favor of the historical reliability of the empty tomb story *if it had originated early and in Palestine*. But, they claim, it had a later, Hellenistic origin. Hence those who created the empty tomb story and their first readers would not have found the witness of women necessarily embarrassing or counterproductive. Obviously a key feature in this debate concerns the dating and background for the composition of Mark's Gospel. Many scholars propose a date around 70 CE or even earlier. Richard Bauckham has marshaled plausible (internal and external) evidence to rehabilitate the case for Simon Peter being the major eyewitness source behind Mark. The naming of Peter, by a kind of inclusion, holds the Gospel together from 1:16–18 right through to 16:7.[9] That would mean that the Gospel of Mark, while coming into its final form in the late 60s, originated early and drew massively on a witness from Palestine.

The second important question bears on the alleged Hellenistic or Greco-Roman elements detectable in what Mark wrote. The fourth point in the previous section is relevant to this discussion, but it is worth pressing matters further. Could this first-century Christian, deeply committed to the new faith, born most probably into a Jewish family, obviously steeped in the Jewish scriptures, and of no great literary talent, have drawn on Greco-Roman ideas to compose a fictional account of women discovering the tomb of Jesus to be open and empty? Mark 1—15 shows this evangelist setting the story of Jesus in the context of Jewish salvation history; these chapters are permeated with quotations and echoes of the Jewish scriptures, as Mark goes about illustrating how Jesus fulfilled various Jewish (and not Greco-Roman) motifs. Can Greco-Roman thought forms be then invoked to unlock the secrets of what Mark wrote in his final eight verses? One notable supporter of this thesis, Yarbro Collins, has to admit that "it is hard to find" in Mark much influence from Greco-Roman literature.[10] If so, it is scarcely plausible to claim that he changed character and unexpectedly used Hellenistic sources in his final chapter.

FURTHER CONSIDERATIONS

Along with arguments based on the presence of named women in Mark's empty tomb story, apologists for the empty tomb have frequently added other considerations. First, late first-century polemic, reported by Matthew and rejecting the message of the resurrection, supposed that the tomb of Jesus was known to be empty. This Gospel tells of the posting of a guard at the tomb (Matt 27:62–66) and the subsequent report by members of the guard (Matt 28:11–14). Matthew states that some of the soldiers were bribed to say that the disciples of Jesus, under cover of night, stole the body. The evangelist ends the story by referring to the time of his writing and something his readers know only too well: "This story is still told among the Jews to this day" (Matt 28:15). Whatever the origin and the historical status of Matthew's story about the setting of the guard and their subsequent actions,[11] the closing remark from the evangelist points to Christians and Jews arguing with one another over the tomb of Jesus at the time Matthew wrote (around 80 CE). The debate presupposed that both parties knew Jesus' tomb had been found to be empty. They agreed on this datum but interpreted it in radically different ways. Naturally the opponents of the Christian movement explained the absence of the body as a plain case of theft (Matt 28:11–15).[12] What was in dispute was not whether the tomb was empty but *why* it was empty. We have no early evidence that anyone, either Christian or non-Christian, ever alleged that the tomb of Jesus still contained his remains.

Second, we have no evidence that any first-century Jews or Christians ever embraced a belief in resurrection that did not involve the body that had been buried. Of course, there were some who expected the kind of glorious transformation suggested by Daniel 12 and others who thought of resurrection in a material way, as the earthly body being reassembled or reconstructed (for example, 2 Macc 7). Nevertheless, despite their differences, all who expected resurrection agreed that the bodies in the graves would be involved when the dead were to be resurrected. They neither imagined nor anticipated a personal resurrection that did not include the bodies that had been buried. For first-century

Jews, no empty tomb meant no resurrection. Thus contemporary notions of resurrection were incompatible with accepting (on the basis of the appearances) the resurrection of Jesus while admitting that his tomb was not empty and that his body had quietly decayed there. Unless his body was involved in his resurrection, no one would have accepted the proclamation of his resurrection from the dead (for example, 1 Cor 15:3–5).

This feature of first-century Jewish beliefs disposes of an objection that is sometimes raised: Why did the apostle Paul remain silent about the discovery of the empty tomb in 1 Corinthians 15:3–8?[13] Does this mean that a bodily resurrection from the grave was irrelevant for Paul? For a Pharisaic Jew like Paul, a resurrection that did not include an empty tomb would have been inconceivable. As Wolfhart Pannenberg has written, "For Paul the empty tomb was a self-evident implication of what was said about the resurrection of Jesus."[14] When the apostle talked about Christ as having been "raised from the dead" (for example, Rom 10:9; 1 Cor 15:12, 20; Gal 1:1), this meant being "raised from the tomb."

Such first-century beliefs also support the conclusion that, at least in Jerusalem and Palestine, it would have been impossible to proclaim the resurrection of Jesus unless his tomb was known to be empty. His alleged resurrection could have been dismissed out of hand as blatantly untrue if his tomb was known to have still contained his mortal remains. It was the discovery of the empty tomb that made it possible to believe in and announce the news of his resurrection.

A 1986 Italian film, *The Inquiry (L'inchiesta)*, expressed this argument on the screen. A Roman officer, sent on mission by the emperor Tiberius to investigate and suppress the emerging Christian Church, went to Jerusalem in search of the grave of Jesus. By opening the tomb and producing Jesus' remains for public display, the officer knew that he could strike at the heart of the new faith by destroying its proclamation of Jesus' resurrection. Other things happened as the story unfolded. But what the officer first aimed to do in Jerusalem matches what we know of contemporary belief: unless the tomb of Jesus was empty, his resurrection could not have taken place.

Further Counter-explanations

Another way of approaching the question of the empty tomb is to examine further counter-explanations. If none of them survives scrutiny, that should encourage us to accept the only view left standing: one or more women did, to their astonishment, discover the tomb of Jesus to be open and empty on the first Easter Sunday morning.

First, there is the thesis of the "final insult." On the basis of Acts 13:27–29, some have claimed that the Jewish or Roman authorities gave Jesus a dishonorable burial by throwing his body into a common grave or at least a grave unknown to his followers. But the vague language of this passage in Acts ("They asked Pilate to have him killed....They took him down from the tree and laid him in a tomb") should be read in the light of the passion story, which has already been told by the author of Acts and which ends with Joseph of Arimathea burying Jesus in a tomb known at least to some female followers of Jesus (Luke 23:50–56). The section on Dale Allison in our introduction showed how the historicity of the burial story can be strongly defended.[15] In any case, when Paul quotes early Christian proclamation to say that Christ "was buried" (1 Cor 15:4), this suggests an honorable burial, without any hint of a final insult.

Second, other critics of the empty tomb story have postulated some kind of mistake on the part of the women. At the beginning of the twentieth century, Kirsopp Lake suggested that the women went to the wrong tomb, where they met a young man who told them that Jesus' corpse was not there ("He is not here").[16] They fled, thinking that they had seen an angel who had told them of the resurrection. But exegetes commonly agree that the evangelist Mark intended an angel when he introduced "a young man, dressed in a white robe, sitting on the right side" (Mark 16:5). Moreover, the message, "He has been raised; he is not here. Look, there is the place they laid him" (Mark 16:6), may not be divided in the trivial way Kirsopp Lake proposed.

Some have hypothesized that after the burial Joseph of Arimathea returned and removed the body to another place. When the women visited the tomb, they found it empty and imagined that Jesus had risen from the dead. Apart from the fact that the Gospels nowhere hint that Joseph returned as claimed, there is no evidence that, in defiance of legal sanctions, corpses were ever transferred in this way. Moreover, could or would Joseph have remained silent when the Christians began to proclaim Jesus' resurrection if he knew the real facts?

In the third century Tertullian (*De Spectaculis*, 30) reported a similar story about the removal of Jesus' corpse. Before the women arrived on the Sunday morning, a local gardener had removed the corpse to stop the disciples from trampling on his vegetables when they came to visit Jesus' tomb. In his first book on Jesus, Malcolm Muggeridge advanced the theory that, hearing of Jesus' kingdom and hoping for some gain, grave robbers stole the corpse.[17] It has also been suggested that the body of Jesus disappeared when it fell down a crack opened by an earthquake. The prize for sheer silliness must go to the theory that I once heard developed at a biblical conference in Australia: the corpse had decomposed with unique speed. When the women arrived on the third day, there were simply no remains to be found.[18]

THEOLOGICAL DIFFICULTIES

Debates about the historicity of the issue do not, I believe, reach the heart of the matter. It is not enough to debate whether the discovery of the empty tomb should be accepted as *historically* reliable. Some alert us to other issues when they dismiss the empty tomb as *theologically* questionable and irrelevant for their faith. They may bravely announce, "It would make no difference to my faith if they found the bones of Jesus." (In passing, one might ask, Would such a discovery *improve* your faith? Moreover, what about the faith of others, very many of whom would be deeply shaken by this discovery?) In a more elegant way, Louis Evely put this challenge: "For me personally, it makes little difference whether Christ's tomb was empty or not. I would have exactly the same faith in his resurrection in either case." In a theological vein he questioned, "If...the resurrection of Christ is our resurrection, why should we expect his to take place in a way different from ours?"[19]

This query recalls the case that G. W. H. Lampe developed from "the truth of the incarnation." In stronger tones than Evely, he insisted that Christ's resurrection "cannot be of different order" from our resurrection. By becoming man, Christ entered fully into the human condition, which entails physical corruption after death. Hence his body *must* have decayed in the grave.[20] Some years later Arthur Peacocke put a similar case: if the resurrection of Jesus "consisted of a transformation of his physical body," there would be an "insuperable" gulf between what happened to Jesus and what could happen to us. The "nature of his resurrection would be unique and irrelevant to what might happen to us." Hence, albeit in less vigorous tones than Lampe, Peacocke envisaged the crucified body of Jesus decomposing in the tomb.[21] As I argue later in this chapter, a theology oriented toward the incarnation does not necessarily exclude Jesus' body being speedily raised in a glorious resurrection.

Some other writers moved beyond historical considerations to raise theological objections to the story of the empty tomb. Thus Hans Grass contended that (1) faith is directed toward the person of the risen Christ, (2) God did not need an empty tomb, and in any case (3) the Easter faith of Peter and the other disciples arose when they encountered the risen Lord, not when they found the tomb to be open and empty.[22] Points 1 and 2 are theological, point 3 historical. In debating with those like Evely, Lampe, Peacocke, and Grass, the real challenge is to offer some insight into the role played by the empty tomb in a full resurrection faith. That will make it possible to clear up the difficulties that these and other such authors raise.

NEW TESTAMENT RESERVATIONS

The New Testament warns against exaggerating the value of the empty tomb. In Mark 16:1–8 the three women who find the tomb open and empty must hear the resurrection message ("He has been raised; he is not here") before they come to believe. The reality of the resurrection is asserted ("He has been raised") before the body's absence is noted ("Look, there is the place where they laid him"). The explanation of resurrection is not deduced from the physical fact of an empty tomb. The angel, in announcing the resurrection, does not answer some such question coming from the women as, "What has happened to the body?" Mark has no particular apologetic for the empty tomb, nor does he assign it any independent status for proclamation. The message that the women are to carry back to the disciples is not "Come and see Jesus' empty tomb," but rather "He is going ahead of you to Galilee; there you will see him."

Luke adds that the women's message about discovering the empty tomb and hearing of the resurrection from two angels met with incredulity: "These words seemed to them [the apostles] an idle tale, and they did not believe them" (Luke 24:11). Reporting the finding of the empty tomb, along with what angels had said about the resurrection, proved insufficient to bring others to faith.

In John, however, the empty tomb has gained enough importance that it can trigger faith in those perfectly disposed to believe. It has become a Johannine sign, a means for grasping an otherworldly truth. Neither an angelic message nor an appearance of the risen Christ is required before the beloved disciple, a model of the authentic believer, comes to faith (John 20:8). As a type of those who believe without seeing the risen Christ, he stands in sharp contrast with the doubting Thomas, who makes faith dependent upon physical contact with the risen Christ. Readers are meant to value highly the faith of the beloved disciple, precisely because he has not yet understood any hints from scripture that Christ must rise from the dead (John 20:9). Even so, he believes.

Nevertheless, the fourth evangelist recognizes that the sheer fact of an empty grave remains ambiguous (John 20:2, 13–15). He puts into the mouth of a follower of Jesus the objection of nonbelievers that unidentified grave robbers unwittingly provided the basis for Easter faith. Mary Magdalene states this view: "They have taken the Lord out of the tomb, and we do not know where they have laid him." A similar (but not identical) explanation involving grave robbery, as we have seen, appears in Matthew's reference to the chief priests and elders alleging that Jesus' disciples had stolen the body. John seemingly wishes to give the lie to any notion that the tomb had been robbed. He notes that the grave cloths remained neatly in the tomb—something that would not have happened if thieves had been at work: "Simon Peter...went into the tomb. He saw the linen wrappings lying there, and the cloth that had been on Jesus' head, not lying with the linen wrappings but rolled up in a place by itself" (John 20:6–7).[23]

To sum up: the New Testament maintains the fact of the empty tomb but freely admits its ambiguity. What theological value does the empty tomb enjoy? What part does it play in Easter faith? Will we be left in the odd position of accepting the fact of the empty tomb but failing to integrate it into our overall understanding of the resurrection?

THE SIGN OF THE TOMB

First, in the New Testament the empty tomb stood for a return from the dead and all that such a return implied. The burial of people signified that they were removed from the land of the living and had fallen into the power of death. The stone or earth that covered their corpses separated them from the living. To be dead was to be in the underworld (Ps 49:14–15; Luke 16:22–23). Hence Christ's resurrection as a victory over death (1 Cor 15:54–57) was understood to have broken the bonds of death and deprived death of its power (Acts 2:24). Christ now possessed the keys of the underworld (Rev 1:18), so that he could guarantee that the forces of death would not prevail against his church (Matt 16:18).[24]

Where tombs express the finality and irrevocable loss of death, Jesus' open and empty tomb symbolized the fullness of the new and everlasting life into which he had risen. Here the emptiness of the tomb, paradoxically, indicated the fullness of life into which the risen Jesus had entered. Graves naturally suggest the quiet decay of an existence dissolved by death. The empty tomb of Jesus symbolized the opposite, the complete life that had overcome the silence of death.

Second, the emptiness of Jesus' grave reflects the holiness of what it once held: the corpse of the incarnate Son of God, who lived totally for others and died to bring a new covenant of love for all people. This "Holy One" could not "experience corruption" (Acts 2:27).

Third, the empty tomb expresses something vital about the nature of redemption: namely, that redemption is much more than a mere escape from our world of suffering and death. Still less is it a kind of second creation "from nothing" (*ex nihilo*). Rather it means the transformation of this material, bodily world with its whole history of sin and suffering. The first Easter began the work of bringing our universe home to its ultimate destiny. God did not discard Jesus' corpse but mysteriously raised and transfigured it, so as to reveal what lies ahead for human beings and their world. In short, that empty tomb in Jerusalem forms God's radical sign that redemption is not an escape to a better world but a wonderful transformation of this world. Seen that way, the open and empty tomb of Jesus is highly significant for anyone who wants to appreciate what redemption means.

Thus the empty tomb acts as a safeguard against overspiritual, docetic, or Platonizing interpretations that would expound the resurrection as an escape from "here" to "there." In such explanations the real world lies elsewhere. By his death and resurrection Jesus leaves this illusory world of decay behind him. He took on the human condition but eventually gave it up as irredeemably hopeless. His body can only be abandoned to the corruption of the grave.

"OVERSPIRITUALIZING" INTERPRETATIONS

Those who dispense with an empty tomb can readily finish up asserting what looks scarcely distinguishable from the immortality of Jesus' soul. Thus Lampe may explicitly refuse to introduce such a doctrine into his discussion of the resurrection.[25] But he erodes this position seriously when he writes of "we" and "our personality" continuing to exist, although not "in the mode of physical being." He even admits, "If my relationship to God continues, then I must continue as my self or my soul (I take these terms as synonymous), not in this present bodily mode of existence, but living because the God on whom my life depends will maintain his grace towards me."[26] In these terms, the victory of the resurrection becomes a continued existence outside "the mode of physical being" of Jesus' personality.

It has become conventional to remark that a dualistic anthropology is no longer self-evident. Modern people, at least in the Western world, are supposed to have ceased believing that immortal souls inhabit their bodies. But Platonism may be hardier than some allege. Perhaps it is in the nature of things that there should always be attempts to interpret the resurrection as the survival of Jesus' inner self that makes a break with his old bodily existence. A resurrected and transformed body that promises a transformed world presents imaginative difficulties that are almost too much to take. It is easier, either overtly or covertly, to deal with an immortal soul and deck out the long-standing Platonic model with new plausibility. In a private conversation, one of my former students, George Hunsinger, expressed this trend as follows: for those who believe in such immortality, the hope is that time will be left behind, not redeemed; that death will be surpassed, not destroyed; that evil will be eluded, not defeated. In this scheme God allows the believer to transcend the old creation through an immortality to be enjoyed beyond the grave in "another world."

Acknowledging the empty tomb guards us against the continual temptation to allow our interpretation of Christ to become docetic. Too easily we can play down the bodily reality of the risen Christ, portray the resurrection as some kind of liberation of the spiritual Christ, and treat the physical world as ultimately illusory and incapable (or at least unworthy) of salvation. It was no coincidence that Rudolf Bultmann's demythologized view of the resurrection both omitted the empty tomb[27] and promoted an existentialist theology that failed to do justice to our physical and social nature. For Bultmann it is only in radical loneliness that human beings find themselves. In responding to his critics, he significantly remarked, "The chief aim of every genuine religion is to escape from the world."[28]

To appreciate the theology of the empty tomb, two complementary affirmations call for our attention. This doctrine asserts something about the redemptive activity of God as well as something about our material world and its possibilities. On the one hand, God intends to save human beings as wholes along with their world (Rom 8:18–25) and has begun to transform the world and redeem human history by raising up and transforming Jesus' dead body. God does not "throw away" the past by saving Jesus' soul and perhaps joining it to a new bodily existence that has no continuity whatsoever with his former bodily life on earth. On the other hand, the world is neither an illusion from which we must awake nor an evil that will prove irredeemable. God reveals this by starting his work of re-creation in favor of Jesus' crucified corpse. The past can be recovered as "raw material" for the future kingdom; matter enjoys a higher, glorious destiny.

BACK TO LAMPE AND GRASS

Let us return to the classical objections against the empty tomb raised by Lampe and Grass, theological objections that turn up over and over again. As we saw, Lampe starts from the doctrine of the incarnation: "That the Word of God was truly made man is the heart of the gospel. God incarnate entered our condition."[29] From this central truth, as we have seen, Lampe deduces the conclusion: the body of Jesus *must* have decayed in the grave.

First, St. Paul would question the opening assertion that we should take the incarnation as "the heart of the gospel." For the apostle the heart of the gospel is found in the death and resurrection of Jesus. For these saving events the sending of the pre-existent Son of God formed a prerequisite (Gal 4:4–5). In Pauline theology the incarnation as such does not redeem us. We may not assume the incarnation-oriented theology of John and the Greek fathers to be indisputably the central point from which we can deduce other truths.

Second, it remains a questionable procedure to deduce a particular fact (about the bodily fate of Jesus) from a principle, even the principle of the incarnation. Teaching about Christ has often been disfigured by theologians taking some general principles and deriving—by some logical necessity that may no longer seem either logical or necessary—specific facts about such matters as the extent and nature of Christ's human knowledge. In any case, the principle involved in Lampe's argument leaves aside such differences between Jesus and ourselves as his sinlessness. One can argue that it is precisely such differences that make it appropriate and intelligible that Jesus' resurrection should not be precisely the same as the resurrection that Christians hope for. His sinlessness militates against his sharing the normal human destiny of undergoing bodily corruption in the grave. Yet here again any straightforward deduction of a particular fact (the empty tomb) from a principle should be rejected as a dubious procedure. At best the principle of sinlessness serves to illuminate an already accepted belief in the empty tomb.

Third, another of my former students, Daniel Harrington, pointed out to me in a personal communication that even an incarnation-oriented theology need not lead us to reject the empty tomb. Lampe formulated the doctrine this way: the Son of God has become *man*. We could reverse the emphasis: *the Son of God* has become man. While Lampe takes it to be necessary that Christ should fully share our fate, I could argue that he came to elevate us and summon us to what is beyond our powers. In other words, we should respect the redemptive purpose of the incarnation. That goal can throw light on the empty tomb, or at least stop us from misinterpreting the aim of the incarnation as sharing, more or less totally, in the normal human condition. Here too we need to remember the personal identity of Jesus as the Son of God. The body buried by Joseph of Arimathea had the unique identity of being the body of the incarnate Son of God, the One who hung upon the cross to save humankind.

Fourth, apropos of objections coming from Grass, we gain nothing by capitulating to his assertion that "we do not believe in the empty tomb, but in the risen Lord." Such an antithesis remains foreign to New Testament faith. To strike out the empty tomb would be to tamper seriously with the Easter witness of the first Christians. As I have argued, the story of the empty tomb was an historically reliable part of what they announced about Christ's resurrection. They testified to what the women discovered on the third day but did not propose this as some alternative to belief in the risen Christ. Such belief had first been triggered by his appearances to some individuals and groups of disciples. The independent discovery of the empty tomb served as a negative sign confirming what they knew through the Easter appearances.

Karl Barth responded magisterially to the Grass-style antithesis. Although "Christians do not believe in the empty tomb but in the living Christ," this does not imply that "we can believe in the living Christ without believing in the empty tomb." It forms "an indispensable sign" that "obviates all possible misunderstanding." It excludes misinterpreting the existence of the risen Christ as something "purely beyond or inward. It distinguishes the confession that Jesus Christ lives from a mere manner of speaking on the part of believers. It is the negative presupposition of the concrete objectivity of his being."[30]

I also challenge the assertion from Grass that "God did not have to make the tomb empty in order to effect the Easter miracle." Is it arrogant presumption to allege what God had to do or did not have to do in order to achieve some desirable result? Instead of speculating about "alternate scenarios," it seems preferable to accept what has taken place (the discovery of the empty tomb) and to reflect on its meanings. In any case, what kind of "Easter miracle" would we face if such a "miracle" did not involve the raising from the grave of Jesus' body? One should call it rather the survival of his soul in heavenly glory or his soul's transmigration into a heavenly body, but not his resurrection from the dead. As I argued in chapter 2, the two verbs that recur in the New Testament language for the resurrection involve raising a dead body from the grave.

Chapter 5

THE RESURRECTION AS REDEEMING AND TRANSFORMING

After two chapters dealing with the major signs that prompted the Easter faith of Jesus' followers (his appearances and the discovery of the empty tomb), one option would be to take up some further events that strengthened and nourished that belief in him as risen from the dead: the outpouring of the Holy Spirit and the success of their mission to the world. These events, not to mention other factors that affected particular individuals and communities, continued to support the Easter faith of the first Christians. In chapter 6 I return to this theme: the cumulative range of causes that feed into faith in the risen Jesus both then and now.

At this point we reflect on the self-communication of God that the first Christians found in the resurrection of the crucified Jesus. Along with redemption, revelation is one distinguishable, if inseparable, dimension of this self-communication. What divine self-revelation came through the events of the first Good Friday and Easter Sunday? How, according to the Gospels and Paul, did these events mediate a new knowledge of God, now encountered as Father, Son, and Holy Spirit? But having recently dedicated many pages to the revelation coming through the crucified and resurrected Jesus,[1] I examine in this chapter the other, inseparable dimension of the divine self-communication: redemption or the saving activity of God.

Faced with claims about the resurrection, many people spontaneously ask, "Did it happen?" But, first of all, what is "it" that is supposed to have happened? If, primarily, the resurrection claim involves a transformed, embodied life for Jesus himself, what did the resurrection bring for human beings and their world? For New Testament Christians, the resurrection of Jesus is inextricably linked to a new creation that touches the entire universe. This resurrection is nothing less than a (new) creative activity of God that initiates the end of all things (Rev 21—22).

We can speak here of three stages in the divine self-bestowal: creation, the incarnation, and the crucified Christ's resurrection from the dead, which opens up a new existence for human beings and anticipates a glorious transformation of all that is to come. The created humanity of Jesus, transfigured and "divinized" to the ultimate degree possible, ushers in liberating consequences for human beings and their world now and at the end.

Eastern icons of the "Anastasis"—such as the one in the monastery of Chora (Istanbul)—indicate the deeply relational nature of Christ's resurrection and its universal impact. They introduce Adam, Eve, and crowds of people standing behind or near them and show vividly that the resurrection of the crucified Jesus is not merely an individual victory for Christ alone but also *the* saving event for all humanity. In liberating and raising Adam, Eve, and their companions, Christ, the Second Adam, raises all humanity. Such icons also imply the cosmic impact of what has happened. Huge rocks, which have been shattered to open Christ's passage down to the "limbo of the fathers," suggest that the Easter transformation includes the whole world. As corporate figures, Adam and Eve[2] foreshadow Christ, *the* corporate figure *par excellence*, whose work of redemption already has its impact on the entire human race and the cosmos.

The narrative theology of the four Gospels offers one approach to the redemptive nature of Christ's resurrection. I take up first Mark's brief Easter chapter, which presents or at least hints at some major aspects of God's redeeming activity. Then I attend to three redemptive themes in Matthew, Luke, and John: the divine victory over evil and injustice; the reconciliation of sinners; and the power and centrality of love.

MARK'S EMPTY TOMB NARRATIVE

At least three themes deserve retrieval from Mark 16:1–8.[3] First, while never formally named in Mark's concluding chapter,

God has triumphed over the evil and injustice that struck Jesus down. Glorious new life and not death has the final word. Two verbs in the passive voice point to the divine activity that has utterly transformed the situation brought about by the crucifixion and burial of Jesus. The link between the crucified Jesus and the risen Jesus is the victorious power of God. The great stone blocking the entrance to the tomb has been "rolled away," and one understands that this has been done "by God." Jesus has "been raised," and once again one understands "by God." Even before the three women arrive, the divine power has dramatically reversed the situation of death and injustice.

Matthew and Luke will picture the victorious and liberating divine action of the resurrection in a fuller context by adding, for example, inclusive elements. The Easter action of God at the end recalls some saving divine action at the start of their Gospels. In doctrinal terms, the divine activity in the resurrection evokes what was already involved in the incarnation. I take this up again later in the chapter.

Second, many commentators find a firm hint of redemptive rehabilitation in the angel's words to the women: "Tell his disciples and Peter that he is going ahead of you to Galilee; there you will see him..." (Mark 16:7). The male disciples sinfully failed when Jesus was arrested. They never showed their faces at the crucifixion and burial of Jesus. Peter denied on oath that he even knew Jesus. When the disciples came to Gethsemane with Jesus, they were called "disciples" (Mark 14:32). But after that point they are named as a faceless "all" who ran away into the night when Jesus was arrested (Mark 14:50). Now in the light and power of the resurrection, they are once again called "disciples." Along with Peter's, their failures are forgiven, and their discipleship is restored with a view to their meeting the risen Lord in Galilee. Through the promise of a rendezvous with the male disciples, Mark hints at the way in which redemption involves the reconciliation of sinners. We see more of this reconciliation later in this chapter.

Third, the angelic figure in the tomb offers a subtle hint of the redemptive power of love. Let me explain in detail. Almost inevitably, attentive readers of Mark's Gospel, when they come to the "young man dressed in white robe" (*stolē* in Greek, Mark 16:5) remember another young man who left his linen cloth/shroud (*sindōn* in Greek) in the hands of those who had come to arrest Jesus and fled naked into the night (Mark 14:51–52). In chapter 14, the nakedness of the young man, his linen cloth/shroud, and the darkness of the night convey the sense of Jesus now being led away defenseless and facing imminent death and burial. Three days later a young man clothed at dawn in the white robe of the resurrection also symbolizes what has happened to Jesus, who has been executed, buried in a linen cloth/shroud (*sindōn*, Mark 15:46), and now raised gloriously from the dead. The shroud of death has given way to the shining robe of resurrection.

The Markan young man of the death and resurrection narratives serves as a symbolic counterpart to Jesus himself. The young man in the tomb also personifies some aspects of *redemptive love*. Here I go beyond the conscious intentions of the evangelist himself. But there is a "plus value" in his text that opens itself to several reflections on how divine love works to save human beings.[4]

I feel encouraged to do so by a feature of all three Synoptic Gospels. The three evangelists never explicitly report Jesus as saying that his heavenly Father has *agapē* or love for human beings and rarely attribute to Jesus himself the explicit language of love (in Mark only at 10:21 and 12:30–31). Yet the universal kindness and mercy of God (for example, Matt 5:45 and Luke 6:35–36) and Jesus' continual care for the sick, the sinful, and the lost make no sense if we fail to recognize how love motivates and empowers the whole story in the Synoptic Gospels. The fact that the articulation of love remains largely implicit earlier in Mark's Gospel prompts me to spell out the redeeming love of God implied in the final chapter. Seven points call for attention.

First, the angelic messenger shows divine love through accepting and affirming the three startled women. To love others is to approve of them, and God's redemptive love means a fundamental divine approval of our "being there." Through the angelic young man, God expresses affirming, loving approval of the three women and of those to whom they are to bring the wonderful message of the resurrection. If we agree that love most radically means approval, we find such approving love of God embodied in Mark's Easter chapter.

Second, love entails active good will toward the other. The angel takes the initiative in reaching out to the three women and with a benevolent and practical concern for their welfare shares with them the good news of the resurrection that will change forever their life and that of other disciples of Jesus. This gift of love will become the self-gift of love, when they keep the rendezvous in Galilee ("There you will see *him*") and meet the risen Jesus himself. The divine giving will then become the self-gift of the Son of God in person.

In all situations, love as gift includes also a trusting disclosure. When we make a gift of ourselves, we do so by revealing ourselves to those whom we love. This third element is suggested by the angel's promise, "There you will see him." The risen Jesus will make himself visible and available to them. That promised self-disclosure will transform their existence.

Fourth, love as gift does not merely bless and bestow value on those who already exist; it brings them into existence. Through what begins with the women's encounter in the tomb, divine love is starting to bring about a new creation. The women and then the men will be created anew by sharing in the transformed life of the risen Christ. In his love Christ will bless them forever with a new and definitive identity and relationship (through him and the Holy Spirit) to the Father.

Authentic love puts those who love at risk—a fifth dimension of love that can be retrieved from Mark's spare account. The angelic messenger knows that the women are looking for Jesus of Nazareth who was *crucified*. The saving love of Christ, like all generously authentic love, has made him vulnerable, cost him much, and even put him on a cross. In various languages a wise choice calls Jesus' suffering and death his "passion," a term that combines intense love with the mortal suffering it brought the lover. Second to none in its dramatic intensity, Mark's Gospel has tracked the steadfastness of Jesus' commitment, which made him vulnerable right to the end, even when one of his male disciples betrayed him, another denied him, and the rest fled in terror. The terrible suffering that his self-forgetful love brought him is evoked and recalled when Mark's text identifies Jesus as he "who was crucified."

Reciprocity comes up as sixth item that an account of redemptive love may find implied in Mark's Easter story and that deserves fuller treatment. Without such reciprocity, love remains radically incomplete, a "disinterested" love that is at best a kind of unilateral generosity or outgoing beneficence. A giving without receiving, even more a giving that deliberately excludes any possibility of receiving and initiating a reciprocal transformation, can hardly be deemed love. Love is an essentially relational reality.[5] By its very nature love aims to establish and maintain in mutual freedom a relationship. To express love is in effect to hope that this love will be returned, but not in a selfish fashion that simply exploits the other to fulfill one's needs and yield one some desired benefit. Whenever the openness and desire for a reciprocal relationship and a mutual giving and receiving are missing, one must wonder whether the lover deals with the beloved as a personal agent and respects the integrity of the other. As Vincent Bruemmer observes, we find our very identity in the *mutual* relationship of love: "Our identity as persons" is not determined by ourselves alone, but is "bestowed on us in the love which others have for us....Our identity is equally determined by the love we have for others. In both senses we owe our identity as persons to others."[6]

The reciprocity that belongs essentially to God's redeeming love surfaces repeatedly in Jesus' ministry, when he invites others to become his disciples (for example, Mark 10:21). He desires a loving relationship with others, and that means he treats them as free agents. Their redeemed identity as persons will be bestowed upon them by the love that he has for them and by the love with which they respond to him. In Mark's closing chapter, the risen Christ invites his disciples to meet him in Galilee. Mark's readers know that they will freely keep this rendezvous and thus find their lasting identity in a mutual relationship of love with the risen Christ.

A seventh characteristic of God's redeeming love shows up, albeit briefly, in the final eight verses of Mark's Gospel: the divine beauty that rouses our love and so redeems us. In his *Confessions*, St. Augustine of Hippo classically linked human love and divine beauty: "Late have I loved you, Beauty so ancient and so new, late have I loved you!" (10.27).[7] At present the divine beauty of the risen Lord that stirs our love remains hidden and is revealed only indirectly. In the final chapter of Mark, that indirect revelation of Jesus' saving beauty comes through the presence of the angelic messenger. As I recall following, Matthew takes a hint from Mark and presents more robustly the brilliant and powerful angelic beauty that transforms a situation of death into one of redeemed life. But something of that is already there in the youth and beauty of God's messenger whom we meet in Mark's empty tomb story. The (presumably handsome) young man, who speaks and in a discreet way serves as a double for Jesus, exemplifies the truth of Dostoevsky's dictum that "beauty will save the world."

Such then are seven aspects of redeeming love that can be gleaned from Mark's final chapter: the divine approval; the gift of God's love that will become a self-gift when the disciples "see" Jesus; the disclosure of the risen Jesus that will transform the lives of the disciples; the new creation that the resurrection initiates; the vulnerable love of Jesus that has effected this new situation; the reciprocity of love to be found in the lasting relationship that the disciples will form with Jesus; and his risen, divinized beauty that will transform their lives.

In reflecting thus on the final chapter of Mark's Gospel, I have aimed to bring out its rich treasure of thought for those who want to move beyond merely historical arguments about the empty tomb of Jesus and catch something of its theological significance. Mark's narrative creates possible ways for understanding human redemption. I turn now to the other Gospels. The final chapters from Matthew, Luke, and John also let us glimpse themes we have detected in Mark 16:1–8.

THE VICTORY OF LIFE

Matthew's Narrative

In Matthew's penultimate chapter, an earthquake had marked the *death* of Jesus and opened the tombs of many holy people (Matt 27:51–53). Now in the final chapter an earthquake works, with the Angel of the Lord who "descends from heaven," to roll away the massive stone blocking the entrance to Jesus' tomb and reveal the *resurrection*. The angel acts with the divine power and authority that overcome death—a theme symbolized by the way he removes the stone and "sits on it."

In his Easter story Matthew draws a large contrast between Jesus' friends (Mary Magdalene and "the other Mary") and the deadly forces of injustice (represented by a group of soldiers set to guard the tomb).[8] The evangelist skillfully shifts focus from the two women who witness the burial of Jesus and mourn at his grave (Matt 27:61), to the stationing of the guard (Matt 27:62–66), back to the women who come at dawn to visit the grave (Matt 28:1), again to the soldiers who at the sight of the Angel of the Lord "become like dead men" (Matt 28:4), and then back again to the women who receive the Easter news (Matt 28:5–7).

Against the unjust powers of the world, represented by the squad of soldiers, those who stand with Jesus seem helpless. Pontius Pilate and the chief priests have sealed the tomb of Jesus and set a guard to watch over it. There is to be no monkey business. Through the power of the Roman Empire and the religious establishment in Jerusalem, Jesus is dead and buried. His corpse now lies in a tomb that is sealed and guarded. Nothing more can happen. His body is locked away and will quietly decay. But then through the magnificent Angel of the Lord, God acts to change dramatically the whole situation, vindicate Jesus (and the two women), and shift the balance of power. In a stroke of delicious irony, the soldiers become themselves like helpless corpses. They thought that they were guarding a dead body. Now it is they who fall to the ground and resemble dead men.

The two women run to share with the male disciples the astonishing news of the resurrection and on their way meet Jesus himself (Matt 28:8–10). Like the wise men from the East, who were "overwhelmed with great joy" when they found the Christ Child and worshiped him (Matt 2:10–11), the women have left the tomb with great joy and now kneel before the risen Jesus in worship.

Meanwhile some of the guards go into Jerusalem and report to the religious authorities "everything that had happened." They receive a large sum of money to spread the false story that the disciples had come by night and stolen the body of Jesus (Matt 28:11–15). Apart from the Parable of the Talents (Matt 25:18–27), Matthew nowhere mentions money except in connection with Judas (Matt 26:14–15; 27:3–10) and with the soldiers who had been at the tomb. The resurrection of Jesus from the dead prompts a second betrayal for money. Judas had been "bought" to make use of what he knew: where Jesus would be found when the Temple police came to arrest him. The soldiers are bought off to suppress what they know through the startling action of the angel at the tomb of Jesus. Something sadly venal about Judas and the soldiers serves as a negative foil to highlight the sheer grandeur of Jesus' self-sacrificing death, the truth of his powerful and glorious resurrection from the dead, and the status of the two holy women who become the first human witnesses to the new life of Jesus' resurrection from the dead.

The friends of God, represented by the holy women, may feel themselves to be weak and helpless when opposed to the apparently overwhelming might of a great political power. But God can and will redemptively change everything and prove victorious over betrayal, injustice, death, and lies. Thus a large pattern links the two concluding chapters from Matthew. This pattern speaks of the power and life of God, who vindicates not only his Son but also the two women who represent faithful discipleship. This pattern at the end of Matthew's Gospel recalls something similar at the beginning: an example of inclusion that serves to hold together the entire text.

Matthew's story of Herod the Great, the visit of the Magi, the death of the Holy Innocents, the flight of the Holy Family into Egypt, and their return (Matt 2:1–23) shows how the birth of Jesus makes it possible to hope that God will bring stunning reversals in situations of sinful horror.[9] There have been few tyrants who surpassed the ruthless standard of vicious brutality practiced by Herod the Great. Without doubt he deserved a place on the short-list of the ugliest despots in history. Within his own family circle he murdered his favorite wife and three of his sons. At home and beyond he dealt out death and so prompted the bitter comment attributed by Macrobius (d. 423 CE; in *Saturnalia*, 2.4.11) to the

Roman emperor Augustus Caesar: "Better to be Herod's pig than Herod's son." A treacherous and cunning man, Herod plays true to form when the Magi call on him. On the pretext of wanting to pay his own homage to the baby, he tries to trick them into revealing the identity and location of the child born to be "King of the Jews." When the Magi fail to return, Herod cannot tolerate the thought of a possible rival and, possessed by a paranoid fear, orders the massacre of all the baby boys in and around Bethlehem. Painters who have depicted this slaughter bring out the hatred and wickedness that motivate the killing.

Matthew's story features a key figure in an Angel of the Lord (Matt 2:13), the agent of God in saving the Holy Family. God also acts to warn and save the Magi. Those who stand obediently with God in the story—Mary, her child, Joseph, and the Magi—seem utterly weak and defenseless against the power of a wicked tyrant. But God effortlessly changes the situation and rescues them. The figure of the Angel of the Lord, who also comes on the scene before and after the flight to Egypt (Matt 1:20–25; 2:19–20), turns up in Matthew's Gospel only here at the beginning and then, much later, at the end (Matt 28:2–7).

Herod represents death, lies, hatred, and wickedness. The Christ Child (at the start of Matthew's Gospel) and the risen Jesus (at the climax of the Gospel) reverse all that by overcoming death with life, lies with truth, hatred with love, and wickedness with God's gracious goodness. Both at the beginning and at the end, the Angel of the Lord can prompt us into acknowledging what God does in bringing about the redeeming victory of love.

At the very end, the male disciples keep rendezvous with Jesus in Galilee and are commissioned to evangelize the world (Matt 28:16–20). The Gospel of Matthew closes by emphasizing the comprehensive authority of the risen Jesus: "*All authority in heaven and on earth* has been given to me. Go therefore and make disciples of *all nations*, baptizing them in the name of the Father and of the Son and of the Holy Spirit, and teaching them to obey *everything* that I have commanded you. And remember, I am with you *always*, to *the end of the age*" (italics mine). In this totalizing way, Matthew concludes his account of the resurrection of Jesus by putting it into a perspective that embraces not only the whole world but also the entire universe (heaven as well as earth) or, as we might say, all space and all time.

The victorious and life-giving impact of Christ's resurrection, the evangelist indicates, affects everyone and everything that make up the entire cosmos and its total history. It is no wonder that he introduces here the rite of baptism in the name of God, now known to be Father, Son, and Holy Spirit. The tripersonal God, who has created all things and rules all things, is revealed in the new creation initiated by Christ's resurrection from the dead and disclosed through the life and worship of the baptized faithful.

Luke's Narrative

In his Easter chapter,[10] Luke does not abandon the language of resurrection (Luke 24:7) but shows a particular liking for the language of victorious life. At the tomb of Jesus the two interpreting angels speak with one voice in challenging the party of women: "Why do you look for the living among the dead?" (Luke 24:5). Then, at the heart of the Emmaus story, this challenge is recalled by the two disciples. They inform the mysterious stranger about a vision of angels who told the women, "He is alive" (Luke 24:23). The language of life in the Easter context is no Lucan monopoly; other New Testament authors apply it to the risen Jesus (for example, Rom 14:9; Rev 1:18). Nevertheless, the explicit use of this language sets Luke's Easter chapter apart from the Easter chapters of the other evangelists.

Since Luke's primary audience was probably Gentile rather than Jewish, this might have been one of his reasons for introducing alongside the language of resurrection that of life. The terminology of life, which is in any case biblical, could communicate better with non-Jewish readers. It continues to do so today. Modern advertising uses not only images of life but the very language itself. For years I have collected examples of the role of "life" in selling products of all kinds. My latest example was a TV ad for fashionable bathrooms. A somewhat goofy teenager looks around with amazed joy at the new bathroom his parents have installed. The accompanying caption ran, "Your bathroom. Your life." Two thousand years ago Luke chose a word that continues to communicate well.

Luke may have had other reasons for using the language of life. It sets out the present situation of Jesus: he has been raised from the dead and therefore he is victoriously alive. Life represents the permanent condition into which the resurrection has brought Jesus. Moreover, "life" suggests very well what Jesus wishes us to share here and hereafter. He is risen from the dead so that we might live with and in God now and forever.

Before leaving what Luke contributes to this first way of understanding the redemptive impact of the resurrection, it is worth noting an inclusion found in his text. Angels turn up at the beginning and the end of Luke's Gospel (on the one hand, Luke 1:5–22, 26–38; 2:8–14; and, on the other hand, 24:4–7, with possibly an angel in 22:41). Along with the stress in chapters 1—2 and 24 on events being "in accordance with the scriptures," an angelic presence forms an inclusion that links the opening and close of the Gospel and, in particular, associates the virginal conception and birth of Jesus in chapters 1 and 2 with his being raised from the grave in chapter 24.[11] A unique divine initiative brought about his being conceived in the womb of a virgin, even as a similar initiative bought it about that he emerged gloriously alive from the tomb-womb. By associating angels not only with the conception and birth of Jesus but also with his rising from the grave, Luke's text hints at a certain (asymmetrical) parallel between the earthly life into which Jesus came from Mary's womb and the heavenly life into which he rose from the tomb. The evangelist's use of angels to form an inclusion prompts recognizing this parallel.

THE RECONCILIATION OF SINNERS

All four Gospels describe how the passion and crucifixion of Jesus uncover the nature of sin. But the Easter chapters of Matthew, Luke, and John, even more than those of Mark, contribute to a sense of the resurrection of Jesus effecting the reconciliation of sinners with one another and with God.

By inserting in his final chapter what was to become the lasting formula for baptism (Matt 28:19), Matthew gave forgiveness its context in Jesus' resurrection from the dead. At the start of his Gospel, he had told of John baptizing in the Jordan those who confessed their sins and announcing the coming of One who would baptize "with the Holy Spirit and with fire" (Matt 3:1–12). The ministry of John the Baptist prefigured the ministry of Jesus' followers, who were to baptize for the forgiveness of sins and "in the name of the Father and of the Son *and of the Holy Spirit*" (Matt 28:19). For the final scene on the mountain in Galilee, Matthew presupposed the outpouring of the Holy Spirit and the reconciliation of sinners who were to come from all nations and become the disciples of Jesus.

In his Easter chapter Luke pictures the risen Jesus announcing that "repentance and forgiveness of sins" are "to be proclaimed in his name to all nations." This promise is associated with the coming of the Holy Spirit (Luke 24:47–48). The promise is fulfilled at Pentecost when the outpouring of the Holy Spirit occurs and Peter, speaking for the other Easter witnesses, invites the crowd (who represent all nations) to accept reconciliation with God: "Repent, and be baptized every one of you in the name of Jesus Christ so that your sins may be forgiven; and you will receive the gift of the Holy Spirit" (Acts 2:38). This baptism for the forgiveness of sins brings believers from all nations into the new community that emerges at Pentecost.[12] The gathering of repentant sinners, which completes the resurrection and the coming of the Spirit, has been exquisitely foretold in the words of John about the death of Jesus "gathering into one the children of God who have been scattered" (John 11:52).

To gather human beings who have been alienated from God and from one another includes but goes beyond the forgiveness of sins to prove itself preeminently a work of *love*. Matthew, Luke, and, even more, John help us to appreciate the centrality of love in the redeeming work of Christ.

REDEEMING LOVE

The three evangelists all yield pointers for those who appreciate the resurrection of the crucified Jesus, with its aftermath in the outpouring of the Holy Spirit, as the climax of that loving salvation that comes from our gracious God. The radiantly beautiful Angel of the Lord (Matt 28:3), who acts as a heavenly double for the risen Jesus, reminds us of the connection among beauty, love, and redemption. Beauty rouses our love and inspires us to act. We desire and give our hearts to what is good and beautiful. The incomparable divine beauty and goodness revealed in the risen Christ can trigger our love and transform our lives. In Luke's story of the meeting on the road to Emmaus, Cleopas and his companion experience the presence and teaching of the risen Jesus that set their "hearts burning" within them (Luke 24:32)—a further hint of the way in which the beauty and truth of the risen Lord have a transforming impact.

But it is John who sets out even more clearly the redemptive power of divine love at work through the death and resurrection of Jesus. The evangelist has already repeatedly signaled this theme of saving love in the farewell discourse of Jesus and, not least, through an inclusion that links the start of chapter 13 with the close of chapter 17. At an introduction to the farewell discourse, John tells us about Jesus: "Having loved his own who were in the world, he loved them to the end [or uttermost]" (John 13:1). At the end of a long prayer, Jesus prays that his dying and rising will bring his followers into the communion of love that is the life of the Trinity (John 17:26).

When we move to the two Easter chapters of John,[13] many themes can speak to us of the redeeming love deployed by the risen Jesus. The observations of Vincent Bruemmer about reciprocal love and our owing our identity as persons to others are wonderfully exemplified in the meeting between Mary Magdalene and her risen Lord. In that encounter we see her lasting identity bestowed on her through the love that Jesus has for her and through her love for him. I dwell rather on the closing chapter of John's Gospel.

JOHN 21 AND HEALING LOVE

Many readers of John notice the theme of Peter's sin and forgiveness. Three times in the courtyard of the high priest Peter denies being a disciple of Jesus (John 18:15–27). That somber episode ends when the cock crows, but without any repentant tears from Peter (as in Luke 22:62). After the resurrection he visits the open and empty tomb (John 20:2–10). He is there with the other disciples when Jesus appears, breathes the Holy Spirit into them, and gives them the power to forgive sins (John 20:19–23). Finally, Peter's threefold declaration of love reverses his denial of a few days earlier and brings the commission to feed the Lord's lambs and sheep (John 21:15–17).

Beyond question, John's final chapter recalls Peter being lovingly forgiven for a recent act of cowardice. But the text says much more about love than that. It shows us the risen Jesus bringing up a buried past and with loving delicacy healing painful memories for Peter *and for the reader*. As so often in John's Gospel, the text invites us to identify with the men and women who meet and experience Jesus deeply. In this case our identification with the disciples in John 21 involves remembering situations into which we have been drawn right from the first chapter of the Gospel. This is an exercise that can recall and heal our own buried pasts. The final chapter of John can lovingly bring about such a healing redemption.

After chapter 20, the situation we come across in the final chapter seems astonishing. Summoned by Mary Magdalene's unexpected discovery, Peter has visited the empty tomb of Jesus (John 20:3–10). On Easter Sunday evening, along with the other disciples, he "rejoices" to see the risen Lord, receives the Holy Spirit, and is sent on mission by the risen Jesus (John 20:21–22). Thomas "called the Twin," who was absent on Easter Sunday evening and expresses his crass doubts about the resurrection, a week later meets the risen Christ and blurts out his confession, "My Lord and my God" (John 20:24–29). Then we suddenly find Thomas, Peter, and five other disciples out fishing, almost as if Jesus had never existed and had never turned their lives around. Peter's announcement, "I am going fishing" (John 21:3), makes it seem as if he is ignoring the association with Jesus that has shaped his recent past. At the least it suggests some uncertainty about the future and the way Peter and his fellow disciples should begin their ministry to the world. Nevertheless, the text evokes what we already know, not from John but from the other Gospels: Peter and "the sons of Zebedee" (John 21:2) were fishermen when Jesus first called them (Mark 1:16–20). Something of their past is showing through.

John's final chapter opens by stating that it will describe how the risen Jesus disclosed himself again to the disciples (John 21:1), his "third" self-disclosure after the resurrection (John 21:14)—actually his fourth when we include the appearance to Mary Magdalene alone (John 20:11–18). Three times in John 21:1 and 21:14, we find the verb *disclose*, the same word used to close the story of water being changed into wine: "Jesus did this, the first of his signs, in Cana of Galilee, and disclosed his glory; and his disciples believed in him" (John 2:11). The narrative of chapter 21 encourages the reader to remember that episode in Cana by noting that one of the seven fishermen, Nathanael, comes from "Cana in Galilee" (John 21:2). Once again the past is being recalled. Just as Galilee saw Jesus working his first sign that disclosed his glory, so now in the same Galilee the risen Christ discloses himself as "the Lord" (John 21:7, 12).

He does this "just after daybreak" (John 21:4). He is there on the beach when darkness slips away and dawn comes. The scene evokes the cure of the blind man who says, "Now I see" (John 9:1–41) and the claim of Jesus to be "the light of the world" (John 9:5). The spring dawn in the final chapter can also take the reader back even to the very beginning of the Gospel and the light that shines in the darkness to enlighten and give life to every man and woman (John 1:4–9). In the closing chapter of John, the disciples have fished all night without catching anything. Now the stranger on the lakeside tells them to cast their net on the right side of the boat. They do so and make a catch of 153 large fish (John 21:6, 8, 11)—a symbol of fullness[14] and an echo of "life in abundance" (John 10:10) that the Gospel, right from its prologue, has promised that the light of the world will bring (John 1:4).

The extraordinary catch of fish, the only such miraculous or semi-miraculous event of its kind in the Easter stories of all four

Gospels, recalls the multiplication of the loaves and fishes (John 6:1–11). In the discourse that follows that sign, Jesus speaks of people being "hauled" (*helkuō*) or drawn to him (John 6:44), a verb that turns up later in the promise, "And, I, when I am lifted up from the earth will draw [literally "haul"] all people to myself" (John 12:32). Now in the closing chapter of the Fourth Gospel the same verb recurs when Peter hauls ashore the unbroken net containing the 153 fish. Symbolically Peter the fisherman is now engaged in the work of "hauling" others to the Lord (see Mark 1:17) or helping to "gather into one the dispersed children of God" (John 11:52).

The remarkable way in which the net remains unbroken, despite its enclosing so many large fish, brings to mind the unity of believers promised by Jesus through the image of gathering all into "one sheepfold" (John 10:16). The images of fish and sheep differ, but the meaning is the same.

When the disciples reach land, they see that Jesus has already prepared for them some fish and bread (John 21:9). In providing a meal Jesus (the cook?) has done something that none of the Gospels ever reports him doing during his lifetime. But then with words and gesture that evoke what he has done when multiplying the loaves and fishes (John 6:8–11), Jesus asks his disciples to bring some of the fish that they have just caught (John 21:10). He "takes" and "gives" them bread and fish (John 21:13), just as he had done earlier (John 6:13). Readers are being lovingly challenged to recall an earlier story. Once more the text works to summon up a past grace by which we can be touched again.

Many readers readily link the "disciple whom Jesus loved" (John 21:7, 20) with the figure repeatedly characterized in this way from the Last Supper in John 13:23 to the visit to the empty tomb in 20:2. Some readers likewise link the charcoal fire (John 21:9) around which the disciples take their breakfast with the charcoal fire in the high priest's courtyard, the scene of Peter's denial (John 18:18, 25). The morning scene on the beach prompts a new evaluation of Peter and ourselves. A broken past can resurface and be lovingly redeemed.

However, despite the explicit recalling of the Last Supper in John 21:20, what may pass unnoticed is the way the lakeside breakfast works to heal the memories of earlier meals in John's narrative. Those earlier meals proved occasions of deadly threats against Jesus (John 12:1–11), disputes about "wasting" precious nard to anoint the feet of Jesus (John 12:4–8), the betrayal of Jesus (John 13:21–30), and a misunderstanding when the wine ran out during a marriage feast (John 2:3–4). The miraculous feeding of the five thousand is also significant here. It led to a discourse on the bread of life, which ended with many disciples leaving Jesus and the first warning of Judas's treacherous betrayal (John 6:25–71). In a loving and healing way, the Easter story at dawn evokes those earlier meals and the crises associated with them and promises Jesus' saving presence through eucharistic meals to come.

Many readers have a sense of what the Gospel says through Peter's threefold profession of love (John 21:15–17). Peter must acknowledge and come to terms with his sinful failure. He renounces his threefold denial (John 18:15–17) and is lovingly forgiven and rehabilitated. Undoubtedly the professions reverse the denials. But the story conveys a richer sense of healing than just that.

Right from the start of the Gospel, Jesus has put questions to various individuals and groups: "What are you looking for?" (John 1:38); "Do you also wish to go away?" (John 6:67); and so forth. The final chapter of the Gospel features the only question Jesus ever repeats, and he puts it three times to Peter: "Do you love me?" In the closing chapter the old habit returns and is intensified. Peter faces Jesus, the loving questioner, from whom he receives forgiveness and a lasting commission.

At their very first meeting Jesus had spoken to Peter as "Simon, son of John" (John 1:41), an address repeated three times at their last, postresurrection encounter (John 21:15–17). In the imagery of the Good Shepherd and his sheep, the Good Shepherd calls his sheep by their names (John 10:1–8). Simon Peter is now commissioned to feed the Lord's lambs and sheep. The great catch of fish with which chapter 21 opens might have shaped the missionary charge as "Cast my net, catch my fish." Yet in John's imagery it is not fishing but shepherding that entails danger and even death (John 10:11–15, 17–18). Peter's commission will lead him to martyrdom (John 21:18–19) in the service of the Lord's flock. No longer will it be a question of Peter deciding whether or where to go or stay (John 6:67–68). He will be carried where he does not wish to go (John 21:18–19). Like Philip at the beginning of the Gospel (John 1:43), Peter at the end hears the simple but radical call to faithful discipleship, "Follow me" (John 21:19, 22).

John's narrative shows us Peter recovering his past before he begins the pastoral work that will eventually bring him to martyrdom. As we have just seen, the final chapter of John recalls much of Jesus' ministry and story, right back to the very prologue. Peter is taken through all this, down to his shameful failure during the passion. The past is not denied, but recalled, forgiven, and lovingly redeemed. A healing through love becomes the basis for Peter's new future.

John 21 opens with Peter going out for a night's fishing. He is, as it were, taking time off while he seeks for a pattern of meaning in his life and particularly in his recent experiences. It is almost as if, for the moment at least, the great design has eluded him. But the Lord appears at dawn to heal Peter's past and enroll him in an heroic mission that will lead to a martyr's death (John 21:18–19).

Something of the redemptive process can also come true for readers of John's Gospel. To the extent that they have allowed themselves to become involved with Jesus in the whole of John's story, the final chapter will have its saving impact on them. It will bring up memories of Jesus and past encounters with him, so as to heal and redeem that past. For the readers, no less than for Peter, the "Follow me" of the last chapter can evoke and heal their memories as the basis for a new future.

This way of reading John 21 accounts for the deeply haunting quality that many readers find in it.[15] Somehow we have heard and experienced it all before. There is an affinity and a continuity between our lives and what we read at the end of John's Gospel. The closing chapter works to bring back to the surface painful and sinful memories. But they can become the starting point for a fresh future—through the loving presence of the risen Lord, who is our goal (because we have accepted the "Follow me") and our necessary support.

Thus far, this chapter has explored the Easter narratives of the four Gospels and seen what they might offer for someone who asks, What do they say about the resurrection and its saving impact on human beings and their world? In particular, the evangelists indicate possible approaches to redemption as the victory of life, the reconciliation of sinners, and healing through love. A coherent pattern of deliverance, atonement, and transforming love emerges from the Easter texts.

OTHER WITNESSES ON THE NEW CREATION

As was said at the start of this chapter, New Testament Christians understood the resurrection of Jesus Christ to usher in the new creation. Having reflected on the narrative theology of the Easter chapters in the four Gospels, I now address further biblical witness to the way in which the resurrection of the crucified Jesus provided a basis for repairing and transforming a disturbed and suffering world.

"Reconciling all things" (Col 1:20), "gathering up all things" (Eph 1:10), or "making all things new" (Rev 1:5) puts the resurrection and redemption in a cosmic context. The resurrection of Christ had not happened without, and certainly not against, creation. It brought a new world in which not only human beings but also all living creatures and the Earth itself would share. This reconciling, gathering up, and renewal of all things inaugurated a "new heaven and a new earth" (Rev 21:1; see 2 Pet 3:13). God will renew, deliver from imperfections, and transform all things (Rom 8:19–21).

It was to inaugurate a history of love with human beings and their world that God first created the universe. Creation expressed a love that initiated a relationship that invited men and women, in the name of all creation, to reciprocate the love that had brought them and all other things into existence. The transforming re-creation initiated by the resurrection carried an invitation to share in an even richer relationship with the creating and now re-recreating God.

Creation fulfills its deepest purpose in a love that glorifies God. It aims at human beings responding to God's creative love with loving worship. This orientation of creation shows itself in the institution of the Sabbath, the day set aside for peacefully acknowledging God. Likewise and even more, the new creation is oriented toward divine adoration—a theme disclosed by the two women and then the male disciples when they worship the risen Christ (Matt 28:9, 17). The Book of Revelation exuberantly shows the worship called for by the new creation when it portrays the heavenly liturgy in which angels, human beings, and all animate life join. With magnificent poetic imagery Revelation evokes the glory of God and the heavenly entourage who gather to worship around the divine throne (Rev 5:6–14).[16]

The new creation, which opened with the events of the first Good Friday and Easter Sunday, produced a state of affairs that anticipated the consummation of life in the new Jerusalem conveyed by Revelation 21—22. The risen and transformed Jesus was the first installment of what would come at the end (1 Cor 15:20). The resurrection and the new presence of the risen Christ and his Holy Spirit anticipated the final and full presence of God. We live now in the situation of the already present kingdom that anticipates, in reality and not merely in thought, the final fullness of the kingdom.

The table fellowship that Jesus shared during his ministry with many, and especially the marginalized members of his society (for example, Luke 15:2), was a real fellowship symbolizing the utterly satisfying fellowship with God to be enjoyed at the "banquet" in the future kingdom (for example, Matt 8:11). In the post-resurrection situation of the inaugurated new creation, Christians meet at the Eucharist for a sacred eating and drinking that "proclaims the death of the [risen] Lord until he comes" (1 Cor 11:26). Their real fellowship now symbolizes and anticipates life in the final kingdom of God. As St. Thomas Aquinas put it in an antiphon he wrote for the new feast of Corpus Christi, in this "sacred banquet [*sacrum convivium*]" "we receive a pledge of the glory that is to be ours [*futurae gloriae nobis pignus datur*]."

FURTHER REFLECTIONS ON
THE NEW CREATION

As "Creator of heaven and earth," God was and is responsible for everyone and everything that has come and comes into existence. The whole created world rests in the divine hands; God holds sway over everyone and everything. As the product of divine intelligence, freedom, and love, the original creation was pure gift and in no way the product of human activity or work. Likewise and even more, as the Creator of "the new heaven and the new earth," God is responsible for everyone and everything that is blessed with new existence. In the final kingdom, a pure gift of the divine intelligence, freedom, and love, God will hold sway over everyone and everything.

The original creation and the new creation parallel or differ from each other in several ways. A powerful hymn in Colossians (1:15-20) takes the form of a diptych as it celebrates the supremacy of Christ over creation and over the church, the sign of the new creation. His universal relevance in both spheres comes through the repeated use of "all" (six times) and the use of some broad and equivalent expressions: for instance, "things visible and invisible" (Col 1:16). Encouraged by this hymn, let me sketch some of the parallels and some of the differences.

First, a parallel. The story of creation found in the Book of Genesis assumed its final form at the time of the Babylonian captivity, a time when the God of Israel seemed defeated.[17] Apparently God could not defend his people and all those who worshiped him. But the book of the consolation of Israel (Isa 40—55) announces deliverance. Incomparably great and powerful as the Creator (Isa 40:12-31), God will bring his people home from the penal servitude of their exile (Isa 40:1-11); he will restore and redeem them (Isa 43:8-21). The story of the new creation took shape and was known at the time of the seeming defeat of the crucifixion. Jesus had worshiped his "Father" and proclaimed the divine kingdom as already present in his own person and work. When Jesus was arrested and condemned to death on Calvary, it seemed that God could not defend him. The vindi-

121

cation of the resurrection showed otherwise as it ushered in the power of the new creation.

Second, the "how" of the original creation and the "how" of the new creation are both shrouded in mystery and are, to all appearances, extremely unlikely. As regards the original creation, life did not have to evolve. In fact, the probability of life, so scientists assure us, was close to zero.[18] A glorious resurrection from the dead flouts the existing laws of nature and looks even more unlikely. Jesus' rising from the dead transformed the laws of nature. He is the first example of the new laws of nature that will guide the world in God's new heaven and new earth.

Third, one can say that the "being of creation" is good, even very good (Gen 1:10–31), while the "being of the new creation" is better. Let me explain. God made humankind in the divine image and likeness (Gen 1:26–27). We are all godlike but "earthy." We share a humanity that was formed from the earth (Gen 2:7; 3:19). We are related to God because of our (past) origin. New creation involves being related to God because we all share the same destiny, that of being shaped in the image and likeness of the risen Christ. The definitive unity of humankind comes not from its past but from its future, found in and through Christ. Paul interprets the scope of the new creation as that of "taking on the form" of the crucified and risen Christ (Phil 3:10). That "transformation" into Christ is what "being *transformed* by the renewing of your minds" (Rom 12:2) involves.

Fourth, drawing inspiration from Paul's scheme of "Adam and Christ as the second or last Adam" (Rom 5:12–21; 1 Cor 15:45–49), Christian writers and artists, along with various liturgical texts, developed a picture of the two Adams: the first represents creation and the second represents the new creation. A long tradition connected and contrasted the two corporate figures: the first Adam who, with Eve, triggered the whole story of human sin, and the Second Adam who brought the blessings of the new creation leading to eternal life.[19]

In the first part of this book on Christ's resurrection, four chapters have been of more "apologetic" nature (chapters 1–4), whereas one (chapter 5) reflected on the larger (theological) meaning that New Testament Christians found in Christ's victory over death. In part II of this book we move to a more "apologetic" chapter (What justifies believing in Jesus as risen from the dead?) and two more theological chapters (on the nature of risen life, and then on the moral and sacramental theology that can and should be drawn from Easter faith).

PART II

CONTEMPORARY ISSUES

Chapter 6

JUSTIFYING EASTER FAITH TODAY

This chapter brings us to the first and most basic of the contemporary issues about the resurrection: its credibility. Is believing in Christ as gloriously risen from the dead a rational option today? Why accept the notion that after his crucifixion and burial the dead Jesus rose bodily from his tomb to enjoy a new, gloriously transformed existence, shapes through the power of the Holy Spirit the lives of all human beings and their world, and will be the goal of all things in the final kingdom of God?

Such Easter faith is undoubtedly a personal matter that shows endless variations. Here we might appeal to and adapt the famous remark of Blaise Pascal, "The heart has its reasons."[1] Different hearts have their different reasons, which sustain and nourish their particular beliefs. The journey of faith of each individual, Christian or otherwise, remains a particular mystery, sometimes even to the individual himself or herself. But, if we stand back from individual hearts and individual reasons, we can see how the making (or unmaking) of Easter faith persistently involves three areas: philosophy and science, history, and personal experiences.

PHILOSOPHY AND SCIENCE

Chapter 1 of this volume has already alerted readers to the role of background theories, repeatedly of a philosophical or scientific nature, that come into play when facing the question of the resurrection. Worldviews can, in advance, rule out or rule in the possibility of Easter faith. Obviously philosophies that deny the existence of an all-powerful and all-loving God exclude in advance the possibility of Jesus being raised from the dead. There is no God, and hence there can be no resurrection. Such a background theory dismisses out of hand claims about God raising Jesus from the dead.

Chapter 1 addressed the position of those who profess belief in God but view the created universe as a closed, rigidly uniform system of causes and effects. In such a universe there can be nothing new under the sun, certainly not a bodily resurrection from the grave. Thus Arthur Peacocke (1924–2006) insisted on the "irreversibility of death." When anyone has died, any reversal of the chemical processes of decay is "highly improbable," even to "the point of appearing to be impossible as breaking the Second Law of Thermodynamics which formalizes such irreversibility in general in natural processes." The Laws of Thermodynamics describe the general direction of change in the universe. According to the Second Law, in a closed system the energy will inevitably tend to become distributed in the most disordered pattern.[2] What he called "the general bearing of science" seemed to control anything that Peacocke was ready to imagine about what had happened to Jesus' body after death and burial.[3]

But John Polkinghorne (b. 1930), another Anglican scientist who like Peacocke entered the ordained ministry, argues that God is not bound to maintain unchanged the Second Law of Thermodynamics and other laws of nature. For good reasons and in appropriate circumstances (for example, the death of the incarnate Son of God), God can suspend or change some laws, which after all depend from moment to moment on God for their continuing existence and operation. In the process of transforming the material universe and its laws, God began by raising Jesus from the tomb to an embodied life of glory, through a resurrection in which an identity-in-transformation was preserved between the earthly and risen states of Jesus.[4]

Two items repeatedly shape such philosophical or scientific background theories: one's image of God and one's view of matter. First, the Book of Acts and then St. Augustine of Hippo can guide our thinking about God to open up the possibility of envisaging Christ's resurrection from the dead. In the account of his visit to Athens, St. Paul says that it is in God that "we live and move and have our being" (Acts 17:28). The apostle pictures God as the One on whom, along with our world, we depend from moment to moment. This is an image of an ever-present, all-powerful, and all-loving God who is our total environment—a nourishing, maternal situation that finds a certain counterpart in the first nine months of existence for human beings within their mothers' wombs. For those months we lived, moved, and had our being within our mother; she was our total environment. Such an image of God differs sharply from the view of an "outsider" Creator who does not or cannot suspend, let alone change, the operation of the closed system of causes and effects once they have come into being.

In his *Confessions*, Augustine wrote of God, or rather said to God, "But you were more inward than my inmost self [*tu autem eras interior intimo meo*]" (3.6.11). We might join with those who have paraphrased this remark as "You were closer to me than I was to myself." God, being so inward and "within" human beings and all creation, can be readily imagined as communicating glorious new life to his crucified Son. Augustine's image of God is worlds away from that of a creator who has brought everything into existence but then acts like an "absentee landlord" and allows natural causes to take care of the running of the universe.

Second, one's view of the nature and destiny of matter also proves decisive for the making of Easter faith. Here Pierre Teilhard de Chardin (1881–1955), a priest and paleontologist, exemplifies brilliantly a background theory that opens itself up to Easter faith. With his vision of "the progressive spiritualization of Matter," Teilhard resisted all those who interpreted the universe, either here or hereafter, in terms of a separation between matter and spirit. "Matter," he maintained, "is the matrix of Spirit. Spirit is the higher state of Matter." He could sing a "Hymn to Matter," when he contemplated the unfolding and evolving cosmos, as it moves toward the Omega Point—through what he called *cosmogenesis, biogenesis, noogenesis,* and *Christogenesis.* Hence he saw the resurrection as "Christ's effective assumption of his function as the universal centre."[5] So far from the resurrection leaving behind Christ's crucified corpse, it made that material body into the proper and perfect vehicle of the Spirit and mediated God's creative power in moving the world toward the final unification of matter and spirit.

Teilhard called love "the most universal, the most tremendous and the most mysterious of the cosmic forces."[6] With Christ's resurrection from the dead, the energy of love was released in a qualitatively new way to organize the "noosphere" and bring it to the Omega Point. After 1930, Teilhard worked out a view of love as *the* most universal force in a world that is dynamically converging toward the risen Christ, the unifying goal of everything. He saw the resurrection as the cosmic event in which Christ overcame matter's resistance to spiritual ascent, effectively assumed his function as the center and focus of the created universe, and guaranteed the upward and forward development of everything that exists. As the "Personal Heart of the Cosmos," the risen Christ released the basic energy of love that progressively carries both humanity and the entire material universe toward the final goal.[7]

Such a vigorously positive view of the nature and destiny of matter allowed Teilhard to make full sense of Jesus' resurrection from the tomb. It was very different from the one-sidedly "spiritual" view of our human existence and future that Peacocke developed. He expressed, as we saw in chapter 2, the hope that the purposes of God may "finally achieve their fulfillment *beyond space and time* within the very being of God himself."[8] This future existence "beyond space and time" will involve the Creator in bringing our "created personalness *out of materiality* into the divine life."[9] Peacocke fell back into an ultimate dualism. The matter of Christ's crucified body was left behind, just as our matter and our material world will be left behind when finally we will be brought "out of materiality" and "beyond space and time" into "the very being of God." As it was for Jesus, so it will be for us: we face a transition *from* the created, material world into "a state of unity" with God and an existence in "an *entirely new* mode of being."[10]

The difference between Peacocke and Teilhard turned on their radical disagreement about matter, its relationship to spirit, and its possibilities in the final world of God. Their irreconcilable worldviews shaped their Easter faith and took them to different positions about the nature and function of Christ's resurrection.

HISTORICAL CONSIDERATIONS

Earlier chapters of this book have argued the case for the historical reality of (1) the appearances of the risen Jesus and (2) the discovery of his empty tomb. The appearances to some individuals and groups formed the primary reason for the first followers of Jesus to accept his resurrection; the empty tomb constituted a confirmatory, secondary sign of his resurrection.

Admittedly in the cases of both (1) and (2) the witnesses were a relatively small number of people. But it would make little or no difference if there were many thousands of such witnesses. Stubborn skeptics, like David Hume, would still argue that it is *never rational* to believe such witnesses and accept that a resurrection from the dead has happened. His (philosophical) background theory excludes in principle that God performs remarkable deeds, or at least that we could ever be sure that such deeds had happened even if there was a God to perform them. According to Hume, in principle there could never be enough historical evidence to justify accepting Christ's resurrection from the dead.[11]

Hume's position has its value by reminding us that Easter faith is never decided simply on the basis of historical evidence alone. Even if millions of witnesses had claimed to have seen the risen Jesus and left abundant written testimony to support that claim, and even if Mary Magdalene and other women had left many authenticated letters about their discovery of the empty tomb, there is more to believing in the risen Christ than such evidence from history. Before returning later to this point, I review some of the historical arguments for the resurrection.

Over the centuries the historical case for the truth of Christ's resurrection has included considerations that press beyond the New Testament witness to the Easter appearances and the discovery of the empty tomb. Often such an apologetic approach argues from demonstrable *effects* in history to the event of the resurrection as the only adequate or plausible *cause*. One typical argument of this kind runs as follows.

After a public career that lasted at most three or four years, Jesus was abandoned by nearly all of his close followers, crucified as a messianic pretender, and apparently rejected by the God whom he had proclaimed as "Abba" or "loving Father." Yet within a few years the reform movement he had led within Judaism spread explosively to become a world religion. How can one account for this documented effect without accepting an adequate cause, namely, Jesus' resurrection from the dead?

Hans Küng broached this argument by comparing Jesus with three other founders of religious movements: the Siddhartha Gautama, Confucius, and Muhammad. In the case of these three founders, time was on their side. Buddhism originated with Gautama, who spent most of his long life teaching the way of enlightenment. The Chinese sage Confucius also passed many years spreading his wisdom and attracting disciples, until he died and was buried with great pomp outside Kufow. A wealthy wife and then military victories helped Muhammad to propagate his teaching. As the recognized prophet of Arabia, he died in Medina and was buried there. In these three instances we can point to publicly verifiable causes that furthered the spread, respectively, of Buddhism, Confucianism, and Islam: the long careers of the founders, financial resources, success in battle, and widespread public esteem right through to their deaths and beyond. In the case of Christianity, the founder had none of these advantages: his public career was very short; he lacked military and financial support; and, despite some initial success in attracting followers, at the end he was left alone to face the hostility of both civil and religious authorities. His life ended in a humiliating and shameful death on a cross. After all this, the subsequent "almost explosive propagation" of Jesus' "message and community" remains an "historical enigma," unless we admit a proportionate cause, his resurrection from the dead.[12]

The argument from publicly documented effects to the only adequate cause (Christ's resurrection) may also appeal to novelties found at the very origins of Christianity. When Christ was crucified as a messianic pretender and even as a blasphemer (Mark 14:61–64), what options were available for those who, despite running away at the time of his arrest, still remained in some sense his followers? Could they have modified their messianic belief in him (Mark 8:29; 11:1–10) and proposed him to be another martyred prophet like John the Baptist? Hardly, it seems to me. To be crucified was not only to suffer an utterly cruel and humiliating form of execution but also to die under a religious curse[13] and "outside the camp" of God's covenanted people (Heb 13:12–13). In other words, crucifixion was seen as the death of a criminal, godless person who perished away from God's presence in the place and company of irreligious men. To honor anyone put to death in such a way was an awful and profound offense (1 Cor 1:23). Given that the crucifixion was such a disgrace, could the disciples of Jesus have proclaimed him *even as a martyred prophet?*

In fact, they began preaching the crucified Jesus as the divinely endorsed Messiah risen from the dead to bring salvation to all. The notion of a messiah who failed, suffered, was crucified, and then rose from the dead was simply foreign to pre-Christian, Jewish belief. Since their previous religious beliefs could not have led Jesus' disciples to make such startlingly new claims about him, what triggered this religious novelty? Where did it come from, if not from the very event of Jesus' resurrection and his subsequent Easter appearances?

In the introduction to this book we saw that Tom Wright and Richard Swinburne have fashioned similar "effect-to-cause" arguments. First, Wright argued that Christian faith in resurrection had no strict precedent even in Judaism. That faith proclaimed one individual (Jesus) to have been raised from the dead in anticipation of the general resurrection that would come at the end of all history. What caused this radical change in expectations held by a significant group of first-century Jews about the fulfillment of human life through resurrection? Neither prior Jewish beliefs nor the study of biblical texts could have generated this new belief in resurrection. The only plausible cause seems to have been the resurrection of Jesus himself. Second, Swinburne named the new celebration of Sunday as the change to be accounted for. Why did the first, Jewish disciples of Jesus no longer give priority to Saturday, the Sabbath understood to have been appointed by God, and turn "the first day of the week," or Sunday, into *the* day for meeting and worshiping together? What made them value this day so highly that they not only changed their day of worship but also their manner of worship by celebrating the Eucharist (see 1 Cor 11:23–26; 16:2)? An obvious reason is close at hand: Sunday was the day when the tomb of Jesus was discovered to be empty and the day when they first encountered the risen Lord.

Without being strict proofs, both arguments enjoy a certain plausibility. Those who reject them need to produce alternate explanations as to why the first disciples of Jesus proclaimed a new, unprecedented hope for resurrection (a general resurrection inaugurated by the glorious resurrection of one individual) and changed their special day of worship from the Jewish Sabbath to the Christian Sunday.

Yet, apropos of these and other historical arguments, there is a story about Bertrand Russell, a nonbelieving philosopher, that enjoys its relevance. On being asked what his reaction would be if after death he found himself in the presence of God, Russell replied, "I would say that God should have given me more evidence." Russell would undoubtedly have said something similar if the question had been phrased in terms of finding himself after death in the presence of the risen Christ. Presumably Russell would have replied, "I would say that Jesus should have given me stronger historical evidence in support of his resurrection."

Here Maurice West wrote something that comments helpfully on a Russell-style position. In his novel *The Clowns of God*, he described a conversation between a French pope and his skeptical German friend, Carl Mendelius. After debating some issue of faith, the pope remarks, "Carl, old friend, there is never enough evidence." Applying this to the theme of the present chapter, we can say that there is never enough evidence for the resurrection, or—put positively—that there is more to faith in the risen Jesus than knowing the (historical) evidence for the resurrection. Such faith does not remain within the limits of the evidence alone. Merely knowing the evidence and even finding it very persuasive does not yet mean knowing him personally in faith.

To those who seek to base Easter faith on historical arguments *alone*, one can fairly object that, if they are right, historians should be much more prominent among the ranks of people who accept the resurrection of Jesus. Through their profession, historians should be peculiarly competent to assess the evidence in favor of the postresurrection appearances and discovery of the empty tomb as actual events in the past. This should put historians in a privileged position to conclude that the resurrection of Jesus is an event that truly happened. But, in fact, we do not find historians featuring disproportionately high in the ranks of believers.

Is the problem that too many historians approach the question of Jesus' resurrection with the prior conviction that the dead cannot rise? Do they rule out in advance the resurrection, since they are convinced that any such resurrection from the dead is simply excluded by the laws of nature? In that case the debate turns on philosophical and scientific background theories rather than on the right assessment of the available historical evidence supporting the resurrection of Jesus.

To be sure, historical considerations can and do help to show how Easter faith is not irrational but rather a reasonable and credible option. Such considerations can both illustrate the strength of evidence supporting the resurrection and point up serious weaknesses in alternative explanations of what happened in the immediate aftermath of Jesus' death and burial. Repeatedly, counter-explanations come across as downright implausible. Yet faith, prompted by spiritual experiences and the grace of the Holy Spirit, goes beyond the evidence and does not remain simply the well-founded conclusion of historical arguments.

Here the case of Malcolm Muggeridge is illuminating. As we saw in chapter 4, he once toyed with the notion that a grave robber had removed the body and so led the followers of Jesus into thinking that he had been raised from the dead. But then Muggeridge came to accept that Jesus had truly risen from the dead and lives with us today. What had happened to Muggeridge? It was not that he had read more widely the relevant biblical scholarship and examined more closely the historical evidence. Rather he took the step to Easter faith because of various experiences. In the Holy Land he saw pilgrims whose faces "were bright with faith,"[14] and in India he came to know, admire, and love Mother Teresa of Calcutta. Her personal example, friendship, and prayers helped him to find in that faith the answer to his fundamental questions about the nature and destiny of human life. The answer, a fresh relationship with the risen Jesus, gave Muggeridge a coherent, deeply satisfying way of living and construing reality.

THE PERSONAL EXPERIENCE OF FAITH

In chapter 1 of this book I argued in a section on personal relationships that making and maintaining such relationships goes beyond "knowing about" people to involve "knowing them" in a trusting and loving commitment. In personal relationships we always know and trust more than the available evidence. Knowing personally those whom we love cannot be reduced to simply knowing many facts about them, facts that could be established by evidential considerations.

The greatest treasures in human life—in particular, married love and family love—press beyond the evidence with a love that grows through experience and mutual trust. We believe "lovingly" in one another. It is because we see with our hearts that the eyes of love can see and believe things that others will fail to see and believe.

When in family life we go beyond the evidence and put our trust in other persons (living or dead), this can happen in matters that affect us very deeply: for instance, that Frank O'Collins, my deceased father, was in fact my father. Theoretically, it is possible that my mother had a secret lover and I have been mistaken for many decades about my paternal origin. Strictly speaking, it is possible that I have been deluded, but I am confident that it is not so. I would never dream of applying for permission to dig up my father's remains to exclude any lingering doubt by having a DNA test performed. Such "definitive" evidence would betray and not enhance my memory of and love for my dead father. From a legal point of view, the DNA evidence could establish my paternity definitively, but it would effectively diminish or even destroy my personal relationship with my dead parents.

When I lived in Rome, every now and then I spotted advertisements for a private detective agency that enjoyed the splendid name of "Terminal Investigations." Those ads encouraged me to imagine someone, let us call him Giovanni, who allowed himself to become worried about his wife's fidelity and engaged an agent from Terminal Investigations. My fantasy then pictured the agent returning after a month to claim his fee and report, "Look, Giovanni, you have nothing to worry about. When Elena goes out in the morning, she often spends some time looking at what's on sale in the Via dei Condotti and then enjoys a cup of coffee with two girl friends. Here's my full report on where she went and what she did outside your home from Monday to Friday over the last month. There is no evidence that she has a secret lover. As I said, you have nothing to worry about." Would that evidence support Giovanni's love for Elena and form the beginning of a wonderful, new phase in their life together? I think rather that the report would signal a breakdown in Giovanni's loving relationship for his wife, even an end to it. The report from Terminal Investigations could very well prove terminal.

These two examples throw light on what a personal relationship to the risen Jesus entails. Believing in him goes beyond merely accepting on evidence that something (namely, his resurrection) happened nearly two thousand years ago. Believing *in him* involves entering here and now into a trusting, loving commitment to him. It means recognizing in him, with profound gratitude, God's personal self-communication to us: in other words, the Redeemer who saves us and the Revealer who has shown us what God is like.[15]

Ludwig Wittgenstein was on target when he wrote, "It is love that believes the resurrection."[16] We might express this more personally. On the one hand, it is love, our love, that believes in the risen Christ; and, on the other hand, our final, personal identity is bestowed on us by the love he has for us. The example of the risen Jesus meeting Mary Magdalene, which we recalled in chapter 5, remains the paradigm. It is to the risen Lord and his love that we owe our lasting identity as persons.

In the making of Easter faith, the external testimony of Christians and the internal working of the Holy Spirit come together. Depending on an unbroken chain of earlier witnesses who stretch back to the original, apostolic witnesses of the risen Christ, contemporary Christians proclaim his resurrection from the dead. Experiencing and accepting this testimony means being led, invisibly and mysteriously, by the Holy Spirit to allow the crucified and risen Jesus to answer our most fundamental questions about the nature, meaning, and destiny of our own existence and that of our cosmos. He offers us nothing less than a coherent and meaningful vision of the whole of life. Such Easter faith not only transforms the way we construe reality but also involves accepting new ways of living. This faith, along with the baptism that reenacts sacramentally the dying, burial, and resurrection of Christ, incorporates us into him and his community, lets us "walk in newness of life," and anticipates a glorious resurrection to come (Rom 6:3–11; see Gal 3:26–27; Col 3:1–4). We allow his crucifixion and resurrection to create our new identity.

John, the Gospel of revelation *par excellence*, offers a number of case studies of Christ rousing faith in men and women who suffer from a variety of problems: religious doubt (Nicodemus), marital problems (the Samaritan woman), a sickness in the family (the royal official), a longstanding disability (the man born blind), and so forth. This Gospel merges seamlessly memories from the past with present experience. The evangelist wrote his work to share with others, whatever the challenges they faced, something of his own deep personal relationship with the Lord, and to invite them to believe in the crucified and risen Jesus and so find life in him (John 20:31). The one-to-one encounters between a range of individuals and Jesus, which form a distinctive characteristic of the Fourth Gospel, offer vivid and convincing narratives of men and women moving to Easter faith. Far from being simply accounts of what happened back there and then, these stories show how the risen Christ continues to transform people. For the readers of the Fourth Gospel, this is a call to let him transform them by accepting and experiencing his powerful presence in their lives.[17]

Coming to Easter faith initiates a Christian existence of being involved with and shaped by the living presence of the risen Jesus. Community worship forms a privileged context for experiencing his presence and that of his Holy Spirit, who is "invoked" to change the life of the worshipers. We know the risen Christ through what we see, hear, say, sing, do, touch (for example, other believers at the exchange of peace), and smell (for example, incense). Thus we reenact the resurrection not only each year at Easter but also every Sunday and even each day in the liturgy, becoming ourselves part of the ongoing history of the resurrection.

What we say at the Eucharist repeatedly points to the presence of the crucified and risen Christ in our midst. For instance, the acclamations that follow the words of institution express the community's experience of the risen Christ, present in his redeeming and life-giving power. They address him directly and in person: "Dying, you destroyed our death, rising you restored our life. Lord Jesus, come in glory." Over and over again the language used at the Eucharist suggests how we share and grow together in Easter faith by experiencing the presence of the risen Christ.

To conclude: believing in the risen Jesus is bound up with experiencing his living presence in worship, prayer, and the events that make up our lives. By giving a continual coherence and meaning to what we experience, this faith proves itself to us through our dwelling in it.

Chapter 7

RISEN EXISTENCE

What was/is the risen existence of Jesus Christ like? What will our risen existence be like? Putting those two questions together does not mean retracting the position presented in chapter 4. There we argued for a more direct, bodily continuity between the crucified and risen Jesus, a continuity that is presented through the Gospel narratives and sets his resurrection apart from our resurrection. Apropos of risen life, there are parallels, but not total conformity, between his case and ours.

A DIFFERENT CASE

When discussing the empty tomb of Jesus, we emphasized two items constituting the unique quality of the corpse buried by Joseph of Arimathea. First, unlike any other corpses the world has ever seen, this was the corpse of the incarnate Son of God. His personal identity gave this body a unique dignity. Second, the body buried by Joseph was the body of the Savior who had suffered and died on the cross to bring all men and women deliverance from evil. Such a universal saving function, which essentially involved the body of Jesus, *also* signaled something unique about the corpse laid in the tomb on Good Friday evening. Then, in being raised bodily from the dead, only Christ revealed his true divine identity (for example, Acts 2:32–36; Rom 1:4), and only he was disclosed as the effective Savior of the world (for example, Acts 4:12; 1 Cor 15:45). On both counts we can accept some uniquely close connection between the corpse laid in the tomb and the risen, bodily existence of Christ.

A partial reading of Paul could obscure the real difference

between the resurrection of Christ and ours. The apostle's (1) remark about Christ's being raised as "the first fruits of those who have died" (1 Cor 15:20) and (2) attempts to illuminate "the resurrection of the dead" in general (1 Cor 15:42–51) do not bring out how different Christ's case is. Yet Paul does imply that difference. It is true *only* of Christ that his resurrection brought "justification" (Rom 4:25) for human beings. He *alone* will effect the resurrection of the dead: "As all die in Adam, so all will be made alive in Christ" (1 Cor 15:22). Paul does not say of any other risen person that "he must reign until he has put all his enemies under his feet" (1 Cor 15:25). In short, Paul does not present Christ's resurrection in the past as a precise prototype of our future resurrection.

Christ's personal identity and redemptive function make it plausible that, in a dramatically transformed state, his dead body should have been "incorporated" immediately into his risen existence and hence that there would be more bodily continuity between the crucified and the risen Jesus than will be the case with us. His empty tomb expresses, among other things (see chapter 4), a close continuity-in-transformation between his earthly and his risen existence.

Thus Christ's resurrection is analogous to, but not identical with, our resurrection. In what follows, however, I presuppose the differences between Jesus and ourselves and reflect on the earthly body and its relationship with the risen body. Since resurrection means a new, embodied future conformed to the risen Christ, we need to ask, Do we find anything about our present human body that points ahead to or even prefigures the bodily destiny of a risen existence? In what way could the earthly body be related to and continuous with the risen, "spiritual" body (1 Cor 15:44)?

Here there is the obvious danger of filling the postmortem void with science fiction fantasies or worse. Julian Barnes warns us of this through his amusing parody of a heavenly existence that consists in indulging in sex, meeting celebrities, and enjoying unprecedented success in sports.[1] None of us has yet experienced resurrection for ourselves, and that seriously conditions the way we might conceptualize risen life. Nevertheless, we can look beyond the limitations and evils that affect our present existence and cautiously suggest something about the new, bodily existence that we hope for.

MATTER AND SPIRIT

As human beings we are bodily—or, if you like—we are bodies. First of all, our bodies obviously insert us into the material world. Each of us becomes a tiny part of the gigantic cosmos and the cosmos part of us. Once upon a time people naively assumed that the human body enjoyed a far-reaching autonomy and stability. Scientists had not yet discovered that our physical life forms a dynamic process of continual circulation between our bodies and our material environment. To adapt some words of John Donne, no body is an island. Through our bodies we incessantly share in and relate to the universe.

Modern thinkers conventionally stress the spiritual and bodily unity of the human person, our psychosomatic unity. At the same time, a certain dualism remains between matter and spirit. But one should add at once that dualistic thinking about our present existence does not necessarily steer us toward a Platonic conclusion in which "we" (as soul or spirit) are "in" a body or "have" a body. Speaking of our present "matter and spirit" need not suppose that they are utterly disparate realities that, like oil and water, will not mix. All matter has something spiritual about it. A pure materiality that would be totally unspiritual seems impossible. I deal here partly with a question of definition. Matter could be flatly defined in opposition to spirit and, if so defined, would not have something spiritual about it. Yet one can well argue that all *human* matter has something spiritual about it. Moreover, all the atomic material in our universe is at least potentially human matter.

Such spiritualizing of matter continually takes place through breathing, eating, and drinking. By being taken into a human body, matter becomes vitally associated with the functions of a spiritual being. The world of art exhibits a similar phenomenon. Paintings, pieces of sculpture, and stained glass windows are material objects. By being organized and spiritualized in the hands of their makers, such works of art can embody a rich cargo of meaning. Christian believers acknowledge a similar process in the life of the sacraments, above all in the case of the Eucharist. A piece of bread and a cup of wine are spiritualized and personalized though the power of the Holy Spirit to become the most intensely real presence of the risen Christ. The use of material substances (for example, water and oil) in all the sacraments visibly associates the bodies of the worshipers with the material universe. But the rites aim to link them with highly personal realities: the body of the church and the body of Christ himself.

Obviously matter can be understood and interpreted in many ways. Nuclear physicists know it as mainly empty space, the field of several basic forces. Electrons and other particles appear as either mass or energy. Nevertheless, breathing, eating, drinking, painting, celebrating the sacraments, and further human activities disclose another face of matter: its possibility of being spiritualized and personalized.

The resurrection of the dead will mean the full and final personalizing and spiritualizing of our matter, not its abolition. Through the action of the Holy Spirit, the human spirit will "dominate" matter, in the sense that the body will clearly express and serve the glorified spirit of human beings. Accepting this requires a leap of imagination. We can be helped to make this leap by reflecting on one aspect of risen transformation that will affect, in particular, our capacity to communicate.

Here and now our material bodiliness creates the possibility of being *communicators*. With and through our bodies we act, express ourselves, relate, and communicate with others. Without our bodies, there would be no language, no art, no literature, no religion, no industry, no political life, no social and economic relations, and none of that married love in which verbal and nonverbal communication reaches a supremely intense level. In short, without our bodies we could not make and enjoy any human history. Through our bodies we build up a vast web of relationships with other human beings, with the material universe, and with God. Our bodies enable us to communicate, play the human game, and compose our individual, personal stories.

Although our bodies enable us to communicate, at the same time they put limits to our communication. Being subject to the constraints of space and time, our bodies set us apart and restrict our chances of relating and communicating. People talk, hug, kiss, make telephone calls, send e-mails and text messages, write letters, and in other ways try to make up quantitatively for what they lack qualitatively. Through sickness, old age, imprisonment, exile, and other causes, our bodies can bring us radical solitude and terrifying loneliness. That bodily loneliness and breakdown in communications find their final expression when the tomb contains a newly buried corpse or a crematorium the fresh ashes of someone.

Few modern writers have described that irreversible break more poignantly than John McGahern. He wrote of his mother, who died at the age of forty-two, "She was gone. She would never answer to her name again. She was gone for ever…gone where I could not follow."[2]

Our bodies do not merely separate and alienate us from one another, from the world, and from God. Through weariness, physical weakness, sickness, sleep, and death, they alienate us from ourselves. Our present embodied condition can make us feel not fully free to be ourselves and to be with others.

We may usefully imagine the resurrection as maximizing our capacity to relate and communicate. The supreme example here, of course, is Jesus himself. As raised from the dead through the power of the Holy Spirit, he now relates to the Father, human beings, and the whole cosmos in a manner that has shed the constraints of his historical existence. Wherever two or three gather in his name, they experience the risen Lord in their midst (Matt 18:20). Nothing reveals more powerfully the new communicative power of Jesus than the Eucharist. It brings his worldwide presence and his offer to communicate a life that will never end.

To expect resurrection involves hoping that we will be set free to go far beyond the limitations and triviality of so much that passes for communication in this world. We will be liberated to be truly ourselves and to be with others in a new, loving way.

BODILY CONTINUITY AND OUR HISTORY

His empty tomb points to a transformation of Jesus' dead body into a new, risen mode of existence but a transformation that brought no loss of his personal identity. The narratives of Matthew, Luke, and John make it credible that, when Jesus appeared to individuals or groups of disciples, they could recognize him as the same Jesus whom they had known during his earthly lifetime. Some (transformed) material continuity enabled them to identify the risen one as numerically identical with the Jesus they had known. But the preservation of *our* individual, personal identity in a risen existence seems more problematic.[3] Let me explain.

Here and now our bodies ensure our individual continuity and our being recognizable as the same person. To be and to be recognized as the same person, we must remain "the same body." Despite continual and massive bodily changes, our personal continuity and identity are somehow bound up with our bodily identity and continuity. We are and have the same body and therefore remain the same person. Bodily continuity points to the persistence of personal identity. Some question the link between bodily continuity and the continuity of personal identity, understanding the latter in terms of continuity in mental states: in particular, consciousness and memories. Unquestionably, chains of conscious memories have a role in maintaining our *sense* of personal identity. The memory of what I have personally experienced constitutes the evidence within me of my persisting identity. Yet one's enduring personhood cannot simply depend upon one's memory. Otherwise loss of memory would entail loss of personal identity. The case of amnesia rebuts attempts to promote memory as the (sole?) means for constituting and preserving personal continuity or the one, unique life story that is "me."

As I stated earlier, personal identity and continuity remain somehow bound up with bodily continuity. In the second century, St. Irenaeus of Lyons emphatically applied this principle to the personal identity that will be preserved in resurrection. He asked, "With what body will the dead rise? Certainly with the same body in which they died; otherwise those who rise would

145

not be the same persons who previously died" (*Against Heresies*, 5.13.1). But in what sense will we rise with the *same* body? What counts here as bodily sameness or individual identity?

Even in this earthly life the enormous and continuous interchange of matter with our environment can make us wonder how far it is correct to speak of someone being or having the same body at six months before birth and then again at six, sixteen, and sixty. As old matter is discarded and new matter is absorbed into a living body, there is a steady replacement of the matter constituting that body. How do we keep the same, numerically identical body right through our lifetime? We might hesitantly suggest that our unique genetic structure, which our DNA molecules carry, maintains our body as the same body through this life. But at death, with our physical remains dispersed into the environment through the decay or burning of our corpse, how can we speak of any bodily continuity between this earthly existence and our risen life?

One answer could be found by noting the connection between saying "I am my body" and "I am my history." Through our bodiliness, we grow in relation to other persons, God, and the world. Our individual history comes from our body being freely "in relationship." This means that in creating our personal history, our exercise of freedom is intimately connected with our bodies. We create our history by freely deciding to go (not just in our imagination but with our bodies) to our places of work, study, living, and relaxation; when we arrive, we do and suffer such and such things with our bodies. Our bodies establish the possibility of building and shaping our particular histories. As bodies we construct our histories—from conception to death. As human beings, we enjoy bodily or embodied histories.

Thinking this way creates some credibility for understanding resurrection as our particular, embodied history being raised from the dead. In resurrection, that particular, bodily history that makes up the unique story of each person will be brought to new life. In a mysterious, transformed fashion their risen existence will express what they as embodied persons were and became in their earthly life. Put that way, the view of Irenaeus makes good sense: "With what bodily history will the dead rise? Certainly with the same bodily history, at the end of which they died; otherwise those who rise would not be the same persons who previously died." Given the intimate link between our bodiliness and history, we can say, "The same resurrected history means the same resurrected body."

This proposal of mine needs defense. First, if I ask what has made me what I am as a unique individual, it has surely been my embodied history and not the millions of molecules that in a passing parade have at different moments constituted my particular physical existence. Second, my whole bodily history is much more "me" than the physical body that breathes its last, say at eighty years of age. In short, it makes sense to imagine the resurrection as God bringing to a transformed, personal life the total embodied history of dead individuals and so ensuring their genuine personal continuity.

This approach makes very good sense of what happened to Jesus, the (partial) prototype of our resurrection. When he rose from the dead, his whole life rose with him. In his risen state Jesus possesses fully his whole human story. His resurrection and glorification have made his entire life and history irrevocably present. Even if they never explicitly thought in terms of the irrevocable presence of Jesus' earthly history, the four evangelists wrote their Gospels out of a sense that the earthly life of Jesus had risen with him and remains indispensably significant for his followers down through the ages.

This proposal about our continuity being preserved through our embodied history being resurrected must face the question, How can the temporal history of individuals, fashioned through a sequence of events that extended through a stretch of time, be resurrected by God in an existence that is nontemporal but eternal? Any full response would need to come up with a fully argued position on time and eternity and their possible relationships and even convergence. Here Brian Leftow made a notable contribution with his *Time and Eternity*.[4] He has also defended convincingly the traditional doctrine that a timeless God became incarnate and so took on a temporal existence.[5] This is to show that divine eternity (a mode of atemporal existence) and time are not mutually exclusive. God can be both timeless and incarnate.

147

Moving beyond the scope of Leftow's arguments, we can fruitfully maintain an analogy between the incarnation and the resurrection. Where the incarnation involved the timeless Son of God taking on a temporal existence, resurrection from the dead involves temporal beings (that have been embodied in their unique history) becoming eternal, to the extent that created beings can participate in the divine attribute of eternity. On the one hand, the timeless Son of God, by becoming embodied, could develop his unique human history. In a similar but not identical way, on the other hand, the embodied, historical existence of human beings can, through the resurrecting power of God, become eternalized.

Something of this sharing in eternity shows up already in the history of human beings. Time not only involves a succession of earlier and later events (as time moves inexorably and irreversibly on) but also has something cumulative about it. More than a mere stream of fleeting moments that disappear, time entails many things coming together and being preserved: memories in the mind, marks on our bodies, webs of persisting relationships with relatives, friends, and colleagues at work, and the rest. Likewise, and much more so, resurrected life will be a gathering up or coming together of a whole, accumulated past that remains present to us. In resurrection, through the power of God our time and history will be summed up and completed.

My proposal about our embodied history being resurrected finds support from Caroline Walker Bynum's *The Resurrection of the Body in Western Christianity, 200–1336*.[6] She illustrates extensively the persistent conviction of many Christians that resurrection would preserve for all eternity their genders, family experiences, and the other characteristics and events that identified them as unique human persons and constituted their individual history. In particular, they rejected Gnostic-style talk about Jesus himself living "male" but rising "human," and, more generally, views about themselves living as male or female but rising as human, with some kind of unisex, spiritual body. Such views detached the risen Jesus from the particular characteristics and circumstances that helped to shape his individual history and, in effect, denied that his particular history rose with him. In rejecting such views

148

about the resurrection of Jesus and their own resurrection, rank-and-file Christians were, in effect, insisting that the whole of our history rises with us.[7]

My proposal goes beyond what Bruno Niederbacher has suggested with reference to St. Thomas Aquinas. The same body will rise when the same rational soul or individual substantial form of a deceased human being comes to form or inform matter. In Niederbacher's words, "If the same individual substantial form comes to form matter, there will also be numerically the same body."[8] What makes the risen body numerically identical with the earthly body will be substantial form or rational soul. Wherever and whenever this form is once again embodied, it will be the same body.

This view is attractive, not least because it moves away from long-standing but tedious efforts to find plausible ways for alleging that God somehow gathers together in the risen body some of the matter that has composed the earthly body. (It could not be all the matter that during a lifetime at some point constituted the body of the deceased. If so, the risen body of someone who died, say over the age of twenty, would emerge in a giant, bloated form.) I agree with Niederbacher that the same bodily person who existed on earth will exist in the afterlife, albeit under radically transformed conditions. But what will make the risen body numerically identical with the earthly body will come from the individual soul with its new embodiment existing in continuity with a previous, unique, embodied existence in history. The one who will rise will be *this* bodily person, who in a complete lifetime experienced (through his or her freedom and body) a unique set of relationships upon earth.

THE TRANSFORMATION OF THE UNIVERSE

If resurrection involves the raising of human persons in all their historical relationships, that includes relationships not only to other persons but also to the created world. Our future environment will be radically new, and this calls for a radically new form of divine action. Much more than an extraordinary event *within* the ordinary background of fully "natural" events, this new creation will involve God changing nature itself.

Some join the late Arthur Peacocke in admitting, as we saw in chapter 6, no alteration to such basic laws of the universe as the Laws of Thermodynamics. These laws describe the general direction of change in the universe. One can express the Second Law of Thermodynamics in terms of entropy, which represents the degree of disorder or randomness of the constituents of any closed system. The entropy of an isolated system can only increase and never decrease. Peacocke could not imagine changes in such laws.[9] But his fellow scientist and Anglican priest, John Polkinghorne, recognizes that God does not have to leave unchanged the laws of nature, which were created like everything else in the universe. God can and will bring about not only the future risen life of human beings but also the transformation of the material universe in which they live.[10]

Here Polkinghorne and others (including myself) acknowledge that the empty tomb of Jesus, which involved his body being transformed into a new, glorious body, remains supremely important in dramatically illustrating the destiny of our material world. The matter of our future environment comes from "the transformed matter of this world." The creation of the new and final universe, initiated and symbolized by the resurrection of Jesus from the grave, entails "the divine redemption of the old [creation]," its "transformation" and not its "abolition." Thus the empty tomb of Jesus is uniquely significant in prefiguring the transforming activity of God that will affect the entire created universe. The present cosmos, regulated by various laws chosen and created by God, is the raw material from which the new creation will come.[11]

Thus God's intention to transform human beings *and their world*, or the work of re-creation, first manifested itself in what happened to the crucified body of Jesus. If that corpse represented the old creation, God did not discard it or leave it behind so as to substitute a new, nonmaterial creation (in Jesus' "spiritual," risen existence). With Jesus' resurrection from the tomb, a qualitatively new way of organizing the cosmos broke through and carried both humanity and the material universe toward the future and final transformation.

Even before the life, death, and resurrection of Jesus, the psalmist invited the stars, animals, trees, and other created things to join human beings in praising God (Ps 148:3–10). In another psalm, the hills, meadows, and valleys "shout and sing for joy" (Ps 65:12–13). The song of the three young men, which Greek versions of the Book of Daniel contain (after 3:23 or after 3:24), develops this theme at greater length. The Prayer of Azariah calls on rivers, seas, the earth, mountains, cattle, fish, and all created things to unite in cosmic praise of God. Such hymns suggest that if all created reality joins now in praising God, it will also (and even more) do so in a transformed universe to come.

Faced with a world damaged by sin, some Jewish prophets dreamed of a future, messianic harmony between human beings and the whole of nature, a time when "the wolf shall live with the lamb, / and the leopard lie down with the kid, / and the calf and the lion and the fatling together, / and a little child shall lead them" (Isa 11:6; see Ezek 47:1–12). This poetic vision has encouraged many Christians to share again the biblical sense that their final redemption embraces the transformation of the world and not an apocalyptic destruction of the material universe.

Ecologists have fastened on Paul's vision of all "creation" (the nonhuman created world) groaning in travail, waiting for liberation from "futility," and hoping to be "set free from its bondage to decay" and so to share intimately in "the freedom of the glory of the children of God" in the coming resurrection of humanity (Rom 8:19–22). Here I agree with those commentators who interpret the apostle's reference to "creation" as going beyond human beings to include the entire created universe.[12] A similarly broad vision turns up when a New Testament hymn celebrates the "reconciliation," through the death of Christ, of "all things, whether on earth or in heaven" (Col 1:19–20): the whole of creation will be transformed, not annihilated.

The Book of Revelation, through a wealth of exotic imagery, invites its readers to contemplate the victory of the risen Christ, a victory that involves the created world as well as the whole of human history. It sums up the goal of God's resurrecting and redemptive activity as "a new heaven and a new earth" (Rev 21:1). The Book of Revelation fills paradise with the leafy trees and rich fruits found on either side of the river of life (Rev 22:1–2). Christian artists took up this theme: for instance, by the wonderful mosaics in Ravenna that picture animals in verdant landscapes, peacocks (representing immortality), stags (representing souls), and doves drinking from the fountain of life. In Ghent, the *Adoration of the Lamb* by Hubert and Jan Van Eyck shows a blossoming meadow in which carefully arranged groups of angels and saints adore Christ enthroned on an altar. This theme of a heavenly garden, symbolizing the transformed world to come, recurs in many Christian paintings, mosaics, and tapestries.

In the introduction to this book we summarized some of the major assessments of the material universe and its future that emerged from a dialogue between scientists and theologians. Astonishing advances in modern science have generally rendered obsolete determinist views of the world as a rigidly closed system of causes and effects. A growing sense of wonder at the material universe, its immense size, and the stunning interaction of its forces has often produced a new willingness to admit the exercise of the special divine causality required by the resurrection of Jesus from the tomb.

God has created and respects the natural order of the world and its functioning. Yet, for good reasons and in the appropriate circumstances (for example, the death of Christ), God can suspend the operation of some laws. After all, those laws need not have existed at all, nor did they have to be precisely the way they are. Created as they are, they depend from moment to moment on God for their continuing existence and operation. In raising Jesus from the tomb, God acted in a way that was qualitatively distinct and different from the "ordinary" divine work in creating and sustaining the world. At the end of history, God will be free to change the laws of nature so as to raise the dead and transform the material world.

In chapter 6 we spoke of the progressive spiritualizing of matter, a theme that shaped the fourfold scheme of Pierre Teilhard de Chardin: *cosmogenesis, biogenesis, noogenesis,* and *Christogenesis.* These terms referred, respectively, to the creation of the material world, the emergence of life, the emergence of mind, and the coming of Christ (his incarnation leading to his resurrection and its results). Teilhard, as we saw in chapter 6, would not accept any strong dualism between matter and spirit. He understood matter to be progressively spiritualized through the risen Christ, until matter and spirit are finally unified in the resurrection of the dead and the transformation of the universe.

Chapter 8

THE RESURRECTION'S IMPACT ON SACRAMENTAL AND MORAL THEOLOGY

The first author presented in the introduction to this book, Tony Kelly, deplored the strange neglect of Christ's resurrection by those who write in the areas of sacramental and moral theology. This complaint could also be directed against many writers in other areas of theology. Here I limit myself to the theology of the sacraments and moral theology (perhaps better named "Christian ethics"). First, have authors in these two fields failed to reflect on the resurrection and to develop their thinking in terms of this unique event that should "saturate" (Kelly) the whole of Christian faith and should transform the life and thought of believers? Second, how does Jesus' resurrection from the dead provide the broadest horizon within which we can recognize what the sacraments mean and how we should live?

RESURRECTION AND THE SACRAMENTS: A STRANGE NEGLECT

Bernard Leeming's *Principles of Sacramental Theology*, a work of nearly 750 pages, proved a classic text in the years leading up to the Second Vatican Council (1962–65). Its references to the resurrection were limited to a few references embodied in a critical evaluation of the "mysteries-presence" theory of Odo Casel.[1] The resurrection of the crucified Jesus was missing in the sacramental theology of Leeming. Did an appropriate attention to the

Easter mystery grow and flourish in sacramental theology during the postconciliar years?

Louis-Marie Chauvet has been rightly valued for the broad theological culture that he brings to the study of the sacraments. He draws upon twenty centuries of theological thought and enriches what he writes with exegesis, philosophy, history, and anthropology.[2] In particular, he has broken new ground by using the thought of John Langshaw Austin to elucidate the sacraments.[3] But, despite proposing "the Paschal mystery of Christ" as his "point of departure," Chauvet does not allow the resurrection of the crucified Jesus to focus clearly his reflections; his account of "the Paschal Mystery" embraces everything from the incarnation to the Parousia.[4] Of course, the resurrection looks back (to creation and not merely to the incarnation) and looks forward (through the time of the church to the final coming of Christ). But I searched in vain for Chauvet's developing such themes as the crucified and risen Christ being personally present and active in the celebration of the sacraments.

Susan Ross has produced a feminist sacramental theology that challenges some positions that need to be challenged: for instance, conceptions of atonement that "have questionable scriptural roots as well as potentially harmful effects on people's lives."[5] This made me think of penal substitution theories that have been bolstered by unacceptable exegesis of passages (coming from the Jewish scriptures, Paul's letters, and the "cry of abandonment" in the passion story of Jesus) and have encouraged the image of an "angry God."[6] Nevertheless, in Ross's book, I found the resurrection sadly missing. She writes of the sacraments being "'saving events' rooted in the life and death of Christ."[7] But surely the sacraments are *also* essentially rooted in the resurrection of Christ and his co-sending of the Holy Spirit? She includes the "central significance of the life and death of Jesus Christ" among "the basic principles" of "Christian feminist theology."[8] Once again she passes over the resurrection and its aftermath at Pentecost. Surely the role of Mary Magdalene and other women as major witnesses to the resurrection and the presence of Jesus' mother in Jerusalem for the coming of the Holy Spirit (Acts 1:14) have something, or even much, to contribute to a "Christian feminist theology"?[9] Such a theology should extend its "basic principles" to include the resurrection and the sending of the Spirit among the events that enjoy "central significance" for sacramentality.

Kelly alerted me to two scholars whose admirable learning has shaped their books in sacramental theology but who remain strangely quiet about the resurrection: Kenan Osborne and David Power.[10] Because Osborne had published a book on the resurrection,[11] his silence about the resurrection when writing a sacramental theology seems even more remarkable. One contemporary writer, German Martinez, who examines sacramentality from the perspective of freedom, manages, however, to incorporate the resurrection into a pastoral presentation of the seven sacraments.[12] It is no accident that the cover of his book carries a representation of the risen Jesus and the book ends with a reflection on the "signs of the liberating presence of the risen Lord."[13] By not neglecting the resurrection in his sacramental theology, Martinez stands out as a welcome exception. But what would I expect to find in a sacramental theology that systematically embraces the crucified Christ's resurrection from the dead?

LETTING THE RESURRECTION SHAPE SACRAMENTAL THEOLOGY

One should cry out against any approach to the sacraments that drifts away from the Easter mystery. Neither the life of Jesus nor his death was enough to set going the sacramental life of the church. Let us look first at the foundational sacraments of baptism and the Eucharist.

Baptized into the Risen Christ

Given the way the resurrection grounds and focuses baptism, Matthew naturally associates the baptismal formula "in the name of the Father and of the Son and of the Holy Spirit" (Matt 28:19) with the solemn appearance of the risen Jesus that brings the whole Gospel narrative to a close. Paul assures us that neophytes enter the Christian community precisely by being baptized into the crucified and risen Jesus (Rom 6:3–12; Gal 3:27; Col 2:12–13). Jesus had referred to his coming death as a "baptism" (Mark 10:38–39; Luke 12:50). The baptized know themselves to be assumed once and for all into the once-and-for-all dying and rising of Christ. They are "given a new birth" through their baptismal sharing in "the resurrection of Jesus Christ from the dead" (1 Pet 1:3; see John 3:5; Titus 3:5). They are immersed in the reality of Christ's death, burial, and resurrection to new life. On the occasion of their being baptized, they confess their faith in Jesus as risen from the dead (Rom 10:9).[14] Their new life means existing "in" the risen Christ, the inclusive figure into whom believers know themselves to have been incorporated (for example, Rom 8:1; 16:7; 1 Cor 15:22; Phil 3:8–9).

By being spiritually washed clean from sin (1 Cor 6:11) and born again through baptism, individual Christians form a single body with the risen Christ (1 Cor 12:12–13) and are engrafted into the life of the glorified Son (John 15:5).[15] Both these images—the head with its members and the vine with its branches—imply that by means of baptism the unifying force of divine life and love, the Holy Spirit, flows not only through the risen Lord of the *Ecclesia* but also through those who enter into the ecclesial community. Furthermore, since Christ and his Father are one (John 14:9–10), those who are rejuvenated with water and anointed with the Spirit also share in the being of the Father.

Baptism means, however, more than passively participating in the existence of the risen Christ who was exalted by the Spirit of the Father (1 Pet 3:18). While the "indicative" of Christian faith announces that the baptized share in a new way of being, the "imperative" of this faith challenges the baptized to share in God's saving mission in history. How can we best describe what this mission involves?

When we say that Jesus was raised up, we mean that his entire life and ministry were vindicated or justified by the Holy Spirit (1 Tim 3:17). Jesus had allowed himself to be baptized by John, for it was "proper in this way to fulfill all righteousness" (Matt 3:15). He preached the righteousness of God's kingdom and led a totally righteous life from his first baptism in the Jordan to his final baptism on Calvary (Mark 10:38–39). For this reason,

Christians, being baptized with the Spirit of the risen Christ, are to be guided by the Spirit of the righteous Jesus (Gal 5:25). Baptismal grace enables them to serve others by becoming signs and sacraments of the invincible justice won by the glorified Jesus. Being baptized into the resurrection of the crucified Jesus calls for the interior renewal conferred by the sacrament to be translated into action on behalf of all humanity (which is in principle already liberated from injustice by the Easter mystery).

The Eucharist and the Resurrection

As for the Eucharist, the disciples would never have begun "doing this in remembrance of the Lord Jesus" (1 Cor 11:23–24) if Jesus had not risen from the dead. Paul and the Synoptic Gospels report the origin of the Eucharist "on the night when the Lord Jesus was betrayed" (1 Cor 11:23)—that is to say, right before the events of the crucifixion and resurrection took place. John expressly links the Eucharist and our participation in the resurrection of Christ: "Those who eat my flesh and drink my blood have eternal life, and I will raise them up on the last day" (John 6:54). In the Eucharist, Christians receive the risen Lord and through him they too will move to resurrected life. In this direct way the Eucharist and the resurrection illuminate each other. The resurrection of the crucified Jesus has already taken place. Through visible signs, the Eucharist makes powerfully present the final resurrection that will come to human beings and their world.

Yet the Eucharist makes the resurrection present in an even fuller sense when Christians recognize the risen Jesus not only in his sacramental body on the altar but also in his ecclesial body gathered in worship and prayer. For the Eucharist, as transubstantiated bread and wine, cannot be properly understood apart from the transfigured body of Jesus who not only "sits at the right hand" of the Father but also mystically unites himself to the community of Christian worshipers. Hence St. Paul castigates those Corinthians who limit encountering the glorified Jesus to the reception of his sacramental body without also receiving him in the poor and hungry members of his ecclesial body. The words "without discerning the body" (1 Cor 11:29) convey therefore two meanings: we can fail to recognize the risen Jesus *either* in the transformed Eucharistic elements *or* in those who have nothing to eat.[16]

The practice Paul encouraged had, of course, been anticipated by the scandalous table fellowship that Jesus offered to sinners during his earthly lifetime (for example, Luke 5:27–32). The risen Lord is the same person who once sat at table with tax collectors and other notorious outcasts and gave himself to them by pardoning their sins, nourishing their broken bodies and spirits, and transforming their alienation into fellowship. Jesus made them "bread sharers" with each other and with the Father.

Likewise today, belief in the risen Lord present in the Eucharist challenges Christians who live in a self-centered society to engage in prophetic acts of solidarity that recall Jesus who poured himself out for others. The words "take and eat" spoken in the upper room (Matt 26:26) can be properly linked to some words of the final judgment scene: "I was hungry and you gave me food" (Matt 25:35). Just as at baptism the Spirit engrafts believers into Christ the vine in order that they produce the fruit of justice, so at the Eucharist the Holy Spirit unites them to Christ the bread of life in order that they produce the fruit of love (John 15:18). At the Eucharist a first *epiclesis* (invocation) (before the words of institution) asks the Spirit to descend upon the gifts to change them into the body and blood of the risen Christ. A second *epiclesis* comes after the consecration and prays that the communicants be changed. Communicating with the risen Jesus and acting in his name, they provisionally participate in his resurrection and look to the day when he will raise them and the cosmos to share unendingly in his life and glory.

It is at the Easter Vigil that the sacraments of initiation—baptism, confirmation, and the Eucharist—come together brilliantly—in the light, so to speak, of the Easter candle, a towering symbol of the risen Christ's presence in the believing community. Baptism, as expounded by Paul, signifies dying, being buried, and rising with Christ (Rom 6:3–5); the Eucharist, the apostle explains, means proclaiming the death of the risen Lord "until he comes" (1 Cor 11:26). Recognizing that profound meaning in baptism and the Eucharist illuminates the climax of the Rite of Christian Initiation of Adults, when the catechumens receive baptism and anointing before sharing for the first time in the body and blood of the risen Lord. The whole community takes part in the Easter Vigil by welcoming the newly baptized, renewing their own baptismal promises, and receiving the Eucharist.

The Other Sacraments

The other sacraments also offer their specific means for participating in the person and mission of the risen Christ. At confirmation, those who have been baptized into the priestly people of God share more fully in Christ the eternal high priest and are called to assume a more active role in witnessing to the risen Christ and spreading the faith by word and example. The sacrament of penance announces that the forgiveness of sinners takes place because "God, the Father of mercies, through the death and resurrection of his Son, has reconciled the world to himself." Through the anointing of the sick, Christians who are weak or at the point of death are more deeply united with the crucified and exalted Jesus, and along with the whole community witness to his rich compassion and healing power. The particular symbolism and rites of confirmation, penance, and the anointing of the sick show how these three sacraments make sense and draw their power from the crucified and risen Jesus who, together with the Father, sends us the Holy Spirit.

The vocational sacraments of orders and marriage link ordained and married persons, respectively, to the glorified bridegroom who cherishes his bride, the church (Eph 5:29). These sacraments commission them to build up the domestic and local Christian communities in anticipation of the eternal wedding feast. Once again the glorious, living Christ reveals what these two sacraments involve and promise.

The Priestly Presence of the Risen Christ

A further vital theme for sacramental theology is the presence of the risen and living Christ in the celebration of the sacraments, a presence that assumes differing forms and intensities.[17] Whenever the sacraments are administered, the risen and eternal high priest is personally and effectively present. It is primarily the invisible Christ (made visible in his Body that is the church) who performs the baptizing, the ordaining, and the dispensing of all sacramental graces. It is at our peril that we neglect the powerful presence of the risen Christ in and through all the sacraments. His presence makes the saving acts of his life, death, resurrection, ascension, and co-sending of the Holy Spirit into present realities.

It was with reference to baptism that St. Augustine of Hippo summed up the sacramental ministry of the risen Lord: "When Peter baptizes it is Christ who baptizes. When Paul baptizes, it is Christ who baptizes" (*Homilies on the Gospel of John*, 5.18; see 6.7). Augustine upheld the principle (which had some roots in the teaching of St. Cyprian and St. John Chrysostom) that "Christ is the only true minister of the sacraments."[18] For Augustine, in "the sacraments of baptism and the Eucharist" the "saving work of Christ, who is both priest and sacrifice, is actualized for the individual."[19] All the sacraments involve personal encounters with the living Christ. He is the real, even if invisible, minister of each and every sacrament. We see and hear the visible ministers of the sacraments: for instance, the ordained priests who administer the sacrament of reconciliation to those who confess their sins or the married couples who give each other the grace of matrimony through their bodily and personal union. But, invisibly and really, it is the risen Lord who heals sinners and reconciles them with God and the community. It is Christ who brings the sacrament of matrimony to husband and wife and helps them grow in mutual love.

Any adequate vision of the active presence of Christ in administering the sacraments involves reflection on his eternal activity as high priest. His priesthood continues forever, since he never ceases to intercede for the world (for example, Rom 8:34; Heb 7:25) and bless the world (Eph 1:3). The risen and exalted Christ remains forever the priestly mediator of divine blessings and benefits. To appreciate the active presence of the Christ in the sacramental life of the church necessarily calls for reflection on his priesthood.[20]

Christ's priestly intercession takes the form, above all, of his eternal self-offering. Augustine pointed to Christ's self-offering that continues: "As our Priest risen from the dead and established in heaven," he "now offers sacrifice on our behalf" (*Expositions of the Psalms,* 26.2). Here we might appeal to the Book of Revelation and its picture of the heavenly liturgy, with the Victim being the Lamb who was slain and who forever faces the presence of God.[21]

That this self-offering of Christ the high priest takes place through the Holy Spirit to the Father develops the theme of Christ being consecrated by the Spirit for his whole mission (Acts 10:38; see Luke 3:22; 4:14). The Holy Spirit enabled Christ to make a perfect and eternal self-offering to the Father (Heb 9:14).[22] The risen and exalted Christ remains forever victim and priest. Through the Spirit the heavenly consummation of Christ's sacrifice continues for all eternity.

Apropos of the eucharistic self-offering of Christ into which the visible ministers and the faithful are drawn, few have put more powerfully its Trinitarian nature than Tom Torrance. He wrote about participation in the Eucharist, "We worship and pray to the Father in such a way that it is [the risen and exalted] Christ himself who is the real content [and agent] of our worship and prayer." Torrance added, "In the Spirit the prayer that ascends from us to the Father is a form of the self-offering of Christ himself."[23]

Christ the eternal high priest continues to pour out the Holy Spirit on the church and the world. This emerges through the Johannine testimony to the Spirit in the words of Jesus: "When the Advocate comes, whom I will send to you from the Father, the Spirit of truth who comes from the Father, he will testify on my behalf" (John 15:26). The evangelist associates the Spirit not only with witnessing to Jesus but also with new birth and life (3:5–8; 4:10, 14; 7:37–39), with truth and teaching (14:16–17, 26; 16:13–15), and with mission and the forgiveness of sins (20:22–23). Such witnessing, giving new life, teaching the truth, and commissioning on the part of the Spirit are ongoing activities that involve a continual sending by the eternal high priest.

Thus the Holy Spirit universalizes the priestly presence and work of Jesus. Here we can deploy the theme of presence. The universal presence of the Spirit accompanies the presence of the exalted Christ that is a universal presence. Since the co-sender of the Spirit (the risen one) is always inseparably and intimately linked with the Sent (the Holy Spirit),[24] and since Christ is present everywhere and in every human life, the Spirit must also be present everywhere and in every human life. Thus the notion of the Spirit universalizing the priestly work of Christ implies a universal presence of both the Spirit and Christ.[25] Here, to avoid misunderstanding, we should add at once: people do not have to be aware of living in the presence of Christ and the Holy Spirit for this to be the case. *Being present* does not, as such, imply *being known to be present.*

To hold that the eternal high priest incessantly acts as the primary, if invisible, minister in the sacramental life (and, we should add, preaching) of the church obviously makes more precise what is left more general in the New Testament. The Gospel of Matthew closes with the risen Christ's command to evangelize and baptize all nations and with the promise: "I will be with you always" (Matt 28:19–20). But the risen Christ does not particularize matters by promising, "When you preach, I will be with you always as the invisible preacher; when you baptize, I will be with you always as the invisible minister." The longer ending of Mark pictures the Lord Jesus being "taken up into heaven" and sitting "at the right hand of God" after commissioning "the eleven" to preach and baptize everywhere. They, then, "went out and proclaimed the good news everywhere, while the Lord *worked with them* and confirmed the message by the signs that accompanied it" (Mark 16:19–20). Unlike Matthew, the author of this additional ending to Mark witnesses more concretely to the belief and experience of early Christians: the exalted Christ was not absent but dramatically present and at work in their mission to preach and baptize.

The Book of Acts, without expressly qualifying the activity as priestly, tells the story of Jesus being with those who preached the gospel, working with them, and confirming what they did in his service through the power of the Holy Spirit. In the Lucan scheme, the risen Jesus needs to be withdrawn from the visible scene before the Holy Spirit comes. But the ascension does not mean that Jesus has gone away, as if he were on a very long sabbatical leave in another universe. He remains powerfully, if invisibly, present in the life of the church. Here distinctions may seem to become a little blurred. Luke can move from instances of faithful guidance by the risen and exalted Christ (Acts 9:10–16; 18:9–10;

22:17–21) to instances of guidance by the Holy Spirit (Acts 8:29; 10:19; 16:6), without distinguishing clearly among them. At least once Luke reports guidance by "the Spirit of Jesus" (Acts 16:7) in parallelism with "the Holy Spirit" (Acts 16:6). Does he mean here the Holy Spirit who comes from Jesus, the Spirit who somehow is identified with Jesus, or the Spirit who brings us to Jesus?[26] As regards the initial outpouring of the Spirit, Luke distinguishes Jesus as divine co-sender from the divine Spirit who is sent or poured out (Luke 24:49; Acts 2:33). But when witnessing to the spread and life of the Christian community, Luke often refers to the powerful guidance of Jesus and that of the Holy Spirit in a seemingly undifferentiated manner. Both are continually present "in, with, and under" the ministry of the church.

Luke's narrative puts flesh and blood on what the Letter to the Hebrews states about human beings being enabled through Christ the high priest to approach God's "throne of grace" (Heb 4:16). One could sum up what Hebrews conveys about the place and means of salvation: "Outside Christ the risen and exalted high priest and his ongoing priestly self-offering and intercession there is no salvation." To avoid misunderstanding, one should add, "But there is no way of being 'outside Christ' and no zone beyond him and his priestly activity."

It was Augustine who classically expressed his faith in the risen Christ as the real, albeit invisible, minister of any and every baptism, no matter who was the visible minister of that baptism. Later, Augustine's principle was extended to the Eucharist, the administration of other sacraments, preaching, and the celebration of the divine office. The Second Vatican Council in its Constitution on the Divine Liturgy (*Sacrosanctum Concilium*) spelled out the multifaceted presence of the risen Christ in the celebration of the liturgy (no. 7), preaching the word (no. 33), and praying or singing the divine office (no. 83).[27]

Among modern theologians few have expressed more eloquently than Torrance the active, priestly presence of the risen Christ whenever the Eucharist is celebrated. He wrote, "When the Church worships, praises and adores the Father through Christ and celebrates the Eucharist in his name, it is Christ himself [in the Spirit] who worships, praises and adores the Father in and through his members, taking up, moulding and sanctifying the prayers of the people."[28]

The Sacraments and Our Resurrection

In the early church Tertullian stood out for insisting that the sacraments promise and assure our future sharing in the life of the risen and exalted Christ. After naming "the flesh" as "the hinge of salvation" (*caro cardo salutis*), Tertullian expressed this hope for "the resurrection of the flesh" in the larger context of Christian initiation and sacramental life.

Through the indissoluble link between, on the one hand, *bodily* baptism, confirmation, and reception of the Eucharist and, on the other, the cleansing, consecrating, fortifying, illuminating, and nourishing of their *souls*, human beings are enabled to live a life of faith and service. Such a life prepares their entire existence, flesh and spirit, for the glorious reward of bodily resurrection. Tertullian wrote:

> The flesh is washed [baptism], so that the soul may be cleansed. The flesh is anointed, so that the soul may be consecrated. The flesh is signed [with the cross], so that the soul may be fortified. The flesh is overshadowed by the imposition of hands [confirmation], so that the soul may be illuminated by the Spirit. The flesh feeds on the body and blood of Christ [the Eucharist], so that the soul likewise may feed on its God. They [the body and the soul] cannot then be separated in their reward, when they are united in their service. (*On the Resurrection of the Flesh*, 8.2)[29]

In the Middle Ages, St. Thomas Aquinas, when writing (among other texts) an antiphon for the Feast of Corpus Christi (instituted in 1264), classically linked the future hope of resurrection conferred by the Eucharist with eucharistic experience and memory: "O sacred banquet in which Christ is received, his suffering is remembered [past], (our) mind is filled with grace [present], and we receive a pledge of the glory that is to be ours [future] [*O sacrum convivium, in quo Christus sumitur, recolitur memoria passionis eius, mens impletur gratia, et futurae gloriae nobis pignus datur].*"

When describing the Eucharist as a "pledge" of the glorious resurrection to come, Thomas stood in a long tradition that led back through Tertullian to St. Ignatius of Antioch. In a passage that would become famous, Ignatius linked the Eucharist and resurrection when he wrote of "breaking one bread, which is the medicine of immortality [and] the antidote against death and which gives eternal life in Jesus Christ" (*Epistle to the Ephesians,* 20.2). Thus Ignatius associated, albeit briefly, the reality of the Eucharist with the future resurrection for which believers hope.

St. Irenaeus of Lyons took further this theme initiated by Ignatius and expressed the impact of the Eucharist on our coming resurrection this way: "Our bodies, after partaking of the Eucharist, are no longer corruptible, having the hope of eternal resurrection" (*Against Heresies,* 4.18.5). Against those who denied "the salvation of the flesh" and alleged "the flesh incapable of immortality," Irenaeus maintained that our "flesh" can enjoy "eternal life," since it is "fed on the flesh and blood of the Lord" (ibid., 5.2.2–3).

Linking the hope of resurrection with the Eucharist goes back to the New Testament (for example, John 6:54). This sacrament, even more vividly than the others, prefigures and anticipates the coming glory of resurrection. But in their differing ways, the other sacraments (above all, baptism) confer their "pledges" of our future resurrection. Any sacramental theology that neglects the promise of the resurrection communicated by all the sacraments remains desperately impoverished.

RESURRECTION AND MORAL THEOLOGY: A CONTINUING NEGLECT

In its Decree on the Training of Priests of October 1965 (*Optatam Totius,* 16), the Second Vatican Council anticipated what it would say three weeks later in the Constitution on Divine Revelation (*Dei Verbum,* 24): the study of sacred scripture should be "the soul of all theology." In particular, Vatican II expected that moral theology should be improved by drawing "more fully on the teaching" of scripture (*Optatam Totius*, 16). But has such an improvement happened? And, specifically, has the message of Christ's resurrection, around which "the New Testament revolves,"[30] had its appropriate impact on moral theology or Christian ethics, the systematic reflection on Christian moral life and on what a truly "good" life should be?

At an ecumenical, interdisciplinary symposium held in New York in 1996, Brian Johnstone documented the way in which leading Christian ethicists have neglected the resurrection of Jesus from the dead, "the fundamental belief of Christians." He added, "That belief does not seem to have left any mark on Christian ethics and moral theology, at least as this is portrayed in the standard texts." Johnstone could name only "one major work in the field of moral theology dedicated to the resurrection: Oliver O'Donovan's *Resurrection and Moral Order*."[31] Yet Johnstone had to admit that even in this book, "the resurrection functions as a reinstatement of order in the world, which sustains the objective status of ethics. The resurrection belief itself does not shape or illustrate the form of the moral life."[32] Johnstone's essay on the relation of resurrection faith to Christian ethics was singled out by reviewers as "perceptive" and "very informative" (John Galvin) and "one of the most important in the book" (Stephen Barton).[33] But has the essay enjoyed the impact it deserved in Christian moral thinking?

In 2008 Tony Kelly cited this seminal article by Johnstone, noted that Christian "reflection on the moral life" had continued to "remain unaffected by the resurrection event and the hope it inspires," and outlined some ways in which "the resurrection effect" might work in moral theology.[34] Since Kelly's book appeared in 2008, nothing much seems to have changed. In 2010, for instance, Patrick Nullens and Ronald T. Michener published *The Matrix of Christian Ethics: Moral Theology in a Postmodern Context*, a work in which the resurrection receives hardly any attention. In passing they mention something of what the resurrection has taught ("The resurrection teaches the value of God's creation and of the body") and has initiated ("Jesus' bodily resurrection has initiated the redemptive healing of the human being into complete wholeness, including the body").[35] In a book on Christian ethics, the resurrection, as the central belief of all Christians, surely deserves much more than two brief mentions that remain undeveloped.

To document further the neglect of Christ's resurrection in moral theology, or at least in Catholic moral theology, I cite three books. First, in *A History of Catholic Moral Theology in the Twentieth Century*, James Keenan devotes more than half of his excellent study to the post–Vatican II situation. As far as I could see, he could report only one (very passing) reference to the resurrection, when he summarized the scope of Jon Sobrino's theology.[36] In 2002, Keenan had collaborated with Daniel Harrington in publishing *Jesus and Virtue Ethics*, in which the resurrection received only a brief paragraph and the resurrection of the body less than a page.[37] Yet the resurrection, as we shall see, is highly relevant to some of the issues they treated: for instance, social justice, sexual ethics, and human responsibility for the environment. Eight years later, the two authors published *Paul and Virtue Ethics*, in which they drew a little more on the resurrection.[38] Nevertheless, the key questions for their virtue ethics ("Who am I?" and "Who or what do I want to become?")[39] took me back, rightly or wrongly, to Aristotle. Surely *Christian* ethics should ask different questions: Who are we as baptized persons who profess faith in the resurrection? Who or what does the risen Jesus want us to become?

I may have done enough to document the way in which Christian ethicists have neglected the resurrection of Jesus and its implications and have left it in the background as a central belief but not one that, from beginning to end, should shape their discipline. In the spirit of "Easter faith seeking moral understanding" (*fides paschalis quaerens intellectum moralem*), I now sketch five themes that might enter into ethical thinking that allows itself to be centered on the resurrection. This is *not* intended to be an exhaustive list, but simply an indication of how I think Easter faith, precisely as such, should enjoy a central, and not a marginal, place in Christian ethics. In doing this, I am conscious of moving out of my disciplines, fundamental and systematic theology. But I offer an honest and, I hope, an informed comment from an "outsider" to friends and colleagues who are specialists in moral theology. How do I think resurrection faith should transform a Christian view of reality and moral behavior?

First of all, the resurrection of the crucified Jesus dramatically challenges any thinking that promotes "my" or "our" interests in a way that involves or may involve victimizing and sacrificing others (see John 11:50). His *self-giving love* meant his own putting into practice that "losing" for the sake of the Gospel (Mark 10:35) to which he called his disciples. A self-giving love, which led him to be victimized on the cross, was vindicated in a glorious resurrection. That victory over death invites others to trust his promise that "losing" for the sake of God's kingdom is not self-destructive but will bring the fullness of eternal life.

Second, the resurrection embodies a *new solidarity* of all human beings. As "the firstborn from the dead," Christ has "reconciled" to God "all things, whether on earth or in heaven, by making peace through the blood of his cross" (Col 1:18, 20). The resurrection of the crucified one has delivered humanity from evil and reordered the world, creating a new humanity that lives now in a universe reconciled to God. This cosmic vision of Colossians puts the question to ethicists: How do you understand and interpret human existence and behavior in a world reconciled to God by the events of the first Good Friday and Easter Sunday?

Third, the common hope for resurrection from the dead (1 Cor 15:12–58) throws new light on questions of *sexual ethics* and *social justice*. Both areas involve human bodies and an enormous range of bodily actions: in sexual relationships, chaste refraining from such relationships, feeding and clothing the bodies of the needy, and practicing "kindness, generosity, self-control," and further virtues listed by Paul (Gal 5:22). The hope inspired by Christ's victory over death raises the question, How should we behave in the areas of sexuality and justice toward other people now that we know that in their bodily existence they are destined for resurrection and transformation? May *our* property interests, for example, continually prevail over *their* needs? The glorious destiny of human beings in their bodiliness must shape the ways we think about them and act toward them in matters of sexuality and justice.

Fourth, what the hymn in Colossians (1:18, 20) says about the reconciliation to God of the whole cosmos ("whether on earth or in heaven") and, even more, what Paul teaches in Romans support human concern for the *well-being of the natural environment* (Rom 8:18–25). Where the Colossians hymn presented what God *has done* in Christ toward reconciling the cosmos, the passage in Romans looks more to the future.

The story of creation in Genesis 1—3 set human beings "in direct relationship to the rest of the world as a key element of their relationship with God." They were "given responsibility for the rest of creation."[40] Now, with the resurrection of Jesus from the dead, the nonhuman created world "waits with eager longing" to be set free from "the bondage of decay" (Rom 8:19, 21) and shares with believers a hope for resurrection. Even more than creation, the new creation of resurrection has put human beings into solidarity with the material world. A common hope stands in judgment over all that human beings have been doing to ravage, pollute, and even destroy their environment. The resurrection provides a new vision to guide our behavior toward the nonhuman created world.

Fifth, Keenan summarizes and rightly praises the great contribution Bernhard Häring made to moral theology—a contribution that recognizes Christ as "the principle, the norm, the center, and the goal" of this discipline.[41] Yet I can only wish that Häring would have more clearly presented the *risen and living* Christ as the principle, norm, center, and goal of moral thinking, judging, and behavior. Brian Johnstone has drawn attention to Häring's failure to offer a specific focus on Christ's resurrection.[42]

The hymn in Colossians 1 understands Christ to be the focal point not only of creation but also of the new creation that his resurrection inaugurated. A moral theology faithful to the vision of this hymn, not to mention Paul in Romans, 1 Corinthians, and other letters, would continually return to the question, What would the risen Jesus want us to think, decide, and do? To be sure, it is not always easy to answer this question. But if we do not raise it, can we hope to discern and practice the kind of fidelity in our moral lives that the living Jesus expects of us?

When sketching a resurrection-centered ethics, Johnstone has suggested that it could lead to a Trinitarian morality of true peace and unity in relationship, not a "peace" created by violence.[43] The way resurrection-oriented morality and Trinity-oriented morality go hand in hand calls for a book-length treatment. Johnstone's suggestion could also alert us to the extraordinary silence in contemporary Christian ethics about the Trinity, the central belief of Christians disclosed in the events of Easter and Pentecost.

But, before developing Trinity-centered ethics, Christian moralists might first ponder Johnstone's proposal about "the threefold role" that "the resurrection narratives and the doctrine that derives from them" should have for Christian ethics: "First, they modify the moral point of view; second, they offer a new and distinctive vision of life, which makes possible a Christian critique of culture; third, the vision provides a principle for interpreting virtue in an authentic Christian way."[44]

EPILOGUE

The resurrection of the crucified Jesus is frequently called "a mystery," but not in the sense of a murder mystery that we might puzzle over and work at. Here *mystery* means a deep and life-giving truth, or rather *the* deep and life-giving truth that works on us. With the resurrection we meet a mysterious truth that draws us into a lifetime of coming to terms with it.

Accepting Jesus risen from the dead means involving ourselves with him not as a memory from the past but as a vital presence in our day-to-day existence. He calls us to a way of life that differs greatly from the goals that others might set before us: for instance, "health, wealth, and prosperity" or "health, wealth, and happiness."

An advertisement I used to see on buses in Rome put such objectives more bluntly: *salute, soldi, e sesso* ("health, money, and sex"). Various magicians promised to make life worthwhile by solving all our problems in those three areas. This distorted view of our human reality and desires needed and needs the transformation that allegiance to the risen Jesus offers.

In the first century, Peter, Mary Magdalene, Paul, and the other founding fathers and founding mothers of Christianity proclaimed a new faith. A Galilean preacher who had died shortly before had been raised from the dead and shares in the divine identity and power. With the Holy Spirit, he inspires and determines the future of humanity and of the whole cosmos.

These are astonishing claims and, if true, must shape the way we construe our lives and destinies. When faced with medical issues and, even more widely, the smooth running of all the technological devices available to us, we want to know the truth and the appropriate solutions to the problems we face.

173

Questions of health and, at times, questions of science and technology can be life-and-death matters. What is the truth? And what should we do?

Hearing the proclamation of the risen Jesus, we can do no less than ask, Are there good reasons for believing this to be true? And if the resurrection truly happened, how should that affect and change our lives?

APPENDIX

Easter Appearances and Bereavement Experiences

His interest in the ways in which the pain of bereavement affected people led a Welsh doctor, Dewi Rees, to undertake research in this area. His paper, "The Hallucinations of Widowhood," published in the *British Medical Journal*,[1] came from his MD thesis ("The Hallucinatory Reactions of Bereavement") for the University of London and drew national and international attention. It was based on interviews with 227 widows and 66 widowers about their experiences following the death of a spouse.

Rees found that close to half (46.7%) reported contact with their beloved dead at various times during waking hours; dreams were not considered in the study. The bereaved had "felt the presence of the deceased" (39.2%), "seen" them (14%), "heard" them (13.3%), "spoken" to them (11.6%), and, very occasionally, been "touched" by them (2.7%). Some of the widows and widowers interviewed reported having had more than one type of experience, and in 36.1% of all the cases these experiences of the beloved dead lasted for years.

After Rees's pioneering work, subsequent work in different places more or less replicated his findings. In 1997, Rees reviewed some of this literature and showed the similarities.[2] From the 1970s many further contributions to bereavement studies had come from psychiatrists, psychologists, and sociologists. For instance, in a collaborative study, Colin Murray Parkes examined the grief experiences of 68 widows and widowers under the age 45 who lived in Boston.[3] One could list further publications: for

175

instance, Andrew Greeley's "Religious Stories and Contact with the Dead"[4] and various contributions to the *Handbook of Bereavement: Theory, Research and Intervention*.[5] Rees himself, after some years in general practice, became a senior clinical lecturer at Birmingham University and medical director of St Mary's Hospice in Birmingham. He has now published another book that concerns bereavement studies and, in particular, experiences of the beloved dead.[6]

The research done by Rees and his successors into the experience of widows and widowers came years ago to the notice of biblical and theological scholars. Gerd Lüdemann, for instance, cited the study by Murray Parkes and his colleagues on 49 widows and 19 widowers when making his case against the "objective" reality of the appearances of the risen Jesus. These experiences, he argued, were hallucinations that occurred in the mourning process of the disciples—in particular, Peter.[7] John Hick also appealed to bereavement studies to explain (or explain away?) the New Testament reports of encounters with Jesus after his death and burial.[8]

At a 1996 symposium on the resurrection, I discussed Hick's attempt to "generalize away" the Easter appearances as nothing more than bereavement experiences that repeatedly recur and have been scientifically studied.[9] In his response to my paper, Archbishop Peter Carnley criticized my objections to Hick's argument.[10] This prompted me to examine in more detail the possibility of finding some analogy between the disciples' experiencing appearances of the risen Jesus and the experiences of bereaved persons.[11] Finally, in the Martin D'Arcy Lectures (Oxford, 2002), published as *Easter Faith*, I treated once again this proposed analogy.[12]

Now in his 2010 book, *Pointers to Eternity*, Dewi Rees has engaged with what I wrote in *Easter Faith* about the bereavement experiences that he presented in his original paper, "The Hallucinations of Widowhood,"[13] and movingly argued that the work he and later researchers have done should be recognized as significant for the theological and biblical presentation of the resurrection. He has also distanced himself from the term "hallucination." In this appendix, after discussing what might replace that term, I want to revise somewhat my position on a possible analogy between bereavement experiences and the Easter appearances, and then respond to the question: what are the religious and spiritual implications of the work of Rees and his successors? What might that research contribute theologically and pastorally?

TERMINOLOGY

A study based on interviews with 46 widows in nursing homes in North Carolina showed how 61% were aware of the presence of their dead husband. Most of the widows found this experience good and helpful; a majority of them had not previously mentioned the experience to anyone; 46% felt that their deceased spouse was still with them. This study also suggested that these experiences merited a new name, since a certain stigma was associated with the term "hallucination."[14] In 2001, Klaus and Walter also agreed with the need for a new term.[15]

In *Pointers to Eternity* Rees agrees with this judgment and adds, "I have always realized that the term 'hallucination' is inappropriate…but I could think of no better term to use then and have not been able to coin an acceptable alternative subsequently."[16] After later research confirmed Rees's initial findings and showed that the experiences of the bereaved are "common, normal and helpful," he believes that psychiatrists now generally agree that the term "hallucination" is "not appropriate for an experience that has none of the features of a psychotic illness or that can be linked to any of the other causes of hallucinations." Rees concludes, "A new, generally acceptable terminology is needed."[17] One can appreciate his reservations over "hallucination" as "a misnomer" and his desire to use more neutral expressions, like "the perceptions of the bereaved"[18] or "the bereaved and their perceptions of the dead."[19] "Hallucination," is, as P. H. Wiebe pointed out, "a theory-laden expression. It might appear to be straightforwardly descriptive, but…it conceals many assumptions about what is real and what humans are capable of knowing."[20] In my 2003 book I also took issue with the term "hallucination" and used the generic and less theory-laden language of "bereavement experiences."[21] Or perhaps we might speak of "continuing relationships" with their beloved dead that many bereaved experience.

POINTS OF SIMILARITY

In *Easter Faith* I recognized that "we can make some comparisons between the experiences of Rees's widows and widowers
and those of the disciples after the death and burial of Jesus: in
both cases we learn of contact with the beloved dead, and it is a
contact that is or at least can be helpful and life-giving."[22]

Along with these two items one should also name two further elements in the proposed analogy: first, the grief experienced
by both Rees's bereaved persons and the disciples after the death
and burial of Jesus. Progress in psychology and a knowledge of
"the processes associated with bereavement" have encouraged
Rees to speak of the disciples' "numbness, disbelief and inner
emptiness." Like many bereaved, they "probably would have been
confused, tearful and restless—unable to accept the reality of
what had happened. This disbelief is likely to have been associated with an overpowering sense of anger." Finally, Rees draws on
one of the Gospels to complete the picture: "we also know that
they were afraid (John 20:19)."[23] His general judgment is convincing: "the death of Jesus was an enormous blow to his followers. Their guiding light and hope for the future had been killed in
a most distressing and public manner."[24] To this picture he might
have pointed to further elements in the passion stories that
brought shattering grief to the disciples, at least to the male disciples: their cowardly flight when Jesus was arrested in Gethsemane
(Mark 14:50) and Peter's subsequent denial of his Master (Mark
14:66–72). Grief over the death of some beloved person always
has its particular profile. But, in general, progress in psychology
and bereavement studies allow us to associate the grief of the disciples with that of the widows and widowers interviewed by Rees.

A second addition that I now make to the analogy proposed
by Rees concerns the unexpected nature of the encounters with
the risen Jesus. As far as the brief indications in the Easter chapters of the Gospels go, the disciples did not expect to see Jesus
risen from the dead and gloriously alive. Even less did they try to
initiate or bring about such meetings with him. There is some
comparison here with the bereaved persons interviewed by Rees:
none "had tried to contact the dead; all of their experiences

occurred spontaneously," and were not initiated by the living. Significantly, "no spiritual medium was ever involved in the process."[25] Thus the perceptions of the beloved dead were unexpected and unsolicited, like the appearances of the risen Christ.

There are then four items (two of which I noted already in *Easter Faith* and two new ones) that suggest a comparison between the experiences of Rees's widows and widowers and the experiences of the disciples after Jesus' death. (1) Both groups found themselves immersed in the grief of bereavement. (2) Then they found themselves in contact with their beloved dead. (3) This contact was uninitiated by the living and unexpected on their side. (4) In both cases the experience was enlightening and life-giving—certainly in the case of the disciples and also in the case of very many of the widows and widowers. Rees reports that 68.6% were helped by their experience, a further 25.5% found them neither helpful nor unpleasant, only 6% found them disturbing.[26]

POINTS OF DISSIMILARITY

But how close is the analogy? How many points of dissimilarity can we spot? In my *Easter Faith* I named a number of reasons for not recognizing a close analogy between the experiences of the disciples and those of Rees's widows and widowers. Rees reports me simply as "rejecting the possibility of an analogy."[27] To be precise, what I rejected was the existence of a "close analogy" that could prove "illuminating."[28] Reading Rees's response to what I wrote,[29] I want to introduce some qualifications, add one dissimilarity mentioned by Rees himself, and draw the conclusion that the proposed analogy reveals too many points of difference (eight in all) to be close and illuminating. That does not mean, however, that the findings made by Rees and his successors are religiously and theologically irrelevant. We will come to that issue in the final section of this appendix.

(1) My first reason concerned the point of departure for the analogy: the *person* whom the bereaved disciples mourned and his prior history. But I expressed this reason far too cryptically: the

disciples "remembered him [Jesus] as having made extraordinary public claims about his identity and mission."[30] By naming "the disciples," what I had in mind was, first of all, the fact that the Twelve and others, both women (e.g., Mary Magdalene) and men (e.g., Cleopas of Luke 24:13–35), were disciples and not married partners of Jesus. During the closing years of his life, their relationship to him had become undoubtedly close, but it was not a relationship of marriage as was the case with the 293 widows and widowers interviewed by Rees. Secondly, the disciples had been faced with an extraordinary and repeated assertion of personal authority made by Jesus about his role in mediating the present and future kingdom of God. By claiming to enjoy a unique filial relationship with "Abba," to change on his own authority the divine law about such matters as marriage and divorce, to forgive sins, to be decisive for human salvation, to mediate redemption through his death (and resurrection), and to be the coming judge of all human beings, he gave the impression of putting himself on a par with God and brought upon himself the charge of blasphemy.[31] What the deceased Jesus had done and claimed during his public ministry set him obviously apart from any of the persons who died and left behind the widows and widowers studied by Rees in rural Wales. In short, before their "bereavement," the disciples of Jesus had enjoyed a different kind of relationship with a remarkably different kind of person who made quite extraordinary claims about his identity and mission. This dissimilarity affects the "point of departure" for the proposed analogy.

Apropos of this first reason, one should also recall the case of Paul. Seemingly he never knew Jesus during the time of the public ministry, still less became his disciple. Paul had enjoyed no close relationship with Jesus that would have plunged him into grief at the time of the crucifixion. In the post-Pentecost situation, Paul comes on the scene rather as a dedicated enemy of the Christian movement (Gal 1:13–14; Acts 7:58; 8:1–3; 9:1–2). From the outset, any analogy between his meeting with the risen Jesus on the road to Damascus and the experiences of Rees's widows and widowers seems ruled out.

(2) My second reason for questioning the closeness of the analogy touched the manner of death of the beloved person. Jesus

died a horrible and utterly shameful death on a public scaffold. In the eyes of his contemporaries, the crucifixion involved being cursed not only by human beings (the religious and political authorities responsible for his execution) but also by God.[32] Rees reports no cases of anything like that among his 293 widows and widowers. Apparently all died from natural causes or accidents; he does not report any suicides or homicides, let alone executions. Apropos of the place of their spouses' deaths, 270 out of the 293 died either at home (161 cases) or in hospital (109 cases). The manner and place of death in the cases examined by Rees do not parallel what the Gospels have to report about the dramatic and terrible death on Calvary that took Jesus away in the prime of life.

(3) A third, enormous difference emerges from the fact that, unlike the disciples of Jesus, none of Rees's widows and widowers ever alleged that their beloved departed had been raised from the dead. The bereaved disciples of Jesus abruptly made such a claim about him shortly after his death and burial. Whatever the experiences of the bereaved and those of the disciples were like, they led to strikingly different conclusions.

(4) A fourth reason for differentiating between the Easter experiences of the disciples and Rees's widows and widowers emerges from the New Testament reports about *appearances to groups*, as well as to individuals. Not only named individuals, Peter (1 Cor 15:5; Luke 24:34), James (1 Cor 15:7), Paul (1 Cor 9:1; 15:8) and Mary Magdalene (John 20:11–18), but also groups, such as the Twelve (e.g., 1 Cor 15:5), more than five hundred followers of Jesus (1 Cor 15:6), seven disciples (John 21:1–14), Cleopas and an unnamed disciple (Luke 24:13–35), and Mary Magdalene and "the other Mary" (Matt 28:9–10), are reported to have encountered the risen Jesus. But the widows and widowers of Rees's pioneering study were all *individuals* who "felt the presence of," "saw," "heard," "spoke to," or were "touched by" their dead spouses. The individual nature of these experiences moves the bereavement analogy away from the resurrection witness of the New Testament, for which appearances of the risen Christ to groups are at least as significant as the appearances to individuals.

Rees admits that "a greater group awareness" distinguishes the New Testament record from those recounted by the widows and widowers in Wales. But he insists that "the experiences of the bereaved can also occur within a social context," and cites two letters that he received from people who read a letter about widowhood he published in the *Church Times* (March 2000).[33] Yet the fact remains that his original study of 293 widows and widowers mentioned only experiences of individuals and never a group experience. Moreover, the two letters tell of experiences of the deceased that happened to individuals (one a widow and the other a friend of the deceased) while other people were present, but they were not, strictly speaking, experiences in which more than one person directly shared.[34]

On the question of bereaved people experiencing (or not experiencing) as a *group* some beloved, deceased person, Allison (who knows and values Rees's ground-breaking research[35]) has also taken issue with me. He claims that there are "many firsthand accounts of several people seeing at once the apparition of a person recently deceased."[36] But he cites no examples and gives no references. Notice that he does not say "bereaved people" having such an experience, and *that* is the issue. Is he thinking of parapsychology and alleged cases of the spirits of the deceased being brought back from the dead through mediums? But many scholars, including professional psychologists, find only pseudoscience in the works of parapsychologists. In fact, Allison himself observes: "reports of collective apparitions are...prominent in the literature of parapsychology but not in normal psychology."[37] That silence on the part of professional psychologists might have warned Allison not to introduce, as he does, repeated references to a number of long-discredited parapsychologists.[38]

(5) A fifth dissimilarity arises when we notice that around 40% of Rees's widows and widowers continued to experience their deceased spouses for many years.[39] But the appearances of the risen Jesus to individuals or groups took place over a limited period of time and did not continue for years. Rees raises three objections to this claim of mine about the appearances of the risen Jesus, and begins with the gap between the resurrection and the ascension.[40]

First, what does the New Testament indicate about a time span between the resurrection and ascension? While John (e.g.,

20:17) and Paul (e.g., Phil 2:9) recognize that "ascension" or "elevation" belongs to the event of Christ's resurrection, it is Luke who introduces a "time span" between the resurrection and the ascension. In his Gospel, the ascension seems to take place late on the very day of the resurrection (Luke 24:50–53). His Acts of the Apostles speaks of an ascension after "many days" (Acts 13:31) but this has been specified in the first chapter as an ascension after forty days (Acts 1:9–11). If we want to talk of a "time span" between resurrection and ascension, Luke makes it clear that it is not a matter of years, let alone many years.

Second, Rees knows of two exceptions to the rule of the Easter appearances belonging to a limited period of time. Peter and Paul, long after their "foundational" encounters with the risen Christ, are reported to have experienced him again. Peter, some years after his Easter vision (1 Cor 15:5; Luke 24:34), once heard (but did not see) the risen Lord (Acts 10:14; 11:8); this was in connection with the critical issue of Gentile converts being obliged or not obliged to keep the Mosaic law. For his part, Paul reports some words he heard from the risen Lord (2 Cor 12:9) years after his foundational vision (1 Cor 15:8). Probably drawing on Pauline traditions but composing the stories to fit his theological and literary purposes, Luke tells of three visions experienced by Paul, two by night and one by day (Acts 18:9–10; 22:17–21; 23:11). These visions occur long after the Damascus Road encounter. They do not match that foundational episode when the risen Lord appeared to him, without Paul reporting any words being said (1 Cor 9:1; 15:8; Gal 1:15–16). These later visions do not establish for Paul the risen existence of Christ nor do they give Paul his apostolic role; the emphasis is rather on some particular, difficult situation and what the Lord says to him in that context. To sum up: these later experiences of the risen Christ enjoyed by Peter and Paul set them apart from all the other Easter witnesses, who met Christ only in the period immediately following the resurrection. Even in the case of Peter and Paul, these experiences are much less significant than their foundational encounters with the risen Christ, meetings that first assured them of his resurrection and put them in their roles as leaders of the emerging Church.

Third, Rees maintains that my argument "discounts" reports of Jesus appearing in later centuries and also today to a "wide variety of individuals." He cites Julian of Norwich and William Booth, the founder of the Salvation Army.[41] To this we could well add both the mystical visions of St Teresa of Avila, St John of the Cross, and others and the contemporary visions of Jesus investigated, for instance, by Phillip Wiebe.[42] Rees knows of the research of Wiebe[43] and the visions of Teresa,[44] and devotes an entire chapter to "Meeting Jesus."[45] I certainly do not wish to discount credible reports from the past and from our contemporaries about Jesus appearing to people, whether or not we want to describe them as mystics.

But one should recognize a distinction between (A) the experiences of those disciples who first saw the risen Jesus and came to faith, and (B) the experiences of all those later people, like Julian of Norwich, William Booth, Teresa of Avila, John of the Cross, and innumerable others, who *already* believed in the risen Jesus before they saw, heard, or in other ways met him. With the exception of Paul, those who belong to group (A) were sunk in deep grief over the death of Jesus when to their astonishment they first met him gloriously alive. Empowered by the Holy Spirit, they—and this includes Paul—then became the founding fathers and founding mothers of the Christian Church. While Paul's encounter with Christ on the Damascus Road is probably to be dated around three or four years later, the other meetings with Jesus were limited to the first days or weeks after the resurrection. Those who belong to group (B) may live in any century of Christian history, were not sunk in deep grief over the death of Jesus when they experienced him, and did not become foundational witnesses to the resurrection who helped to launch the Church. Their meetings with Jesus had other purposes: in the case of Teresa of Avila, for instance, her experiences of Jesus strengthened her in the work of religious reformation and supported her in becoming a classical teacher of prayer and the spiritual life. Beyond question, one should accept convincing reports of Jesus appearing to innumerable persons to be listed under (B). But one should discount attempts to play down the differences between them and group (A).[46]

(6) Apropos of the "time difference" between the experiences of groups (A) and (B), Rees himself notes "one difference between the Easter experiences and those reported by the widowed....Widowed people's experiences of their dead spouses tend to occur weeks or months after the person's death; in contrast, Jesus appeared to his friends soon after the crucifixion."[47] This difference is worth noting, even if it is not as significant as the dissimilarity just discussed between groups (A) and (B).

(7) Prior to Rees's study, only 27.7% of the bereaved who experienced their dead spouses had mentioned these experiences to others. The rest (72.3%) had not disclosed what had happened to anyone, not even to relatives and close friends. Rees comments on this by remarking that "people are often wary of sharing their most treasured secrets with others." He adds, in the light of some letters he had recently received, that "people are more willing to discuss these experiences with others than was the case forty years ago. This is due to various factors, particularly to the increased awareness that such experiences are normal and not unusual."[48] Anecdotal evidence from today seems to confirm what Rees adds here. But the question at stake remains: how far can we press the analogy between the experiences of the 293 widows and widowers that Rees studied scientifically forty years ago and the Easter experiences of Jesus' first followers? Nearly three-quarters of Rees's widows and widowers kept their experience to themselves. By way of contrast, those to whom Jesus appeared quickly passed on their experience to others. After Jesus appeared to him, within hours Peter told the other disciples what had happened (Luke 24:34); this seems clearly implied by Luke's narrative. When Jesus met Mary Magdalene, she went at once to bring the good news to the other disciples (John 20:18). According to Matthew, Mary Magdalene and "the other Mary" immediately ran to tell "the disciples" the good news of the resurrection they had received from an "angel of the Lord," and this mission was straightaway strengthened when they met the risen Jesus himself (Matt 28:1–10).

The only seeming exceptions to this "rule" of passing on at once the good news of the resurrection occur in Mark's Easter chapter and in Galatians. Mark ends his Gospel by saying of the three women who had visited Jesus' tomb and heard the good news of the resurrection from a heavenly messenger: "they fled from the tomb, for trembling and amazement had seized them, and they said nothing to anyone, for they were afraid" (Mark 16:8). Such reactions, as we find earlier in Mark's Gospel and in other biblical texts, can form an appropriate human response to the awesome mystery of divine actions and revelations. The silence of the women should be understood as provisional; they said nothing to inappropriate persons before passing on their message to the appropriate audience, the disciples. To explain Mark's text as meaning that the three women never said anything to anyone raises the obvious question: how could he then, the narrator, know about the experience of the women? Their silence can only have been temporary.[49]

As for Paul, he tells us that, after meeting Jesus on the Damascus Road, he "did not confer with any human being...but went away at once into Arabia [= the kingdom of the Nabateans, to the east of Palestine] and afterwards" returned to Damascus. Three years later he went up to Jerusalem to visit Cephas (= Peter) (Gal 1:17–24). Paul does not specify how long he spent in "Arabia," why he went there, and what he did when he returned to Damascus. What Paul writes does not exclude his having spent only a brief time in Arabia and having proclaimed the risen Jesus on his return to Damascus.[50] According to Luke, Paul did not first head for "Arabia" but stayed in Damascus after his meeting with the risen Jesus and then began to proclaim Jesus in the synagogues (Acts 9:19–22; see 26:20).

Provided one faces the seeming exceptions arising from Mark and Paul, I believe it remains accurate to say that, as far as the evidence takes us, those to whom the risen Jesus appeared quickly passed on to others the good news of their experience. This was certainly not the case with the 46.7% of Rees's 293 bereaved persons who claimed to have experienced their beloved dead. Of that group, over 70% had never told anyone of their experience, prior to being involved in Rees's study.

(8) In *Easter Faith* I pointed out an eighth difference: unlike the first followers of Jesus, "none of those whose bereavement experiences are reported by Rees dramatically changed their lifestyle and became missionaries proclaiming to the world their

experience and what it implied."[51] First, Rees rightly remarks that in this context I should have mentioned what Luke indicates about the disciples: "the dramatic change in lifestyle occurred after Pentecost and was the direct result of the descent of the Holy Spirit."[52] Yet one should not separate this descent from the death and resurrection of Jesus, which were integrally connected with the gift of the Holy Spirit—a theme that John, in particular, develops. The Spirit is "handed over" to the little group present at the very death of Jesus (John 19:30) and imparted to the disciples late on the day of the resurrection (John 20:22). To experience the death and resurrection of Jesus was to experience the gift of the Spirit. In any case, as Rees observes, the Holy Spirit should be mentioned. In the Book of Acts, Luke constantly represents the Holy Spirit as empowering and guiding Peter, Paul, and others (e.g., Acts 8:29; 10:19; 16:6) in spreading the message of Jesus whom they had met gloriously risen from the dead.

Second, while some disciples such as Peter and Paul changed remarkably because of their experience of the risen Jesus and became his missionary witnesses to the world, do we have evidence about the subsequent activity of others to whom the risen Christ appeared? James, "the Lord's brother" (Mark 6:3) and not to be identified with any of the Twelve to whom the risen Jesus appeared (1 Cor 15:5), seems to be the same James to whom the risen Jesus also appeared (1 Cor 15:7) and who became the leader of the Christian community in Jerusalem and was martyred there in AD 62.[53] In his case we have some information about how meeting the risen Jesus dramatically changed his life.

Then what of the Twelve? (Luke lists their names [Acts 1:13] and goes on to refer to them normally as "the apostles.") After meeting the risen Jesus and receiving the Holy Spirit, Peter led the Twelve in courageously witnessing to the good news (e.g., Acts 2:14, 32, 37, 42–43). For preaching Jesus and his message, they were arrested, flogged, and released with a warning not "to speak in the name of Jesus" (Acts 5:17–42). As a group, they remained for some time in Jerusalem,[54] exercising there a leadership role (e.g., Acts 6:2) and coordinating the missionary outreach of the early Church (e.g., Acts 8:14). The last time we read of them in Acts comes at the council in Jerusalem which affirmed the admission of Gentiles into the Church, a meeting at which Paul, Peter, and James played decisive roles (Acts 15:1–35). Here "the [twelve] apostles" appear alongside "elders" as leaders in the Church's life and mission.

We read, in particular, of what John (the son of Zebedee) did together with Peter in proclaiming Jesus and how, together with Peter, he was arrested, appeared before the Sanhedrin, and then was released (Acts 3:1–4:22). Later we hear of Peter and John acting together in laying on hands and bringing the Holy Spirit to converts and announcing the good news to many villages of the Samaritans (Acts 8:14–25). Paul speaks of meeting John in Jerusalem (Gal 2:9)—seemingly on the occasion of the council that Luke describes in Acts 15.

If we leave aside later traditions and legends about what Andrew, Thomas, and other members of the Twelve did towards carrying the message of Jesus to the world, we do have, at least from the Acts of the Apostles, some indications of how their experience of the risen Lord, with the associated gift of the Holy Spirit, changed them into courageous witnesses who set about spreading the good news and leading the mission of the early Church. While our reliable knowledge of the work undertaken by *individual* members of the Twelve (apostles) (apart from Peter and John) remains "minimal," what Luke attests about the activity (and suffering) of the Twelve suggests, *pace* Rees, that together they were "all activists in the missionary sense of that word."[55]

Regrettably we have no reliable information on what happened subsequently to Mary Magdalene, "the other Mary," Cleopas and his companion, the over five hundred followers of Jesus (1 Cor 15:6), and others to whom the risen Lord appeared. Some early traditions may contain elements of historical truth. But there is enough evidence to show that their experience of the risen Jesus radically changed the lives of Paul, Peter, John, other members of the Twelve, and James, and made them public witnesses to their risen Lord and founders of the Church's life and mission.

In the case of his widows and widowers who experienced their beloved dead, Rees points out that very many of them were significantly, if quietly, changed through that experience. But, to use his language, none of them went out "and set the world ablaze."[56] That is the precisely the difference which I noted between them and the disciples to whom Jesus appeared.

In this appendix I have drawn attention, in a much fuller form than I did in *Easter Faith*, to serious differences (eight in all) between (A) the experiences of the disciples and (B) those of the widows and widowers reported by Rees to have experienced their deceased spouses.[57] These differences, I believe, support my conclusion that the weight of dissimilarity means that (B) does not offer a close analogy that might throw fresh light on the Easter appearances (A). Yet the research of Rees and his successors into the experiences that many bereaved have of their beloved dead enjoys its pastoral and theological significance.

PERCEPTIONS OF THE DECEASED AND RESURRECTION FAITH

Rees writes of personal contact with deceased relatives. He means contacts that have not been initiated by the living and are unexpected, at least on the occasion when they first begin. He suggests that these contacts provide an "experiential justification for accepting as true…the Easter message that Jesus is risen." He does not propose that such experiences can or should "replace" the biblical and theological bases for Christian belief in Jesus risen from the dead. Rather he is drawing attention to what, through his research into the experiences of widows and widowers, he knows to happen with a substantial number of them.[58] Now a widower, he admits that he himself has never had any such experience of his late, beloved wife, and he reminds his readers that around 50% of the bereaved persons he investigated never enjoyed any perceived relationship with their dead spouses.[59] Nevertheless, for those widows and widowers who experienced their dead to be present to them as "well and happy,"[60] such perceptions could help to confirm their faith in the living reality of the risen Christ and their hope to share in that resurrected existence. As Rees writes, the widowed can find "in their own experiences evidence for Christ's promise of eternal life," evidence which "complements that provided in the Gospel stories."[61]

Believing in the Resurrection

In the light of his research, Rees describes the changes that experiencing their deceased spouses can bring to the bereaved: "These changes may include a sense of being protected, of being guided, of inner tranquility and of no longer being afraid of darkness or loneliness." Add too the basic "assurance that there is more to life than its earthly span."[62] We might sum up what perceptions of the deceased typically bring to the bereaved as a surprising, further experience of love, a love that can dispose them to believe in and hope for resurrection and to continue doing so. "It is *love*," Ludwig Wittgenstein wrote, "that believes the Resurrection."[63]

Rees paints a different picture from Murray Parkes, who speaks of the "searching" and "finding" through which bereaved persons may seek to mitigate the pain of grieving and so enjoy a "sense of presence" and a "bereavement dream" of the deceased loved one. Even if he will not introduce the loaded term "hallucination," Parkes uses "illusions" and writes of the one who is being sought as "absent" and concludes: "No matter how happy the dream, there must always be a 'sad awakening.'"[64] But the research of Rees should have alerted him to the experiences of those who did *not* engage in any "seeking" for special encounters with their deceased spouses; the living did not initiate these experiences; and, at least initially, these experiences were not only unsolicited but also unexpected and not something "found" after a "search." Parkes failed to produce convincing evidence to back up his claim about a "sad awakening"; that was something which he believed "must be." The negative conclusion seems connected with the fact that, unlike Rees, he included in his research dreams and attempts of the bereaved to contact the spirits of the departed. For his part, Rees has nothing to report about sad awakenings. In the case of some of the bereaved persons he studied, their experiences of the deceased did not last very long, but in 40% of the cases such experiences continued for many years. But in neither case were there "sad awakenings." The only negative feature to be reported by Rees was that 6% of those who had such experiences found them "disturbing."

What contribution could Rees's research make to those who have never personally shared the experiences of their deceased spouses reported by nearly 50% of his cases? Rees himself is an "outsider" to such experiences. Even if he was widowed after a long and happy marriage, he has never had such an experience. Nevertheless, his research has clearly fed into his personal faith in the resurrection of Jesus and hope for his own resurrection. Those who read his research or in other ways learn, directly or indirectly, of similar bereavement experiences may well find that this somehow contributes to or confirms their Easter faith and hope.

The stories of individuals coming to faith in the risen Christ and continuing to live by that faith (and the personal hope it involves) can vary a very great deal. Experiences of public worship and private prayer, the testimony of the Scriptures and of Christians through the ages, contemporary proclamation, a huge range of experiences in life, and the interior promptings of the Holy Spirit can all play their role in initiating and sustaining Easter faith.[65] Unquestionably, what Rees and others have investigated and passed on about the experiences of the bereaved could well have a part in bringing some people to such Easter faith or at least in maintaining them in such faith.

NOTES

INTRODUCTION:
SOME REPRESENTATIVE WORKS
ON THE RESURRECTION

1. A. J. Kelly, *The Resurrection Effect: Transforming Christian Life and Thought* (Maryknoll, NY: Orbis, 2008); see my review, *Theological Studies* 70 (2009): 478–80.

2. F.-X. Durrwell, *The Resurrection*, trans. Rosemary Sheed (London and New York: Sheed & Ward, 1960). Years later Durrwell took up again the main themes of *The Resurrection* in *Christ Our Passover: The Indispensable Role of the Resurrection in Our Salvation*, trans. John F. Craghan (Liguori, MO: Liguori, 2004).

3. See, e.g., W. Pannenberg, *Systematic Theology*, trans. G. W. Bromiley, 3 vols. (Grand Rapids, MI: Eerdmans, 1991–98); G. O'Collins, *Jesus Risen: An Historical, Fundamental and Systematic Examination of Christ's Resurrection* (New York/Mahwah, NJ: Paulist Press, 1987).

4. Even if Jon Sobrino has reflected on the resurrection (see O'Collins, *Jesus Risen*, 94–97), the way liberation theologians have generally neglected that theme is reflected by the fact that resurrection is not mentioned in the index to Christopher Rowland, ed., *Cambridge Companion to Liberation Theology* (Cambridge, UK: Cambridge University Press, 1999).

5. On the way moral theologians and sacramental theologians neglect the resurrection, see Kelly, *Resurrection Effect*, 159–68 and 5, respectively.

6. N. T. Wright, *Christian Origins and the Question of God,*

vol. 3, *The Resurrection of the Son of God* (Minneapolis: Fortress, 2003); see my review, *The Tablet* (April 19, 2003): 28–29.

7. Wright, *The Resurrection*, 205; "most" may be too strong, but certainly many Jews at the time of Jesus (like the Pharisees) believed in resurrection.

8. Ibid., 585–615. Kelly was also struck by Wright's theme of the surprising items in the Easter narratives of the Gospels, but he regrets Wright's failure to reflect on the resurrection as a phenomenon that saturates the whole life of faith (*Resurrection Effect*, 4, 61–52).

9. R. Swinburne, *The Resurrection of God Incarnate* (New York: Oxford University Press, 2003).

10. Ibid., 33–34.

11. On divine activity and special divine acts, see G. O'Collins, *Christology: A Biblical, Historical, and Systematic Study of Jesus*, 2nd ed. (New York: Oxford University Press, 2009), 112–18; and id., *Rethinking Fundamental Theology: Toward a New Fundamental Theology* (Oxford, UK: Oxford University Press, 2011), 22–29.

12. Swinburne, *The Resurrection*, 186, 190. On p. 31 Swinburne speaks of "suspending" the laws of nature, but at once returns to the language of "the violation of the natural laws." Kelly is also troubled by the way Swinburne presents the resurrection as a "super-miracle" in a world of natural laws: "The idea of a new creation is not evident" (Kelly, *Resurrection Effect*, 8).

13. Ibid., 174–75. See also G. O'Collins and D. Kendall, "On Reissuing Venturini," *Gregorianum* 75 (1994): 241–54; reprinted in G. O'Collins and D. Kendall, *Focus on Jesus* (Leominster, UK: Gracewing, 1996), 153–75.

14. Swinburne, *The Resurrection*, 184.

15. Ibid., 215.

16. S. M. Schneiders, *Written That You May Believe: Encountering Jesus in the Fourth Gospel*, rev. and exp. ed. (New York: Crossroad, 2003).

17. Ibid., 57.

18. Ibid., 149–70.

19. Ibid., 171–83.

20. A. Schweitzer, *The Quest of the Historical Jesus: A Critical Study of Its Progress from Reimarus to Wrede*, 3rd ed., trans. W.

Montgomery (London: A. & C. Black, 1954; orig. German 1906), 401.

21. T. Peters, R. J. Russell, and M. Welker, eds., *Resurrection: Theological and Scientific Assessments* (Grand Rapids, MI: Eerdmans, 2002).

22. Ibid., 297.

23. "Jesus," in *Encyclopedia of Religion*, ed. Lindsay Jones, vol. 7 (Detroit: Macmillan, 2006), 4843–52.

24. D. C. Allison, *Resurrecting Jesus: The Earliest Christian Tradition and Its Interpreters* (New York/London: T. & T. Clark, 2005).

25. Ibid., 199–213.

26. Ibid., 345–50.

27. G. O'Collins, *Easter Faith: Believing in the Risen Jesus* (Mahwah, NJ: Paulist Press, 2003), 1–24.

28. Allison, *Resurrecting Jesus*, 346–50; see 340–44.

29. Ibid., 341.

30. Ibid., 349.

31. Ibid., 350.

32. Ibid., 352–63.

33. G. O'Collins and D. Kendall, "Did Joseph of Arimathea Exist?" *Biblica* 75 (1994): 235–41.

34. Ibid., 241.

35. Allison, *Resurrecting Jesus*, 269–75, 278–84.

36. Ibid., 279, n. 292.

37. Ibid., 232–69.

38. Ibid., 299–337.

39. Ibid., 269.

40. Ibid., 300–311 and 311–31, respectively.

41. Ibid., 344.

42. Ibid., 342, n. 564; emphasis mine.

43. Ibid., 275–77.

44. Ibid., 364.

45. For a detailed discussion of the similarities and dissimilarities in the analogy proposed by Allison and others, see the appendix to this volume, "Easter Appearances and Bereavement Experiences," and O'Collins, *Christology*, 97–100.

46. Allison, *Resurrecting Jesus*, 372.

47. Ibid., 364–75.

48. Ibid., 375.

49. Toward the end Allison talks about handing the discussion over to "the philosophers and theologians, among whose lofty company" he is "not privileged to dwell" (351). Some dialogue with them might have stopped Allison from dismissing resurrection as "the recovery" of one's "current flesh and bones" (344; see 219–28).

50. Allison, *Resurrecting Jesus*, xi, 352.

51. Ibid., 342.

52. Ibid., 213–19.

53. D. A. Smith, *Revisiting the Empty Tomb: The Early History of Easter* (Minneapolis: Fortress, 2010).

54. R. Bauckham, *Jesus and the Eyewitnesses: The Gospels as Eyewitness Testimony* (Grand Rapids, MI: Eerdmans, 2006).

55. P. L. Danove, *The End of Mark's Story: A Methodological Study* (Leiden: E. J. Brill, 1993).

56. A. Yarbro Collins, "The Empty Tomb in the Gospel According to Mark," in *Hermes and Athena*, ed. E. Stump and T. P. Flint (Notre Dame: University of Notre Dame Press, 1993), 107–40, at 130–31. In her *Mark: A Commentary* (Minneapolis: Fortress, 2007), she wrote of "the possibility of the influence on Mark 16:1–8 of ancient notions of the translation or transference of a body of a favored person to the ends of the earth or to heaven, where he or she is made immortal. Ancient notions of deification or apotheosis may also have influenced the story of the empty tomb." She concluded, "The author of Mark was probably aware of the idea that some Roman emperors had ascended into heaven and become gods. He may also have known that their deifications were modeled on that of Romulus" (791–92, 793). No evidence is cited to show any such "awareness" on the part of the evangelist; what was stated as "possible" becomes "probable"—once again without any evidence being produced.

57. G. Vermes, *Jesus the Jew: A Historian's Reading* (London: Collins, 1973); id., *The Complete Dead Sea Scrolls in English* (New York/London: Allen Lane/Penguin, 1997; orig. ed., 1962).

58. G. Vermes, *The Resurrection* (New York: Doubleday, 2008).

59. K. J. Madigan and J. D. Levenson, *Resurrection: The Power of God for Christians and Jews* (New Haven, CT: Yale University Press, 2008); see also Alan Segal, *Life after Death: A History of the Afterlife in the Religions of the West* (New York: Doubleday, 2004).

60. P. Winter, *On the Trial of Jesus*, 2nd ed. (Berlin: De Gruyter, 1974), 208.

61. Vermes, *Resurrection*, 65.

62. Yarbro Collins, *Mark*, 558–59; J. R. Donahue, "A Neglected Factor in the Theology of Mark," *Journal of Biblical Literature*, 101 (1982): 563–94, at 575–76; J. Marcus, *Mark 8—16* (New Haven, CT: Yale University Press, 2009), 826–36, at 830; J. P. Meier, *A Marginal Jew*, vol. 3 (New York: Doubleday, 2001), 431–44; F. J. Moloney, *The Gospel of Mark: A Commentary* (Peabody, MA: Hendrickson, 2002), 237, fn. 117.

63. Vermes, *Resurrection*, 82.

64. Ibid., 68.

65. Ibid., 153.

66. N. Notovitch, *The Unknown Life of Jesus Christ*, trans. J. H. Connelly and L. Landsberg (New York: G. W. Dillingham, 1894).

67. P. Pullman, *The Good Man Jesus and the Scoundrel Christ* (Edinburgh: Canongate, 2010). On this book see G. O'Collins, *Philip Pullman's Jesus* (Mahwah, NJ: Paulist Press, 2011).

68. Pullman did not first create the "theory" that credited Jesus with a twin brother who faked his resurrection; it had been proposed some years earlier; see Allison, *Resurrecting Jesus*, 213, n. 60.

CHAPTER 1
OUR WORLDVIEWS AND THE LIFE AND DEATH OF JESUS

1. See P. Gwynne, "Why Some Still Doubt That Jesus' Body Was Raised," in *The Convergence of Theology*, ed. D. Kendall and S. T. Davis (Mahwah, NJ: Paulist Press, 2001), 355–67.

2. G. Lüdemann, "The Resurrection of Jesus: The Greatest Hoax in History," *Forum* 10 (1994): 161–75, at 162–65, 168; id., *The Resurrection of Jesus: History, Experience, Theology*, trans. J.

Bowden (Minneapolis: Fortress, 1994), 180–81; id., *What Really Happened to Jesus? A Historical Approach to the Resurrection*, trans. J. Bowden (London: SCM, 1995), 135–37.

3. D. Edwards, *How God Acts: Creation, Redemption, and Special Divine Action* (Minneapolis: Fortress, 2010); see also G. O'Collins, "God's Activity," in *Christology: A Biblical, Historical and Systematic Study of Jesus*, 2nd ed. (Oxford, UK: Oxford University Press, 2009), 112–18.

4. Lüdemann, *The Resurrection of Jesus*, 6, 14–15, 19, 69, 178, 211.

5. J. N. D. Kelly, *Early Christian Creeds*, 3rd ed. (London: Longman, 1974).

6. See A. Baxter, "Historical Judgement, Transcendent Perspective and 'Resurrection Appearances,'" *Heythrop Journal* 40 (1999): 19–40.

7. On the making of (Easter) faith, see G. O'Collins, *Rethinking Fundamental Theology: Toward a New Fundamental Theology* (Oxford, UK: Oxford University Press, 2011), 166–89.

8. On the use of analogies in resurrection studies, see G. O'Collins, *Easter Faith: Believing in the Risen Jesus* (Mahwah, NJ: Paulist Press, 2003), 5–24.

9. On access to the history of Jesus, see further O'Collins, *Rethinking Fundamental Theology*, 97–106.

10. Origen, *In Matt.* 24.7: "Jesus is wisdom itself, justice itself, truth itself, the kingdom itself." Origen said this when recalling the Parable of the Debtors (Matt 18:23–35). On Jesus' preaching of the kingdom and his prophetic, messianic, and filial consciousness, see O'Collins, *Christology*, 54–62, 126–32; id., *Rethinking Fundamental Theology*, 106–28.

11. J. P. Meier, *A Marginal Jew*, vol. 4 (New Haven, CT: Yale University Press, 2009), 126, 128.

12. Ibid., 415.

13. See N. T. Wright, *Jesus and the Victory of God* (London: SPCK, 1996), 489–519.

14. On the Son of Man sayings deriving from Jesus, see O'Collins, *Christology*, 63–65; and Meier, *A Marginal Jew*, vol. 4, 334–35.

15. For more detail see O'Collins, *Christology*, 119–40.

16. See R. Bauckham, *Jesus and the Eyewitnesses: The Gospels as Eyewitness Testimony* (Grand Rapids, MI: Eerdmans, 2006), 193.

17. For further details (and documentation) on all this and on what follows, see G. O'Collins, *Jesus: A Portrait* (Maryknoll, NY: Orbis, 2008), 147–64; id., *Christology*, 67–81.

18. Of course, there are other parables in which Jesus spoke, if less clearly, of himself: e.g., the Parable of the Wise and Foolish Bridesmaids (Matt 25:1–13). On the Parable of the Vineyard and the Tenants, see J. Marcus, *Mark 8—16* (New Haven, CT: Yale University Press, 2009), 801–15.

19. For further reasons for finding authentic sayings of Jesus at the core of the passion predictions, see O'Collins, *Christology*, 70–71.

20. On the final banquet, see G. O'Collins, *Salvation for All: God's Other Peoples* (Oxford, UK: Oxford University Press, 2008), 95–97.

21. On this verse see J. P. Meier, *A Marginal Jew: Rethinking the Historical Jesus*, vol. 2 (New York: Doubleday, 1994), 302–9, 366–71.

22. O'Collins, *Salvation for All*, 79–99.

23. Ibid., 111–20.

24. See Meier, *A Marginal Jew*, vol. 2, 1035–37.

25. See O'Collins, *Salvation for All*, 79–99.

26. See J. Marcus, *Mark 1—8* (New York: Doubleday, 1999), 446–47, 452–61.

CHAPTER 2
THE MEANING OF THE
RESURRECTION CLAIM

1. Special divine action is a modern, rather than a biblical, notion. The scriptures draw no distinction between the "common" activity of God (in upholding and working through/with the general laws of nature) and special divine acts (manifested, e.g., in the resurrection).

2. P. Winter, *On the Trial of Jesus*, 2nd ed. (Berlin: De Gruyter, 1974), 208.

3. For further examples of those who "redefine" the resurrection, see (in chronological order) G. O'Collins, *What Are They Saying About Jesus?* 2nd ed. (Ramsey, NJ: Paulist Press, 1983), 44–51; id., *Jesus Risen: An Historical, Fundamental and Systematic Examination of Christ's Resurrection* (New York/Mahwah, NJ: Paulist Press, 1987), 103–7; id., *The Resurrection of Jesus Christ: Some Contemporary Issues* (Milwaukee: Marquette University Press, 1993), 1–14; and id., "The Resurrection: The State of the Questions," in *The Resurrection: An Interdisciplinary Symposium on the Resurrection of Jesus*, ed. S. T. Davis, D. Kendall, and G. O'Collins (Oxford, UK: Oxford University Press, 1997), 5–9.

4. God was now defined not simply as the Raiser of the dead (as in the Jewish Eighteen Benedictions) but, specifically, as the Raiser of the dead Jesus; see R. Martin-Achard, "Resurrection (Old Testament)," in *Anchor Bible Dictionary*, ed. D. N. Freedman, vol. 5 (New York: Doubleday, 1992), 680–84; G. W. Nickelsburg, "Resurrection (Early Judaism and Christianity)," in ibid., 684–91.

5. On 1 Cor 15:3–5, see J. A. Fitzmyer, *First Corinthians* (New Haven, CT: Yale University Press, 2008), 539–50; and A. C. Thiselton, *The First Epistle to the Corinthians* (Grand Rapids, MI: Eerdmans, 2000), 1186–1205.

6. On the theme of exaltation, see A. T. Lincoln, *The Gospel according to John* (London: Continuum, 2006), 153, 269, 336–37, 352–53, 493–96.

7. A. Peacocke, *Theology for a Scientific Age* (Minneapolis: Fortress, 1993), 279–88, 332.

8. A. Peacocke, *Creation and the World of Science* (Oxford, UK: Clarendon Press, 1979), 353; italics mine.

9. Peacocke, *Theology for a Scientific Age*, 344; italics mine.

10. Ibid., 384.

CHAPTER 3
THE APPEARANCES OF THE RISEN JESUS

1. For some bibliography on the appearances, see G. O'Collins, *Christology: A Biblical, Historical, and Systematic Study of*

Jesus, 2nd ed. (Oxford, UK: Oxford University Press, 2009), 90–100.

2. M. J. Harris, *The Second Epistle to the Corinthians* (Grand Rapids, MI: Eerdmans, 2005), 33–37.

3. G. B. Caird, *The Language and Imagery of the Bible* (London: Gerald Duckworth, 1980), 147.

4. J. A. Fitzmyer, *The Gospel according to Luke X—XXIV* (New York: Doubleday, 1985), 1223.

5. From Celsus's *True Discourse*, cited by Origen in *Contra Celsum* (II.70); trans. Henry Chadwick, *Origen: Contra Celsum* (Cambridge, UK: Cambridge University Press, 1953), 109.

6. G. Lüdemann, *The Resurrection of Jesus*, trans. J. Bowden (Minneapolis: Fortress, 1994); see my reviews of that book in *Gregorianum* 77 (1996): 357–59, and *Theological Studies* 57 (1996): 341–43.

7. See D. Kendall and G. O'Collins, "The Uniqueness of the Easter Appearances," *Catholic Biblical Quarterly* 54 (1992): 287–307, at 293–94.

8. Lüdemann, *Resurrection of Jesus*, 79–84.

9. Michael Grant, *Saint Paul* (London: Weidenfeld & Nicolson, 1976), 108–9.

10. R. P. Bentall, *Madness Explained: Psychosis and Human Nature* (London: Penguin Books, 2004), 97.

11. Ibid., 358–60.

12. Ibid., 588, n. 43.

13. See ibid., 357.

14. On the theories of Graves and other authors, see G. O'Collins and D. Kendall, "On Reissuing Venturini," *Gregorianum* 75 (1994): 241–65.

15. On these and other Jewish and Roman sources, see J. P. Meier, *A Marginal Jew: Rethinking the Historical Jesus*, vol. 1 (New York: Doubleday, 1991), 56–111.

16. D. F. Strauss, *The Life of Jesus for the People*, vol. 1 (London: Williams & Norgate, 1879), 412.

17. For details see G. O'Collins, *Jesus Risen: An Historical, Fundamental and Systematic Examination of Christ's Resurrection* (New York: Paulist Press, 1987), 10.

18. *Reimarus: Fragments*, no. 32; ed. C. H. Talbert, trans. R. S. Fraser (Philadelphia: Fortress, 1970), 199–200.

19. For details see O'Collins, *Jesus Risen*, 11–12.

20. *Theologische Quartalschrift* 153 (1973): 201–83.

21. R. Pesch, "Le genèse de la foi en la resurrection de Jésus. Une nouvelle tentative," in *La Pâque du Christ: Mystère de salut*, ed. M. Benzerath et al. (Paris: Cerf, 1982), 51–74.

22. See D. A. Campbell, *The Deliverance of God: An Apocalyptic Rereading of Justification in Paul* (Grand Rapids, MI: Eerdmans, 2009), 896–911.

23. C. K. Barrett, *The Gospel according to St John*, 2nd ed. (London: SPCK, 1978), 565.

CHAPTER 4
THE DISCOVERY OF THE EMPTY TOMB

1. G. O'Collins, *Jesus Our Redeemer: A Christian Approach to Salvation* (Oxford, UK: Oxford University Press, 2007), 145–46.

2. In Matt 1—27, there are thirteen such fulfillment quotations; see U. Luz, *Matthew 1—7*, trans. J. E. Crouch (Minneapolis: Fortress, 2007), 125–31.

3. Matt 28:1–20 uses "Jesus" three times and introduces no title other than "Son," to be found in the baptismal formula (Matt 28:19).

4. J. Marcus, *Mark 8—16* (New Haven, CT: Yale University Press), 1083.

5. Or is the Mary of Mark 16:1 to be understood as "Mary the wife of James"? See ibid., 1060.

6. R. Pesch, *Das Markusevangelium*, vol. 2 (Freiburg: Herder, 1977), 519–28.

7. For details see G. O'Collins and D. Kendall, "Mary Magdalene as Major Witness to Jesus' Resurrection," *Theological Studies* 48 (1987): 631–46, at 631, n. 7.

8. P. F. Carnley, *The Structure of Resurrection Belief* (Oxford, UK: Clarendon Press, 1987), 60.

9. R. Bauckham, *Jesus and the Eyewitnesses: The Gospels as*

Eyewitness Testimony (Grand Rapids, MI: Eerdmans, 2006), 155–82.

10. A. Yarbro Collins, "The Empty Tomb in the Gospel According to Mark," in *Hermes and Athena*, ed. E. Stump and T. P. Flint (Notre Dame: University of Notre Dame Press, 1993), 107–40, at 130–31.

11. See U. Luz, *Matthew 21—28*, trans. J. E. Crouch (Minneapolis: Fortress, 2005), 585–89, 609–13; Luz judges Matt 27:62–66 and 28:11–15 to be "a narrative fiction, largely created by the evangelist Matthew, perhaps based on a tradition of the guards at Jesus' tomb" (ibid., 609) but ending with something "Matthew's Jewish Christian readers know all too well," the explanation that Jews of their day gave for the tomb being empty (ibid., 611). On these passages see also J. Nolland, *The Gospel of Matthew* (Grand Rapids, MI: Eerdmans, 2005), 1234–39, 1254–58. He defends the basic historicity of the story about the setting of the guard and its aftermath (ibid., 1235), and comments, "Matthew finds it necessary to explain how some of his Jewish contemporaries offer another explanation of the empty tomb" (ibid., 1254). N. T. Wright argues for the essential historicity of the story of the setting and the bribery of the guards: *The Resurrection of the Son of God* (Minneapolis: Fortress, 2003), 636–40.

12. In the introduction to this book, we saw how Philip Pullman endorses this explanation: the corpse of Jesus was missing because it had been taken away at night. This theory of theft has been repeated over the centuries: e.g., in the second century by St. Justin Martyr's opponents in his *Dialogue with Trypho* (no. 108), and in the eighteenth by Hermann Reimarus. The idea that the disciples stole the body of Jesus and invented the story of his resurrection is not compatible with what we know about them; see D. C. Allison, *Resurrecting Jesus* (New York: T. & T. Clark, 2005), 207–9.

13. Was Paul silent about the empty tomb of Jesus? His reference to the burial of Jesus (1 Cor 15:4) suggests that Jesus rose from the grave—something expressed through the symbolism of baptism in which sacramentally the baptized die, are buried with Christ, and are "raised from the dead," so as to leave the tomb of the waters and "walk in newness of life" (Rom 6:4). Apropos of

the tradition cited by Paul in 1 Cor 15:3–5, public incredulity and prejudice may explain why the tradition does not include women in its list of witnesses.

14. W. Pannenberg, *Systematic Theology*, trans. G. W Bromiley, vol. 2 (Edinburgh: T. & T. Clark, 1994), 359.

15. Allison, while putting a strong case for the historicity of Mark's burial narrative (*Resurrecting Jesus*, 352–63), curiously argues that Joseph of Arimathea gave Jesus a "hurried and dishonorable" burial (ibid., 362), probably in "a criminal's grave" (ibid., 363).

16. See K. Lake, *The Historical Evidence for the Resurrection of Jesus Christ* (London: Williams & Norgate, 1907), 148–52.

17. M. Muggeridge, *Jesus Rediscovered* (London: Fontana, 1969), 50–51. Muggeridge later changed his mind and accepted a resurrection from the tomb as part of his faith in Jesus; see his *Jesus the Man Who Lives* (London: Collins, 1976), 184–91.

18. On the theory of rapid disintegration and other theories that involve the disappearance of Jesus' corpse and a subsequent misunderstanding on the part of the disciples, see Allison, *Resurrecting Jesus*, 201–4, 212–14.

19. L. Evely, *The Gospels without Myth*, trans. J. F. Bernard (New York: Doubleday, 1971), 160.

20. G. W. H. Lampe, *The Resurrection*, a dialogue with D. M. MacKinnon (London: Mowbray, 1966), 59, 97, 99.

21. A. Peacocke, *Theology for a Scientific Age*, 2nd ed. (London: SCM, 1993), 279–88, 332.

22. "God did not have to make the tomb empty in order to effect his Easter miracle.…The Easter faith arose far from the burial place and independently of it. The historical reality of the empty tomb is no item by which the resurrection stands or falls.…We do not believe in the empty grave, but in the risen Lord" (H. Grass, *Ostergeschehen und Ostergeschichte*, 2nd ed. [Göttingen: Vandenhoeck & Ruprecht, 1962], 180; trans. mine).

23. As well as showing apologetically that the body had not been stolen (Why would robbers have carefully removed and folded the grave clothes?), the evangelist intends a contrast with the earlier raising of Lazarus: "In the case of Lazarus, at Jesus' command he had come out of the tomb still bound…and his

head still wrapped in a cloth....Lazarus had to be freed to take up life again in this world. But Jesus' own sovereignty over death is shown in the way he has left behind the wrappings associated with death." He "himself has demonstrated that death could not hold him" (A. T. Lincoln, *The Gospel according to John* [London: Continuum, 2005], 490).

24. See Nolland, *The Gospel of Matthew*, 673–76.

25. Lampe, *The Resurrection*, 10: "Easter...has nothing to do...with the idea that there is some part of our being that is inherently immortal: some entity that we might call a soul. No. As far as our human nature is concerned, when you're dead you're dead; and so it was with Jesus."

26. Ibid., 45, 60.

27. Bultmann dismisses the empty tomb as an "apologetic legend" in *The History of the Synoptic Tradition*, 2nd ed., trans. J. Marsh (Oxford, UK: Blackwell, 1968), 290.

28. R. Bultmann, in *Kerygma and Myth*, ed. H. W. Bartsch (London: SPCK, 1972), 113.

29. Lampe, *The Resurrection*, 92.

30. K. Barth, *Church Dogmatics* III/2, trans. G. W. Bromiley et al. (Edinburgh: T. & T. Clark, 1960), 453; and IV/1, trans. G. W. Bromiley (Edinburgh: T. & T. Clark, 1956), 341.

CHAPTER 5
THE RESURRECTION AS REDEEMING AND TRANSFORMING

1. On the revelation communicated through Christ's death and resurrection, see my *Rethinking Fundamental Theology* (Oxford, UK: Oxford University Press, 2011), 136–65.

2. Adam and Eve also prefigure all human families that, while seldom including one son (Cain) who murders another (Abel), are always in various ways dysfunctional and in need of redemption. The future of the human race depends on the health of marriage and the family. The Book of Genesis pictures marriage and the family not only as coming from the creative hand of God but also as requiring redemption from sin and evil.

3. On Mark 16:1–8, see J. Marcus, *Mark 8—16* (New Haven, CT: Yale University Press, 2009), 1079–87.

4. Some readers may react with suspicion to the idea that, like other texts, the concluding chapter of Mark can mean and communicate more to readers than its author ever consciously meant. Of course, we should reject interpretations that are contrary to what the evangelist wished to express. But, provided that does not take place, we should acknowledge how the meaning of his and other texts, when read in new contexts by later readers, can go beyond the original authors' intentions when they wrote in particular situations for specific audiences. See O'Collins, *Rethinking Fundamental Theology*, 253–64; id., *Easter Faith: Believing in the Risen Jesus* (Mahwah, NJ: Paulist Press, 2003), 81–84.

5. On the interdependence of giving and receiving love, see John Rist, *Real Ethics* (Cambridge, UK: Cambridge University Press, 2002), 109.

6. V. Bruemmer, *The Model of Love: A Study in Philosophical Theology* (Cambridge, UK: Cambridge University Press, 1993), 171.

7. See C. Harrison, *Beauty and Revelation in the Thought of Saint Augustine* (Oxford, UK: Clarendon Press, 1992).

8. On Matt 27:57—28:20, see J. Nolland, *The Gospel of Matthew* (Grand Rapids, MI: Eerdmans, 2005), 1225–72; and U. Luz, *Matthew 21—28*, trans. J. E. Crouch (Minneapolis: Fortress, 2008), 576–636.

9. On Matt 2:1–23, see Nolland, *The Gospel of Matthew*, 103–31; and on Matt 1:2—2:23, see U. Luz, *Matthew 1—7*, trans. J. E. Crouch (Minneapolis: Fortress, 2007), 74–124.

10. Curiously little or nothing is said about Luke's important Easter theme of life in such large commentaries as D. L. Bock, *Luke 9:51—24:53* (Grand Rapids, MI: Baker Books, 1996); F. Bovon, *Das Evangelium nach Lukas 19,28—24,53* (Neukirchen: Neukirchener, 2009); J. A. Fitzmyer, *The Gospel according to Luke X—XXIV* (New York: Doubleday, 1985); J. Nolland, *Luke 18:35—24:53* (Dallas: Word, 1993).

11. The two angelic figures in Acts 1:10–11 who "explain" the ascension belong with similar figures in Luke 24:4–7 in constituting the angelic "inclusion."

12. On Luke and the salvation brought by Jesus, see G. O'Collins, *Salvation for All: God's Other Peoples* (Oxford, UK: Oxford University Press, 2008), 142–61.

13. On these two chapters, see A. T. Lincoln, *The Gospel according to John* (London: Continuum, 2005), 487–524.

14. Greek zoologists reckoned that there were 153 different kinds of fish; thus the catch of John 21 symbolizes that with the help of Jesus the disciples will catch "all kinds"; for details, see R. Schnackenburg, *The Gospel according to John*, vol. 3, trans. David Smith and G. A. Kon (Tunbridge Wells, UK: Burns & Oates, 1982), 357.

15. This way of approaching the message of John's final chapter makes me regret the title chosen by Schnackenburg, "The Problems Thrown Up by John 21," in ibid., 141–74. Instead of expounding its spiritual riches, the great biblical scholar seems concerned to demonstrate that John 21 is an "editorial conclusion" rather than a "postscript, appendix or epilogue." I owe much more to the way Rowan Williams expounds John 21 in his *Resurrection: Interpreting the Easter Gospel* (London: Darton, Longman & Todd, 2002).

16. See G. O'Collins and M. K. Jones, *Jesus Our Priest: A Christian Approach to the Priesthood of Christ* (Oxford, UK: Oxford University Press, 2010), 38–43.

17. For years many scholars agreed that the earliest material in Genesis was to be found in non-Priestly material that combined two sources: a "Yahwistic" document (J) from the tenth century BCE and an "Elohistic" document (E) written two centuries later. Recently, however, some scholars date major elements in J to the sixth century and so around the time of the Babylonian exile. See R. S. Hendel, "Genesis, Book of," in *Anchor Bible Dictionary*, ed. D. N. Freedman, vol. 2 (New York: Doubleday, 1992), 933–41, at 933–35.

18. On the origins of life, see J. C. Lennox, *God's Undertaker: Has Science Buried God?* (Oxford, UK: Lion, 2007), 116–26; and A. E. McGrath, *A Fine-Tuned Universe: The Quest for God in Science and Theology* (Louisville: Westminster John Knox, 2009), 127–42.

19. On the two Adams, see G. O'Collins, *Jesus Our Redeemer:*

A Christian Approach to Salvation (Oxford, UK: Oxford University Press, 2007), 37–42.

CHAPTER 6
JUSTIFYING EASTER FAITH TODAY

1. Blaise Pascal, *Pensées*, trans. A. J. Krailsheimer (London: Penguin Books, 1966), no. 424.

2. One can express the Second Law in terms of "entropy," which represents the degree of disorder or randomness in the constituents of any closed system. The entropy of an isolated system can only increase but will never decrease.

3. A. Peacocke, *Theology for a Scientific Age* (Minneapolis: Fortress, 1993), 281.

4. See John Polkinghorne, *The God of Hope and the End of the World* (New Haven, CT: Yale University Press, 2002), 74–76, 113–16.

5. Pierre Teilhard de Chardin, *Science and Christ*, trans. René Hague (New York: Harper & Row, 1968), 27, 35, 63–64, 75–76.

6. P. Teilhard de Chardin, *Human Energy*, trans. J. M. Cohen (London: Collins, 1969), 32.

7. See Christopher F. Mooney, *Teilhard de Chardin and the Mystery of Christ* (London: Collins, 1966), 120, 135; and Robert Faricy, *All Things in Christ: Teilhard de Chardin's Spirituality* (London: Collins, 1981), 13–31.

8. A. Peacocke, *Creation and the World of Science* (Oxford, UK: Clarendon Press, 1979), 353; italics mine.

9. Peacocke, *Theology for a Scientific Age*, 344; italics mine.

10. Ibid., 384; italics mine.

11. See David Hume, *An Enquiry concerning the Human Understanding*, ed. L. A. Selby-Bigge, X ("Of Miracles") (Oxford, UK: Clarendon Press, 1963), 109–31, at 128. On the problems with Hume's version of testimony, see C. A. J. Coady, *Testimony: A Philosophical Study* (Oxford, UK: Clarendon Press, 1994), 79–100; on Hume's unsatisfactory reaction to "astonishing reports," see ibid., 179–98.

12. Hans Küng, *On Being a Christian*, trans. E. Quinn (London: Collins, 1977), 345.

13. On Gal 3:13, see J. L. Martyn, *Galatians* (New York: Doubleday, 1998), 316–21.

14. M. Muggeridge, *Jesus Rediscovered* (London: Collins, 1969), 8; see also ibid., 16–36.

15. On our faith response to Jesus the divine redeemer and revealer, see G. O'Collins, *Rethinking Fundamental Theology* (Oxford, UK: Oxford University Press, 2011), 166–89.

16. Ludwig Wittgenstein, *Culture and Value*, trans. P. Winch (Oxford, UK: Basil Blackwell, 1980), 33c.

17. On the encounters with Jesus in John's Gospel as paradigms of coming to Easter faith, see O'Collins, *Rethinking Fundamental Theology*, 179–88.

CHAPTER 7
RISEN EXISTENCE

1. Julian Barnes, *The History of the World in 10^1/$_2$ Chapters* (London: Jonathan Cape, 1990), 283–309.

2. John McGahern, *All Will Be Well* (New York: Random House, 2007), 136, 138.

3. On personal identity and continuity, see A. C. Danto, "Persons," in *The Encyclopedia of Philosophy*, ed. Paul Edwards, vol. 6 (New York: Macmillan, 1967), 110–14; T. Penelhum, "Personal Identity," in ibid., 95–107; B. Garrett, "Personal Identity," in *Routledge Encyclopedia of Philosophy*, ed. E. Craig, vol. 7 (London: Routledge, 1998), 308–14; M. F. Goodman, "Persons," in *The Encyclopedia of Philosophy*, ed. D. M. Borchert, vol. 7 (Detroit: Thompson Gale, 2006), 237–44; Anthony Kenny (on John Locke and personal identity), *A New History of Western Philosophy* (Oxford, UK: Clarendon Press, 2010), 668–70.

4. B. Leftow, *Time and Eternity* (Ithaca, NY: Cornell University Press, 1991).

5. B. Leftow, "A Timeless God Incarnate," in *The Incarnation: An Interdisciplinary Symposium on the Incarnation of the Son of God*,

ed. S. T. Davis, D. Kendall, and G. O'Collins (Oxford, UK: Oxford University Press, 2002), 273–99.

6. New York: Columbia University Press, 1995.

7. St. Gregory of Nyssa risked being incompatible with the hope of Christians when he suggested that we will rise like angels, without age or sex; see ibid., 83.

8. B. Niederbacher, "Thomas Aquinas on the Numerical Identity of the Resurrected Body," in *Personal Identity and Resurrection*, ed. Georg Gasser (Farnham, UK: Ashgate, 2010), 145–59, at 157.

9. A. Peacocke, *Theology for a Scientific Age*, 2nd ed. (London: SCM, 1993), 281.

10. J. Polkinghorne, *The God of Hope and the End of the World* (New Haven, CT: Yale University Press, 2002), 74–76, 113–16.

11. J. Polkinghorne, *The Faith of a Physicist: Reflections of a Bottom-Up Thinker* (Minneapolis: Fortress, 1994), 163–70; see also his "Eschatology: Some Questions and Some Insights from Science," in *The End of the World and the Ends of God: Science and Religion on Eschatology*, ed. J. Polkinghorne and M. Welker (Harrisburg, PA: Trinity Press International, 2000), 29–41, at 29–30.

12. See B. Byrne, *Romans* (Collegeville, MN: Liturgical Press, 1996), 254–62; J. A. Fitzmyer, *Romans* (New York: Doubleday, 1993), 504–14; D. J. Moo, *The Epistle to the Romans* (Grand Rapids, MI: Eerdmans, 1996), 506–18.

CHAPTER 8
THE RESURRECTION'S IMPACT ON SACRAMENTAL AND MORAL THEOLOGY

1. B. Leeming, *Principles of Sacramental Theology* (London: Longmans, Green & Co., 1956), 305–6, 310–11. On Casel, see "Casel, Odo," in *The Oxford Dictionary of the Christian Church*, 3rd ed. rev., ed. F. L. Cross and E. A. Livingstone (Oxford, UK: Oxford University Press, 2005), 297.

2. L.-M. Chauvet, *The Sacraments: The Word of God at the Mercy of the Body* (Collegeville, MN: Liturgical Press, 2001).

3. J. L. Austin, *How to Do Things with Words* (Oxford, UK: Clarendon Press, 1962).

4. Chauvet, *The Sacraments*, 156–63, at 160.

5. S. A. Ross, *Extravagant Affections: A Feminist Sacramental Theology* (New York: Continuum, 2001), 38.

6. See my rejection of penal substitution theories in G. O'Collins, *Jesus Our Redeemer: A Christian Approach to Salvation* (Oxford, UK: Oxford University Press, 2007), 133–60.

7. Ross, *Extravagant Affections*, 38.

8. Ibid., 46.

9. See G. O'Collins and D. Kendall, "Mary Magdalene as Major Witness to Jesus' Resurrection," *Theological Studies* 48 (1987): 631–46; reprinted in G. O'Collins, *Interpreting the Resurrection* (New York: Paulist Press, 1988), 22–38.

10. K. B. Osborne, *Christian Sacraments in a Postmodern World: A Theology for the Third Millennium* (Mahwah, NJ: Paulist Press, 1999); D. N. Power, *Sacrament: The Language of God's Giving* (New York: Crossroad, 1999).

11. K. B. Osborne, *The Resurrection of Jesus: New Considerations for Its Theological Interpretation* (New York: Paulist Press, 1997).

12. G. Martinez, *Signs of Freedom: Theology of the Christian Sacraments* (Mahwah, NJ: Paulist Press, 2003), 92–101, 136–43, 148–53.

13. Ibid., 307–8.

14. "If you confess with your lips that Jesus is Lord and believe in your heart that God raised him from the dead, you will be saved." Paul clearly cites a confession of faith, possibly connected with the reception of baptism. See B. Byrne, *Romans* (Collegeville, MN: Liturgical Press, 1996), 321–22; J. A. Fitzmyer, *Romans* (New York: Doubleday, 1993), 588–89, 591–92; D. J. Moo, *The Epistle to the Romans* (Grand Rapids, MI: Eerdmans, 1996), 657–58.

15. Baptism involves "washing." But the primary symbolism of the sacrament is not washing but being conformed to the death and resurrection of Christ and so sharing in his triple function as priest, prophet, and king.

16. See J. A. Fitzmyer, *First Corinthians* (New Haven, CT: Yale University Press, 2008), 446; A. C. Thiselton, *The First Epistle to the Corinthians* (Grand Rapids, MI: Eerdmans, 2000), 891–94.

17. For an account of what "presence" involves, see G. O'Collins, *Christology: A Biblical, Historical, and Systematic Study of Jesus*, 2nd ed. (Oxford, UK: Oxford University Press, 2009), 334–57.

18. Gerald Bonner, "*Christus Sacerdos*: The Roots of Augustine's Anti-Donatist Polemic," in *Signum Pietatis*, ed. A. Zumkeller (Würzburg: Augustinus-Verlag, 1989), 325–39, at 338.

19. Ibid., 331.

20. See G. O'Collins and M. K. Jones, *Jesus Our Priest: A Christian Approach to the Priesthood of Christ* (Oxford, UK: Oxford University Press, 2010).

21. See ibid., 38–43.

22. On this verse from Hebrews, see ibid., 48–49.

23. T. F. Torrance, *Theology in Reconciliation: Essays toward Evangelical and Catholic Unity in East and West* (Eugene, OR: Wipf & Stock, 1996), 209; for more on Torrance's view of Christ's living, priestly presence in the liturgy, see O'Collins and Jones, *Jesus Our Priest*, 224–29.

24. See G. O'Collins, *Salvation for All: God's Other Peoples* (Oxford, UK: Oxford University Press, 2008), 142–60.

25. On this universal presence of Christ and the Spirit, see further ibid., 202–29.

26. On these two verses, see J. A. Fitzmyer, *The Acts of the Apostles* (New York: Doubleday, 1998), 577, 578.

27. On the presence of Christ according to *Sacrosanctum Concilium*, see O'Collins and Jones, *Jesus Our Priest*, 234–36. See also Karl Rahner, "The Presence of the Lord in the Christian Community at Worship," *Theological Investigations*, vol. 10, trans. D. Bourke (London: Darton, Longman & Todd, 1973), 71–83.

28. T. F. Torrance, *Theology in Reconciliation: Essays toward Evangelical and Catholic Unity in East and West* (Eugene, OR: Wipf & Stock, 1996), 134.

29. Tertullian himself called baptism and the Eucharist (but not confirmation) "sacraments" (*Against Marcion*, 4.34).

30. Northrop Frye, *The Great Code: The Bible and Literature* (San Diego: Harcourt, 1982), 171–72.

31. Oliver O'Donovan, *Resurrection and Moral Order: An Outline for Evangelical Ethics* (Grand Rapids, MI: Eerdmans, 1986).

32. B. Johnstone, "Transformation Ethics: The Moral Implications of the Resurrection," in *The Resurrection: An Interdisciplinary Symposium on the Resurrection of Jesus*, ed. S. T. Davis, D. Kendall, and G. O'Collins (Oxford, UK: Oxford University Press, 1997), 339–60, at 339, 342–43.

33. Reviews of ibid. by J. P. Galvin in *The Thomist* 63 (1999): 504–7, and by S. C. Barton in *Theology* 798 (1997): 455–57.

34. A. J. Kelly, *The Resurrection Effect: Transforming Christian Life and Thought* (Maryknoll, NY: Orbis, 2008), 159–68, at 159.

35. P. Nullens and R. T. Michener, *The Matrix of Christian Ethics: Integrating Philosophy and Moral Theology in a Postmodern Context* (Colorado Springs, CO: Paternoster, 2010), 168, 183.

36. J. F. Keenan, *A History of Catholic Moral Theology in the Twentieth Century: From Confessing Sins to Liberating Consciences* (London/New York: Continuum, 2010), 200.

37. D. J. Harrington and J. F. Keenan, *Jesus and Virtue Ethics: Building Bridges between New Testament Studies and Moral Theology* (Lanham, MD: Sheed & Ward, 2002), 38, 189–90. Two pages, under the heading of "New Testament Texts" (187–88), also contain some material that situates the life, death, and resurrection of Jesus in a cosmic context.

38. D. J. Harrington and J. F. Keenan, *Paul and Virtue Ethics: Building Bridges between New Testament Studies and Moral Theology* (Lanham, MD: Rowman & Littlefield, 2010), 15–17, 24–27, 36–37, 99–101.

39. Ibid., 21.

40. Byrne, *Romans*, 259.

41. Keenan, *A History of Catholic Moral Theology in the Twentieth Century*, 88–95, at 88.

42. See Johnstone, "Transformation Ethics," 342.

43. Ibid., 349–50.

44. Ibid., 340.

APPENDIX:
EASTER APPEARANCES AND
BEREAVEMENT EXPERIENCES

1. D. Rees, "The Hallucinations of Widowhood," 2 October 1971, 37–41.

2. D. Rees, *Death and Bereavement: The Psychological, Religious and Cultural Interface* (London: Whurr, 1997), 256–81; see D. Klaus and T. Walter, "Processes of Grieving: How Bonds Are Continued," in *Handbook of Bereavement Research: Consequences, Coping, and Care*, ed. M. S. Stroebe et al. (Washington, DC: American Psychological Association, 2001), 431–48, at 436.

3. I. O. Glick, R. S. Weiss, and C. M. Parkes, *The First Year of Bereavement* (New York: John Wiley/Interscience, 1974). In his *Bereavement: Studies of Grief in Adult Life* (London: Tavistock Publications, 1972), 21, Parkes gives the number of these widows and widowers as 68. In *Love and Loss: The Roots of Grief and its Complications* (London: Routledge, 2006), 27, Parkes gives the number as 59. In C. M. Parkes and R. S. Weiss, *Recovery from Bereavement* (New York: Basic Books, 1983), 25, it is explained that 68 widows and widowers completed all three of the initially scheduled interviews, while only 59 were interviewed in a follow-up.

4. A. M. Greeley, *Religion as Poetry* (New Brunswick: Transaction Publishers, 1996), 217–27.

5. M. S. Stroebe, W. Stroebe and R. O. Hansson, eds. (New York: Cambridge University Press, 1993); see also M. S. Stroebe et al., eds., *Handbook of Bereavement Research and Practice: Advances in Theory and Intervention* (Washington, DC: American Psychological Association, 2008). D. C. Allison recognizes the importance of Rees's research and the impulse it gave to other researchers, and adds an extensive bibliography on the experiences of bereaved persons: *Resurrecting Jesus: The Earliest Christian Tradition and Its Interpreters* (New York and London: T. & T. Clark, 2005), 273, n. 306. In footnotes that accompany pp. 296–99, Allison provides a mass of further references. But some of these references are to unreliable popular literature, to outdated works, and to the writ-

ings of parapsychologists that many professional psychologists dismiss or ignore as pseudo-science.

6. D. Rees, *Pointers to Eternity* (Talypon, Wales: Y Lolfa Press, 2010), 167–210.

7. G. Lüdemann, *The Resurrection of Jesus: History, Experience, Theology*, trans. J. Bowden (London: SCM Press, 1994), 97–100, 225, n. 398.

8. *The Metaphor of God Incarnate* (London: SCM Press, 1993), 38; the page reference remains the same in the 2nd ed. of 2005. Without naming Rees or any other researcher, Hick writes here of "the vivid sense, widely reported, that a loved person who has died (usually recently) is invisibly present, comforting or guiding or challenging one in the present situation."

9. G. O'Collins, "Resurrection: The State of the Questions," in *The Resurrection: An Interdisciplinary Symposium on the Resurrection of Jesus*, ed. S. T. Davis, D. Kendall and G. O'Collins (Oxford: Oxford University Press, 1997), 5–28, at 10–13.

10. Ibid., 29–40.

11. G. O'Collins, "The Risen Jesus: Analogies and Presence," in *Resurrection*, ed. S. E. Porter, M. A. Hayes, and D. Tombs (Sheffield: Sheffield Academic Press, 1999), 195–217, at 206–10; id., "The Resurrection of Jesus: The Debate Continued," *Gregorianum* 81 (2000), 589–98, at 596–97.

12. G. O'Collins, *Easter Faith: Believing in the Risen Jesus* (London: Darton, Longman & Todd, 2003), 11–15.

13. Rees, *Pointers to Eternity*, 47–48, 167–210.

14. P. R. Olson et al., "Hallucinations of Widowhood," *Proceedings of the American Geriatric Society* 33 (1985), 543–47.

15. Klaus and Walter, "Processes of Grieving," 436.

16. Rees, *Pointers to Eternity*, 173.

17. Ibid., 187–88.

18. Ibid., 201.

19. Ibid., 202.

20. P. H. Wiebe, *Visions of Jesus* (New York: Oxford University Press, 1997), 195.

21. O'Collins, *Easter Faith*, 12–13.

22. Ibid., 12.

23. Rees, *Pointers to Eternity*, 37.

24. Ibid.

25. Ibid., 170. ˙

26. Ibid., 179.

27. Ibid., 204.

28. O'Collins, *Easter Faith*, 13.

29. Rees, *Pointers to Eternity*, 204–9.

30. O'Collins, *Easter Faith*, 13.

31. For details see G. O'Collins, *Christology: A Biblical, Historical, and Systematic Study of Jesus* (Oxford: Oxford University Press, 2nd edn, 2009), 54–81, 126–32.

32. See G. O'Collins, "Crucifixion," in *Anchor Bible Dictionary*, ed. D. N. Freedman, vol. 1 (New York: Doubleday, 1992), 1207–10.

33. Rees, *Pointers to Eternity*, 205.

34. Ibid., 183, 185.

35. Allison, *Resurrecting Jesus*, 273. On the same page he adds: "There are likewise innumerable accounts of various people [*he does not say "bereaved people"*] seeing an apparition over an extended period of time." Should we think here of "ghost stories" connected with "haunted houses"? That too would be a red herring, since what Rees and others, like Lüdemann and Hick, propose is an analogy between the Easter appearances and the experiences of *bereaved* persons. Later Allison cites some literature (including unreliable, popular sources) which claims that deceased persons have been "seen" by more than one [bereaved?] percipient at the same time (ibid., 279, n. 321; see 275, n. 310).

36. Ibid., 270.

37. Ibid., 270, n. 292.

38. For instance, ibid., 270, n. 293, and 272, nn. 298–300 (featuring, e.g., Sir Oliver Lodge, F. W. H. Meyers, and E. M. Sidgwick).

39. Apropos of this point, Klaus and Walter remark that "there are plenty of examples of the dead appearing to comfort well-adjusted individuals decades later" ("Processes of Grieving," 436).

40. Rees, *Pointers to Eternity*, 208–9.

41. Ibid., 208.

42. Wiebe, *Visions of Jesus*.

43. Rees, *Pointers to Eternity*, 108–11.

44. Ibid., 105–6.

45. Ibid., 93–114.

46. On the distinction between the two groups, see further O'Collins, *Jesus Risen*, 15–23, and G. O'Collins and D. Kendall, "The Uniqueness of the Easter Appearances," *Catholic Biblical Quarterly* 54 (1992), 287–307.

47. Rees, *Pointers to Eternity*, 191; see 180.

48. Ibid., 207.

49. See O'Collins, *Easter Faith*, 74–75, 114.

50. See J. L. Martyn, *Galatians* (New York: Doubleday, 1997), 170.

51. O'Collins, *Easter Faith*, 13.

52. Rees, *Pointers to Eternity*, 206.

53. See J. Painter, *Just James: The Brother of Jesus in History and Tradition* (Columbia, SC: The University of South Carolina Press, 1999); B. Chilton and C. A. Evans, eds., *James the Just and Christian Origins* (Leiden/Boston: Brill, 1999).

54. Luke notes that when a severe persecution drove members of the Church away into the countryside of Judea and Samaria, "the apostles" (= the Twelve) were able to stay on in Jerusalem (Acts 8:1).

55. Rees, *Pointers to Eternity*, 207.

56. Ibid., 207–8.

57. Rees himself introduces two further (significant?) differences by pointing out that, in the case of the disciples to whom the risen Jesus appeared, "for the most part we are dealing with a different gender and age group. Jesus' closest followers were men in the prime of life" (206). One should recall that Mary Magdalene, a very prominent Easter witness, and other women belonged among the closest followers of Jesus (see, e.g., Luke 8:1–3), and that there were unquestionably women among the more than five hundred followers to whom Jesus appeared (1 Cor 15:6) and among the disciples in Jerusalem (Luke 24:36–49; John 20:19–23) to whom Jesus likewise appeared. Rees's expression, "for the most part," allows for this.

Nevertheless, those 46.7% of the 293 bereaved interviewed by Rees who experienced their dead spouses included many older people and far more widows than widowers. In the case of the

Easter appearances of Jesus, the New Testament does not mention (at least explicitly) any older people to whom he appeared, and among the persons explicitly named as those to whom Jesus appeared men are more numerous than women. Early traditions in the East and West, but not the New Testament, spoke of an appearance of the risen Christ to his widowed mother; for some details see G. O'Collins and D. Kendall, *Focus on Jesus* (Leominster, UK: Gracewing, 1996), 130–33.

58. Rees, *Pointers to Eternity*, 167.

59. Ibid., 209.

60. Ibid., 169.

61. Ibid., 204.

62. Ibid., 207.

63. L. Wittgenstein, *Culture and Value*, trans. P. Winch (Oxford: Basil Blackwell, 1980), 33c.

64. Parkes, *Bereavement Studies of Grief in Adult Life*, 59–65, at 62.

65. See O'Collins, *Easter Faith*, 55–65.

Select Bibliography

Allison, Dale C. *Resurrecting Jesus: The Earliest Christian Tradition and Its Interpreters*. New York: T. & T. Clark, 2005.

Barton, Stephen, and Graham Stanton, eds. *Resurrection*. London: SPCK, 1994.

Brown, Raymond E. *The Virginal Conception and the Bodily Resurrection of Jesus*. New York: Paulist Press, 1973.

Charlesworth, James H., et al., eds. *Resurrection: The Origin and Future of a Biblical Doctrine*. New York: Continuum, 2006.

Davis, Stephen T., Daniel Kendall, and Gerald O'Collins, eds. *Resurrection: An Interdisciplinary Symposium on the Resurrection of Jesus*. Oxford, UK: Oxford University Press, 1997.

Dawson, Robert Dale. *The Resurrection in Karl Barth*. Aldershot, UK: Ashgate, 2007.

Gasser, Georg, ed. *Personal Identity and Resurrection*. Farnham, UK: Ashgate, 2010.

Habermas, Gary R. *The Risen Jesus and Future Hope*. Lanham, MD: Rowman & Littlefield, 2003.

Kelly, Anthony J. *The Resurrection Effect: Transforming Christian Life and Thought*. Maryknoll, NY: Orbis, 2008.

Licona, Michael R. *The Resurrection of Jesus: A New Historiographical Approach*. Downers Grove, IL: IVP Academic, 2010.

Lorenzen, Thorwald. *Resurrection, Discipleship, Justice: Affirming the Resurrection of Jesus Christ Today*. Macon, GA: Smyth & Helwys, 2003.

O'Collins, Gerald. *Easter Faith: Believing in the Risen Jesus*. Mahwah, NJ: Paulist Press, 2003.

————. *Jesus Risen: An Historical, Fundamental and Systematic Examination of Christ's Resurrection*. New York/Mahwah, NJ: Paulist Press, 1987.

Perkins, Pheme. *Resurrection*. New York: Doubleday, 1984.

Peters, Ted, Robert J. Russell, and Michael Welker, eds. *Resurrection: Theological and Scientific Assessments*. Grand Rapids, MI: Eerdmans, 2002.

Robinette, Brian D. *Grammars of Resurrection: A Christian Theology of Presence and Absence*. New York: Crossroad, 2009.

Schneiders, Sandra M. *Written That You May Believe: Encountering Jesus in the Fourth Gospel*. Rev. ed. New York: Crossroad, 2003.

Stewart, Robert B., ed. *The Resurrection of Jesus: John Dominic Crossan and N. T. Wright in Dialogue*. Minneapolis: Augsburg Fortress, 2006.

Swinburne, Richard. *The Resurrection of God Incarnate*. Oxford, UK: Oxford University Press, 2003.

Williams, Rowan. *Resurrection: Interpreting the Easter Gospel*. London: Darton, Longman & Todd, 2002.

Wright, Nicholas Thomas. *Christian Origins and the Question of God*, vol. 3, *The Resurrection of the Son of God*. Minneapolis: Fortress, 2003.

———. *Surprised by Hope*. London: SPCK, 2007.

INDEX

Index

Index

Index

Index

Index

Walter, T., 177, 214, 215, 216
Weiss, R. S., 214
Welker, M., 12, 195, 210, 220
West, M., 134
Wiebe, P., 177, 184, 215, 216
Williams, R., 207, 220
Winch, P., 209, 218
Winter, P., 20, 51, 53, 197, 199

Wittgenstein, L. 137, 190, 209, 218
Wright, N. T., 2–4, 12, 13, 22, 71, 81, 133, 193–94, 109, 203, 220

Yarbro Collins, A., 19, 21, 56, 80, 83–84, 87, 196, 197, 203

Zumkeller, A., 212